Lecture Notes in Computer Science   11249

Commenced Publication in 1973
Founding and Former Series Editors:
Gerhard Goos, Juris Hartmanis, and Jan van Leeuwen

More information about this series at http://www.springer.com/series/7409

Achilles Kameas · Kostas Stathis (Eds.)

Ambient Intelligence

14th European Conference, AmI 2018
Larnaca, Cyprus, November 12–14, 2018
Proceedings

 Springer

Editors
Achilles Kameas ⓘ
Hellenic Open University
Patras, Greece

Kostas Stathis
University of London, Royal Holloway
Egham, UK

ISSN 0302-9743   ISSN 1611-3349   (electronic)
Lecture Notes in Computer Science
ISBN 978-3-030-03061-2   ISBN 978-3-030-03062-9   (eBook)
https://doi.org/10.1007/978-3-030-03062-9

Library of Congress Control Number: 2018958965

LNCS Sublibrary: SL3 – Information Systems and Applications, incl. Internet/Web, and HCI

This Springer imprint is published by the registered company Springer Nature Switzerland AG
The registered company address is: Gewerbestrasse 11, 6330 Cham, Switzerland

Preface

The purpose of the European Conference on Ambient Intelligence (AmI) is to promote work that studies how to bring intelligence to our everyday environments in order to make these environments sensitive to us. A further aim is to support scientic exchanges among Ambient Intelligence researchers, practitioners, scientists, and engineers in affiliated disciplines not only from Europe but from around the globe. This year's conference, AmI 2018, sought to maintain the momentum of last year's event to keep the interdisciplinary research community interested in the field of ambient intelligence and related fields such as the Internet of Things, cyber-physical systems, and artificial intelligence. We have approached these areas from points of view ranging from computer science and engineering, to psychology and social sciences to design and architecture. Technologies that once were simply part of the vision of ambient intelligence are now becoming more and more common for our daily lives, with smart devices recognizing our speech and intelligent software agents acting as assistants to provide us with personalized services, leading to new ways for us to interact with our environment.

The formal proceedings of this 14th edition of the European Conference on Ambient Intelligence are collected in Vol. 11249 of Springer's LNCS series. The conference solicited contributions from a number of topics that were presented in the program under the themes of:

- Ambient Services and Smart Environments
- Sensor Networks and Articial Intelligence
- Activity and Situation Recognition
- Ambient Intelligence in Education

As in previous years, we attracted the interest of researchers from academia and industry, who contributed to our varied program on research in ambient intelligence. This year's edition received 36 submissions for the full and short paper track. Each of these papers received at least three reviews by members of our technical Program Committee that comprised experts from industry, academia, and research organizations. This process led to the acceptance of 12 full papers and six short papers, a combined acceptance rate of 50%. These were accepted for a presentation and are included in this volume.

This year's trend toward increasing number of submissions from last year's event indicates that the European Conference on Ambient Intelligence remains highly engaging for the research community, with the respective editions of the proceedings receiving a large number of chapter downloads. This gives us hope that both the research community and industry can benefit from the work and presented get inspiration for future research, designs, and products.

We would like to extend our thanks to all the authors who submitted their research to this conference, contributing to the high-quality program. Most importantly, this would not have been possible without the help of our technical Program Committee and the Organizing Committee. Our Program Committee members and their sub-reviewers dedicated their time to provide high-quality reviews of the submissions, within a very tight schedule. Without their help we would not have been able to offer such an engaging program. We would also like to thank the Steering Committee of the conference in general and Boris De Ruyter in particular, for their initial advice on all stages of the conference organisation. Last but not least, we wish to thank the University of Cyprus, Austrian Airlines, and Springer for sponsoring this event.

November 2018   Achilles Kameas
                                                                Kostas Stathis

Organization

General Chair

George Roussos   Birkbeck, University of London, UK

Program Chairs

Achilles Kameas   Hellenic Open University, Greece
Kostas Stathis   Royal Holloway, University of London, UK

Workshops Chairs

Ioannis Chatzigiannakis   Sapienza University of Rome, Italy
Fariba Sadri   Imperial College, UK

Local Organization Chair

George Angelos Papadopoulos   University of Cyprus, Cyprus

Program Committee

Evgenia Adamopoulou	National Technical University of Athens, Greece
Claudio Ardagna	Università degli Studi di Milano, Italy
Antonis Argyros	University of Crete, Greece
Ahmed Sabbir Arif	University of California, Merced, USA
Alexander Artikis	NCSR Demokritos, Greece
Juan Carlos Augusto	Middlesex University, UK
Elena Bellodi	University of Ferrara, Italy
Sara Bernardini	Royal Holloway, University of London, UK
Antonis Bikakis	University College London, UK
Spiros Borotis	Hellenic Open University, Greece
Andreas Braun	Fraunhofer Institute, Germany
Ioannis Chatzigiannakis	Sapienza University of Rome, Italy
Boris De Ruyter	Philips Research, Netherlands
Kieran Delaney	Cork Institute of Technology, Ireland
Claudia Di Napoli	C.N.R. - Istituto di Calcolo e Reti ad Alte Prestazioni, Italy
Monica Divitini	Norwegian University of Science and Technology, Norway
Babak A. Farshchian	Norwegian University of Science and Technology, Norway
Panos Fitsilis	Technological Educational Institute of Thessaly, Greece

Maria Ganzha	Warsaw University of Technology, Poland
Damianos Gavalas	University of the Aegean, Greece
Nikolaos Georgantas	Inria, France
Paolo Giorgini	University of Trento, Italy
Hristijan Gjoreski	Ss. Cyril and Methodius University, Former Yugoslav Republic of Macedonia
Christos Goumopoulos	University of the Aegean, Greece
Tobias Grosse-Puppendahl	Microsoft, Germany
Sten Hanke	Austrian Institute of Technology, Austria
Otthein Herzog	Jacobs University Bremen, Tongji University, Shanghai, and University of Bremen, Germany
R. Özgür Kafali	University of Kent, UK
Antonis Kakas	University of Cyprus, Cyprus
Achilles Kameas	Hellenic Open University, Greece
Paris Kitsos	Technological Educational Institute of Western Greece, Greece
Kristian Kloeckl	Northeastern University, USA
Andreas Komninos	University of Patras, Greece
Arjan Kuijper	TU Darmstadt, Germany
Zhiyuan Luo	Royal Holloway, University of London, UK
Irene Mavrommati	Hellenic Open University, Greece
Antonio Maña	University of Malaga, Spain
Loizos Michael	Open University of Cyprus, Cyprus
Rob Miller	University College London, UK
Maxime Morge	Université de Lille, France
Petros Nicopolitidis	Aristotle University of Thessaloniki, Greece
Andrea Omicini	University of Bologna, Italy
Theofanis Orphanoudakis	Hellenic Open University, Greece
George Palaigeorgiou	Technological Educational Institute of Kavala, Greece
Theodore Panagiotakopoulos	Hellenic Open University, Greece
Panagiotis Papadimitriou	University of Macedonia, Greece
George Angelos Papadopoulos	University of Cyprus, Cyprus
Yorgos Papagiannakis	University of Crete, Greece
Fabio Paterno	CNR-ISTI, Italy
Dimitris Plexousakis	University of Crete, Greece
Kostas Psannis	University of Macedonia, Greece
Carlos Ramos	Instituto Superior de Engenharia do Porto, Portugal
Alessandro Ricci	University of Bologna, Italy
Silvia Rossi	University of Naples Federico II, Italy
George Roussos	Birkbeck College, University of London, UK
Carsten Röcker	Fraunhofer Institute, Germany

Fariba Sadri	Imperial College London, UK
Albert Ali Salah	Bogazici University, Turkey
Daniele Sgandurra	Royal Holloway, University of London, UK
Stephan Sigg	Aalto University, Finland
Nikolaos Spanoudakis	Technical University of Crete, Greece
Kostas Stathis	Royal Holloway, University of London, UK
Dimitrios Stratogiannis	National Technical University of Athens, Greece
Paolo Torroni	University of Bologna, Italy
Manfred Tscheligi	University of Salzburg, Austria
Kristof Van Laerhoven	University of Siegen, Germany
Lawrence Wai-Choong Wong	National University of Singapore, Singapore
Ioannis Zaharakis	Computer Technology Institute and Press Diophantus, Greece
Arkady Zaslavsky	CSIRO, Australia
Riccardo Zese	University of Ferrara, Italy
Gottfried Zimmermann	Stuttgart Media University, Germany

Additional Reviewers

Achilleos, Achilleas
Kakalou, Ioanna
Katzouris, Nikos
Quinde, Mario
Tsoli, Aggeliki

Contents

Ambient Services and Smart Environments

Predicting User Responsiveness to Smartphone Notifications for Edge Computing

Andreas Komninos$^{(\boxtimes)}$, Elton Frengkou, and John Garofalakis

University of Patras, 26504 Rio, Greece
akomninos@ceid.upatras.gr

Abstract. Edge computing requires the addressing of several challenges in terms of privacy, complexity, bandwidth and battery life. While in the past attempts have been made to predict users' responsiveness to smartphone notifications, we show that this is possible with a minimal number of just three features synthesized from non-sensor based data. Our approach demonstrates that it is possible to classify user attentiveness to notifications with good accuracy, and predict response time to any type of notification within a margin of 1 min, without the need for personalized modelling.

Keywords: Smartphones · Notifications · Attentivity · Responsiveness

1 Introduction

Smartphone notifications are part-and-parcel of everyday interaction with our devices and the services we expect to receive from them. Unfortunately, despite several years of research, managing these notifications remains a mostly manual task, in which the users are unassisted by intelligence embedded in the operating system, or even applications themselves. Recent work has shown that it is possible to assist users by anticipating opportune moments to issue notifications (i.e. moments in which the user is likely to be attentive to the device, and also able to engage with the notification content [1]). Other work has attempted to examine the role of modality in attracting the user's attention (e.g. [2]). Generally, to intelligently manage notifications, Anderson et al. [3] propose a four-stage system approach, starting with acquiring sensor data, processing sensor data, inferring context from sensor data, building interruptibility models and finally managing an incoming notification (selecting modality, or deferring it). However, all previous approaches assume the analysis of large volumes of data in the cloud, collected by a large variety of device sensors and context data sources, placing not just a strain on the device battery but also doubts on the applicability of these techniques, both due to privacy concerns, and device constraints (e.g. network availability): Precisely the challenges that modern *Edge Computing* paradigms aim to address.

In this field of research, the least studied aspect is the issuing of a notification under the selection of an appropriate modality. The choice of modality is a balancing act that requires awareness of the user's context (e.g. social surroundings, time of day, likely activity etc.), and also the notification's context (e.g. the event it relates to, its general

A. Kameas and K. Stathis (Eds.): AmI 2018, LNCS 11249, pp. 3–19, 2018.
https://doi.org/10.1007/978-3-030-03062-9_1

importance, its relative importance to the user's current task, whether the user's immediate attention is required, the cost or impact of not attending to the event etc.).

For any researcher that has even trivially worked in context awareness, it is easy to see that these types of context are difficult to acquire – even if it were indeed possible, it remains entirely plausible that the user might prefer a system not to have such extensive and intimate knowledge about their context for privacy reasons. Thus, on one hand we have today's approach, in which the user is notified immediately using any modality that the service developers consider appropriate to attract attention, and on the other hand, a shift of the locus of control towards a notification management system which determines the appropriate modality to use given the user's and notification's contexts. To give an example, such a system might dynamically alter pre-programmed notification modalities to issue trivial notifications using the device LED only while the user is working, and allow the device to sound and vibrate only if there's an incoming call from a stressed colleague working on the same project.

From the above it is plain to see that both approaches have problems: Leaving the locus of control entirely up to the users causes frequent disruption and frustrations and also leads to missing important notifications, as the users resort to coarse handling strategies such as setting the phone to silent (which affects all notifications). On the other hand, shifting the locus of control towards the system can still have grave consequences when the system doesn't get it right and ends up causing the user to miss important information. In this sense, the situation becomes akin to text entry auto-corrects and the embarrassing moments it has caused, shared across the web – usually it works well, but when it doesn't, the cost to the user can be very serious. In this context, we present here an analysis of real-world notifications, and discuss a model to predict the users' engagement with notifications which aims to use minimal data sources, in order to preserve user privacy and minimize the resources required for predicting user responsiveness in AmI environments using edge computing architectures.

2 Related Work

Predicting interruptibility and opportune times to deliver smartphone notifications is the subject of several recent research efforts. Much of the research is summarized by the excellent recent survey in [3] so we will not repeat it here, however, we lay out the parameters of recent important work related to our topic in Table 1 so that our own contribution may be placed in context with past work.

Our work complements existing approaches in a number of ways. In contrast with most previous work, our analysis comes from user's behaviour with notifications from any app and the OS itself, and not from a notification issued by a single application. We also refrain from using privacy-sensitive features (e.g. user location or application type). Further, all previous approaches consider the just the device ringer mode (e.g. [4–6]), which does not actually equate to the modality with which a notification is delivered, as we explain next. In our work, we algorithmically determine the true actual modality with which the notifications were delivered. Another differentiation is that we employ only opportunistic data collection without sensor sampling, to minimize impact on the user's battery. Lastly, while previous work rests on classification (e.g. is the user

Table 1. Overview of recent notification behaviour prediction research

Paper	Notification source	Users	# Notifications	Context features	Measurement	Performance
Okoshi et al. [1]	Single app	687,840	N/A	387	Response time	49.7% reduction
Pielot et al. [4]	Single app	337	78,930	201	Notification acceptance	0.31 (F_1 score)
Turner et al. [5]	Single app	93	11,396	9	Notification acceptance (multilevel)	~80% prec.
Poppinga et al. [7]	Single app	314	6,581	9	Notification acceptance (binary)	77.48% acc.
Pielot et al. [6]	Messaging apps	24	6,423	17	Attentiveness (binary)	68.71% acc.
Okoshi et al. [8]	Single app	30	2,162	45	Response time	12% reduction
Turner et al. [9]	Single app	93	11,396	9	Notification acceptance (multilevel)	34–65% acc.
Mehrotra et al. [10]	All apps	35	70,000	14	Notification acceptance (binary)	70–80% specificity

reachable, or attentive to their device), we also report the results of a regression-based approach to quantify the reaction time to notifications.

3 Data Collection

3.1 Understanding the Android Notification System

All previous in-the-wild studies that we have found rely on the Android OS, which allows application programmers to specify *desired* notification modalities in their code. Hence a notification may be programmed to request from the device any combination of modality during issue, including the device LED, sound and vibration. Users can specify a ringer mode for their device, either manually, or, in later versions of the OS, via context-driven rules (e.g. set to completely silent between certain hours, or only allow certain applications at these hours). The ringer mode may *suppress, but does not add* beyond the programmed modality requests (thus will not add a LED illumination, vibration or sound to a notification which is not programmed to have one). Furthermore, the Android OS allows users to suppress notification modalities for individual applications. The locus of control in the way a modality is used to issue a notification is shown diagrammatically in Fig. 1. The OS overrides programmed modality requests based on a range of possible user settings.

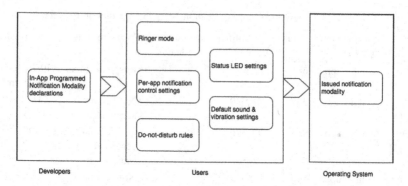

Fig. 1. Locus of control over the actual modality with which a notification is issued in the Android OS. App developers request a combination of modalities, but the OS may not necessarily honour these, depending on the user's individual settings and preferences.

Another point is that some notifications are not dismissible until a task completes or a user performs some action (e.g. showing a downloading progress bar, or a low disk-space event) and that some persist during ongoing events (e.g. a phonecall).

To infer thus reliable conclusions on how a notification modality influenced response time, a study should capture all types of information (what were the pro-grammed notification modalities, user per-app preferences and what was the current ringer mode at the time of notification). If only the current ringer mode, or programmed notification modality are captured, then we cannot know with any certainty what modality was actually used to issue a notification and, consequently, estimate the effect an individual modality might have had on the users' response time.

3.2   Collected Data

To collect data for our analysis, we built a simple logging application which works silently as UI-less background process. Previous works have employed a range of sensors to detect context (e.g. [8]). A downside of this approach is that frequent sensor sampling drains the users' battery. We adopted here a more opportunistic approach, sampling context information *only* at the time when a notification was issued, *without using any hardware sensor* data (e.g. accelerometer, GPS). Another consideration in our approach was the number of features sampled. In [4], the researchers collected data for 201 features, without any justification relating to their use. We believe this indis-criminate collection of data without at least some evidence to support their selection is unnecessary and of course, consists a significant privacy violation with doubtful utility (only a handful of features were shown to have some impact on engagement). The concerns over privacy are mentioned as a challenge in [3] and thus we selected to collect data only for features that relate immediately to the direct perceptibility of a notification. The application subclasses the Android "notification listener" service. The service is triggered, after the user has granted the relevant one-time permission, every time a notification is issued by any application or the OS itself. This service is also triggered upon dismissal of a notification. The callback methods in the service allow access to all the information related to the notification. Therefore for every notification we captured the following features relating either to the notification itself, or the device state at the time of issuing the notification (Table 2):

For later versions of the Android OS, the captured notification shows not the programmed modalities, but the modalities that this notification was allowed to have based on the user's preferences (through the notification channel settings). Thus, this set of features covers the issues identified in Sect. 3.1. The application was installed on the smartphones of 26 participants and was left to log data for a period of 4 weeks (28 days), after obtaining informed consent. The participants were computer science students, aged 18–22, recruited via social media and did not receive compensation. Of these participants, some dropped out of the study, others removed our service's access permissions after some time and some returned only very small datasets. As a result, our analysis proceeded with data from 14 (6f) participants.

Table 2. Captured notification and device state features

	Feature	Description	Values
Notification features	Time posted	Timestamp at issue time	Unix time (seconds)
	Time removed	Timestamp at dismissal time	Unix time or blank (self-cancelling notifs.)
	Package name	Package identifier of the application	String literal
	Sound	Use a custom sound at issue time?	Sound clip URI
	Default sound	Use the device defaults at issue time?	True | false
	LED	Use a custom LED colour and pattern at issue time?	LED on/off time pattern
	Default LED	Use the device defaults at issue time?	True | false
	Vibration pattern	Use a custom vibration pattern at issue time?	Vibration on/off time pattern
	Default vibration	Use the device defaults at issue time?	True | false
	Notification flags	A bit mask with flags related to the notification	1: should use LED 2: ongoing notification 4: insistent notification 8: only-once 16: auto-cancelling 32: no-clear 64: foreground 128: high priority 256: local only 512: group summary

(*continued*)

Table 2. (*continued*)

	Feature	Description	Values
Device features	Ringer mode	The current device ringer mode	0: silent (LED only) 1: vibration & LED 2: sound, vibr. & LED
	Interactive	Whether the device is in a current "interactive" state (ready to interact with the user)	0: device sleeping 1: ready to interact
	Screen state	The current screen state	1: off 2: on 3: dozing 4: dozing - suspended
	Allow lock-screen notifs	Are notifs. allowed to be displayed on the lock-screen of the device?	True | false

4   Data Analysis

4.1   Feature Transformation and Cleansing

As stated above, to determine the actual modality with which a notification was delivered to a user, we need more than just ringer mode information only. Having collected both the requested delivery modalities (programmed modalities and filtering by per-app settings) *and* the ringer mode, it is quite easy to derive simple rules for determining the actual delivery modality used. Hence, in contrast with work such as [10] where these are not combined, we derive the synthetic binary variables "Had LED", "Had Sound" and "Had Vibration". From these values we determine the modality combination that was used to deliver a notification (one of 8 possible combinations). Furthermore, by subtracting the dismissal time from the issuing time, we derive the feature "Response Time" in seconds. Finally, from the issuing time, we calculate the hour of day in which the notification was issued ("Hour").

In terms of the data, we collected 176,195 notifications from the 14 participants. The full dataset can be obtained freely at https://github.com/komis1/ami2018-notifications. For analysis, we removed those notifications which the user could not manually dismiss and all notifications pertinent to ongoing events (e.g. phonecalls, downloads etc). We noticed also that on some devices the OS was generating many notifications which it issued and dismissed at the same time, so any notifications that had a response time of zero were also filtered out. Examining the reaction time, we found that there existed several outliers in terms of reaction time, and since 90% of the sample had a reaction time <1376 s ($\sim$22 min), we pruned the set at that threshold.

4.2 Statistical Processing

In the following description, all statistical tests are chosen based on the distribution of the relevant variables (normal or otherwise). After pruning, the resulting notification set consisted of 12,612 notifications, showing that less than 10% of the notifications received by a user are actually *interactive* notifications, i.e. events for which the user's attention is required by an application or service. These had a mean response time $\mu = 103.30$ s ($\sigma = 220.163$ s). The median was 16.00 s (compared to 6.15 min found in [6]) and 3rd quartile was 75.00 s. As can be seen, the distribution of response time follows a power-law curve (Fig. 2 left).

How Responsive Are Users to Notifications Throughout the Day? Another interesting observation is the diurnal distribution of issued notifications (Fig. 2 right, shaded area), were we can see an increase of interruption after midday (skewness −.908, kurtosis −.357), after which the level of interruption remains relatively constant until approximately midnight, where it starts to decrease. This pattern resembles closely the one in [7] although that result discusses the rate of engaging with content in a notification issued by a single app, where as we could not know whether our participants engaged, or simply dismissed the notifications issued to them. To quantify the disruptiveness of the interruption, we looked at the distribution of response times per hour of day (Fig. 2 right). As expected, notifications issued deep in the night have a visibly longer mean response time compared to the rest of the day. A Kruskal-Wallis H test (owing to the non-normal distribution of response time in each hour bin) reveals that response time is indeed distributed differently throughout the day with statistical significance ($\chi^2_{(23)} = 123.142$, $p < 0.01$). Interestingly, we observe that users seem to respond to notifications with almost the same speed as the day progresses, despite the considerable increase in volume of received notifications. The times of 8 am – 11 am seem to be those when users are least attentive to their notifications, something that may be partly explainable by the fact that they receive fewer notifications at these time, hence do not anticipate having to engage with them and are not proactively attending to their phone.

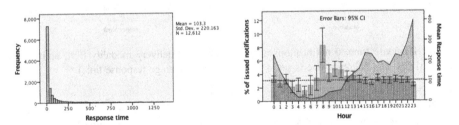

Fig. 2. Distribution of response time to notifications (left) and diurnal notification volume (right). The reference line is set at 103.3 s (overall average response time).

How Is Response Time Affected by Ringer Mode and Actual Delivery Modality? The next step was to examine the effect of modality on response time. We note that the majority of notifications (46.61%) was delivered using the "LED & Vibration (LV)" combination, followed by "LED & Sound & Vibration (LSV)" (35.97%) and "No modality (NM)" (12.71%) (Fig. 3 left). A Kruskal – Wallis H test confirms that the distribution of response time within all the modality categories is different with statistical significance ($\chi^2_{(7)} = 383.757$, p < 0.01). The three modality combinations accounted for >95% of the notifications and thus we selected them for further pairwise comparisons, using Mann-U tests with post-hoc Bonferroni correction, setting the statistical significance level at p = 0.017. In these tests, we find statistically significant differences across all comparisons, showing that NM ($\mu = 133.13$, $\sigma = 239.686$) has the slowest response time compared to LSV ($\mu = 119.49$, $\sigma = 240.058$) (Z = −8.763, p = 0.00) and LV ($\mu = 75.26$, $\sigma = 182.594$) (Z = −16.925, p = 0.00). The difference between LV and LSV is also statistically significant (Z = −9.960, p = 0.00).

The result indicates that users are more attentive to their devices when the modality used is LED & Vibration only, seemingly confirming the findings in [2, 11] where it was found that when the phone was set to "vibration only" ringer mode, the response time to notifications was faster. Further examination of response time by ringer mode in our dataset, also corroborates previous results (Fig. 3 left). A Kruskal-Wallis H test confirms the observed differences are distributed differently with statistical significance ($\chi^2_{(2)} = 50.262$, p < 0.01). Using Mann-U tests with post-hoc Bonferroni correction, setting the statistical significance level at p = 0.017, we can confirm when the device ringer mode is set to "Vibrate only" ($\mu = 81.46$, $\sigma = 189.050$) the response time is faster than "Silent" ($\mu = 117.25$, $\sigma = 234.029$, Z = −6.902, p < 0.01) and than "Sound and Vibrate" ($\mu = 110.27$, $\sigma = 228.993$, Z = −4.693, p < 0.01). We also noted that "Sound and Vibrate" has a statistically significant lower response time than "Silent" (Z = −4.485, p < 0.01).

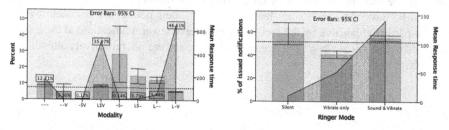

Fig. 3. Response time to notifications according to actual delivery modality (left) and ringer mode (right). The reference line is set at 103.3 s (overall average response time).

Naturally, an assumption could be made here that "silent" mode has the slowest reaction time because it would be a type of mode typically associated with contexts where no disturbance is required. Such a context might be night time, when users go to sleep. On the other hand, we noticed in Fig. 2 (right) that users seem to be, if anything, more attentive to their devices at these hours. We noticed that users place their device on "silent" mode not just at night time, but also frequently during the day too (10 am–5 pm). In fact we also notice increased use of the "vibrate only" mode in these hours. In a sense that can be expected – these are normal class-going hours for students (Fig. 4 left).

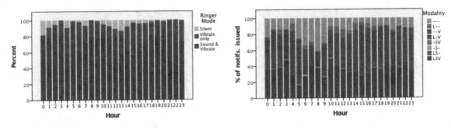

Fig. 4. Distribution of notifications according to ringer mode (left) and actual delivery modality (right).

However, when we plot the diurnal distribution of the actual delivery modality of the notifications, a totally different picture emerges (Fig. 4 right). The discrepancy between user ringer mode and actual delivery of the notification is immediately obvious.

The next question thus becomes, can the ringer mode, or actual delivery modality be used to predict response time to notifications? Bivariate Spearman's rho correlations between the mean response time in each hourly slot and the percentage of notifications delivered under each of the ringer mode settings at that time, reveal no statistically significant correlation (Table 3). On the other hand, a similar analysis between mean response time in each hourly slog and the percentage of notifications delivered with each of the 8 modality combinations, revealed a statistically significant negative correlation with LV (Table 3).

Table 3. Bivariate correlation coefficients and statistical significance between percentage of notifications under specific modality or general ringer mode and response time.

Modality	– – –	- -V	-SV	LSV	-S-	LS-	L - -	L-V
Spearman's ρ	0.237	0.226	−0.25	0.322	0.148	0.176	0.297	**−.524**
p-value	0.266	0.289	0.238	0.125	0.490	0.410	0.159	**0.009**

Ringer mode	Silent	Vibrate	Sound & Vibrate
Spearman's ρ	0.254	−0.283	0.156
p-value	0.231	0.179	0.468

Further analysis with linear modelling shows that using the percentage of notifications delivered under each ringer mode does not sufficiently explain the variability in response time ($R^2 = 0.65$). This finding is in line with [6], where it was found that ringer mode is a rather weak predictor of message notification attentivity. On the other hand, linear modelling with the percentage of notifications under their actual delivery modality, the model fit is quite good ($R^2 = 0.830$), showing that the use of actual delivery modalities is a much better predictor for a population's attentivity to issued notifications (Fig. 5).

What Is the Role of Device and Screen Operational State in Response Time? A further set of features related to the device state ("interactive" or not) and the screen state, as discussed above. To explain this further, a device is in an "interactive" state

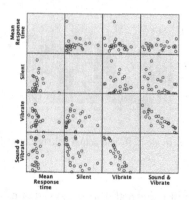 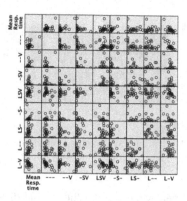

Fig. 5. Correlation plots for mean response time to notifications, and percentage of notifications delivered under given ringer mode (left) or with actual modality (right)

when it is ready to interact with the user. The screen is typically "on" at that time, but might be temporarily turned off (e.g. by the proximity sensor while the user is taking a call). The device is considered to be "interactive" also while at the "dreaming" state (akin to a screensaver mode). If the device is not interactive (i.e. sleeping), it typically requires the device to be woken up by pressing the power button. The actual state of the screen regardless of its "interactive" mode, can be separately captured at any time. Of these two features (interactive and screen state), we are mostly interested in "interactive" because when combined with the screen state ON value, we can be relatively sure that the user is currently engaged with the device, while a non-interactive state shows that the user's attention is away from the device at the time of notification.

We encountered 3 of the four possible screen states in our set. Table 4 shows the distribution of notifications by screen state and interactive state. As can be seen, our participants mostly received notifications while their device was at an interactive state with the screen turned on (69.63% of all notifications) or when the device was not interactive with the screen also turned off (29.25%). Together these represent 98.88% of all cases and can be synthesized into another feature (*Interactive-S*). For these two

Table 4. Distribution of received notifications based on device state. Combinations that synthesize the Interactive-S feature are highlighted bold.

Screen state	Interactive	Frequency	Percentage
Off	**TRUE**	81	0.64%
	FALSE	**3689**	**29.25%**
	Total	*3770*	*29.89%*
On	**TRUE**	8782	**69.63%**
	FALSE	44	0.35%
	Total	*8826*	*69.98%*
Dozing	TRUE	0	0.00%
	FALSE	16	0.13%
	Total	*16*	*0.13%*

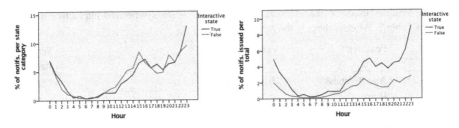

Fig. 6. Diurnal distribution of notifications received in each device interactivity state, as a percentage of each state's total (left) and of the total number of notifications (right)

predominant device states we plotted the diurnal distributions (Fig. 6) and note that the probability of a notification arriving while the device is non-interactive is considerably less in the later hours of the day (after 3 pm and until 4am). This gives an indication of when our users were mostly active on their devices and presumably more likely to respond to a notification quickly.

On one hand, these observations might explain the relatively steady diurnal reaction time observed, as users were mostly engaged with their devices while receiving notifications, thus exhibited similar engagement behaviour. On the other, we might have expected a rather more immediate response than the average 103.30 s given that the participants were already interacting with their device. Indeed, it appears that whether the device is in an interactive state or not, does not give useful insight to the responsiveness to incoming notifications. Linear modelling shows that the variability explained by the percentage of notifications received under either interactivity state is low ($R^2 = 0.087$). This is a unique finding that shows that conceptually, there exists a lower temporal boundary for engagement and that responsiveness to notifications is a matter of conscious decision by the user, and not dependent on whether a notification is immediately noticed.

5   Predicting Reaction to Notifications with Machine Learning

In [6, 7], the researchers attempt to predict whether the user is "likely" to attend to a notification. This is defined in [7] as a binary response to engaging with a notification regardless of response time, and in [6] using the median of response times to notifications as a threshold for classifying the user as having "high" or "low" attentiveness to the messages they receive. Following the latter approach, we selected two thresholds for attentiveness to notifications: "*Extremely attentive*", using our median (T = 16 s) and "*Highly attentive*", using the average response time of T = 103 s and "*Moderately attentive*" using the T = 6.15 min threshold in [6]. Therefore we attempt to answer the question "Will the user respond to a given notification once it has been issued within, or outwith temporal threshold *T*?".

We aimed to examine how predictive modelling using the "*raw*" data set captured from our logging application compared to a synthesized data ("*synth*"), as well as an extended set of our synthesized data containing additional features ("*synth+*") that we thought might be interesting to investigate (Table 5). The synth dataset is directly

Table 5. Features used for classification. "Interactive-S" is the synthesized interactive state as shown in Table 3. Attentiveness is the *target* variable

Data set	Features	Values	Set size
Raw	Attentiveness	High | Low	12,612
	Hour	[0–23]	
	Interactive	True | False	
	LED	True | False	
	Sound	True | False	
	Vibration	True | False	
	Ringer mode	[Silent, Vibrate Only, Sound & Vibrate]	
	Screen state	[Off, On, Dozing]	
Synthetic	Attentiveness	High | Low	12,471
	Hour	[0–23]	
	Interactive-S	True | False	
	Modality	[− − −, - -V, -SV, LSV, -S-, LS-, L- -, L-V]	
Synthetic+	Attentiveness	High | Low	12,471
	Hour	[0–23]	
	Interactive-S	True | False	
	Modality	[− − −, - -V, -SV, LSV, -S-, LS-, L- -, L-V]	
	Lockscreen notifications	True | False	
	Package name	<string value>	
	User ID	[1–14]	

derived from the raw data, which can then be discarded to minimize the privacy risk to the user. For analysis, we used a range of classification algorithms (Naïve Bayes, SVM with Multiquadric kernel, Random Forest, NN). For each algorithm, a 10-fold cross-validation was performed using stratified sampling. The results are shown in Table 6.

The immediate observation from the above is that prediction performance is strongly dependent on the attentiveness level set as the classification target. All classifiers perform exceptionally well (even the computationally inexpensive ones like baseline Naïve Bayes and Decision Tree) at the "moderately attentive" threshold from literature. The result is explainable as this threshold is well above the average response time in our dataset. Interestingly, good performance is obtained for the 103 s "highly attentive" threshold, reaching close to 90% for all classifiers and independent of the feature set used, showing that it is possible to infer whether a user will engage with a notification within 103 s from issuing, with high accuracy. From there on, performance degrades to about 65% for all classifiers for the "extremely attentive" (16 s) threshold. Given that this threshold is the median of our dataset, the classifier's performance is considered to be better than random (50% chance), but still improvements might be possible to make in this regard (Fig. 7).

Table 6. Classification average F_1-score results

Classifier	Raw dataset	Synth dataset	Synth+ dataset
Bayes – 16 s	66.32%	66.40%	65.11%
Bayes – 103 s	71.97%	87.38%	87.57%
Bayes – 369 s	88.41%	95.32%	89.99%
RF – 16 s	66.67%	66.76%	67.03%
RF – 103 s	88.35%	88.35%	88.35%
RF – 369 s	95.42%	95.42%	95.42%
SVM – 16 s	67.12%	67.12%	67.12%
SVM – 103 s	88.35%	88.35%	88.35%
SVM – 369 s	95.42%	95.42%	95.42%
DT – 16 s	68.35%	66.79%	66.16%
DT – 103 s	88.17%	88.25%	88.04%
DT – 369 s	95.30%	95.40%	95.35%

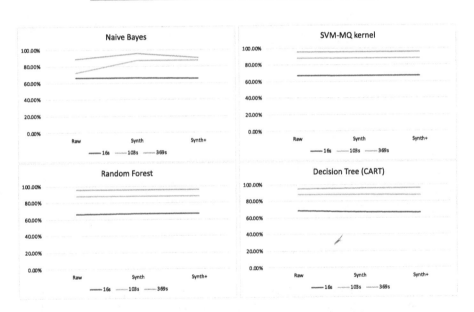

Fig. 7. Classification performance (F-score averages).

Apart from these findings, it should be considered that the obtained results emerge from a very limited feature set, compared to previous literature that presents results based on large feature sets. We show that the baseline performance using the raw feature set is maintained when reducing the features through sensible combination to just four (in the "Synth" dataset). Additional features in the "Synth+" dataset show no significant performance gain. This result hints that application type doesn't seem to strongly affect response times, thereby user responsiveness to notifications seems to be a *behavioral attitude* [3, Table 3] which covers all types of notification, rather than being selectively applied to certain types. We also note that user ID doesn't seem to improve performance, hinting that personalization of predictive models might not be necessary, at least for homogeneous population types such our participants. This result confirms the findings in [5] where it was found that personalized models only have benefits in very specific prediction targets and that general models are overall more successful.

To further investigate, we examine the most interesting case, i.e. the "Highly attentive" threshold on the "Synth" dataset (least features), using the output from the computationally cheap Decision Tree (Fig. 8). We notice that the most important feature is "*Interactive-S*". If the device is not in an interactive state, then the *Modality* is the most important feature. The results show that using all modalities (LSV) the user is attentive to the notifications. When using only vibration-type modality (L-V), the result is dependent on the *Hour* of day. For "silent" notifications (i.e. no modality or LED only) is most likely attentive to the notifications, and for "sound only", users seem not attentive.

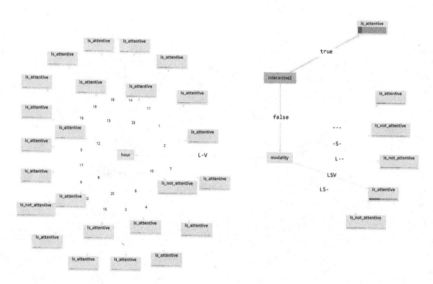

Fig. 8. Decision tree output (Synth dataset, 103 s threshold). The blue proportion is the % of cases labelled as "not attentive" and red are the "attentive" cases. Root node is highlighted blue. (Color figure online)

As a final step, we also used the decision tree modelling procedure with the "Synth" dataset, to perform regression on the dataset and examine the model's ability to predict the reaction time to notifications. With this procedure (10-fold cross validation) we achieve an average root mean squared error of $\mu = 212.857$ s ($\sigma = 11.306$ s), which is about 3.5 min. The mean predicted response time ($\mu = 102.91$ s, $\sigma = 64.77$) is quite similar to the actual response time mean ($\mu = 102.69$ s, $\sigma = 219.45$) but as expected, the distributions are quite different and is skewed towards "later" predictions. When grouping by the feature value combinations, the response time Δ_{RT} (predicted – actual) is greatest for feature values [Interactive-S = 0; modality = -S-; hour = 6]:668 s and [Interactive-S = 0; modality = LS-; hour = 14]: −1137 s. However, we note that these feature value combinations only have one instance. For reference, best performance is observed for feature values [Interactive-S = 1; modality = L-V; hour = 21]: −0.006 s (350 instances). When pruning the result set to include only those feature combinations whose instances make up for 95% of the dataset, and calculate the actual average $\Delta_{RT} = -3.41$ s ($\sigma = 39.68$) and $|\Delta_{RT}| = 20.03$ s ($\sigma = 34.37$ s). Therefore, we can claim that the *usable* prediction result of the regression modelling is actually quite good: We can predict the time of response to notifications of any type an accuracy spanning at most 1 min, using just 3 features (Fig. 9).

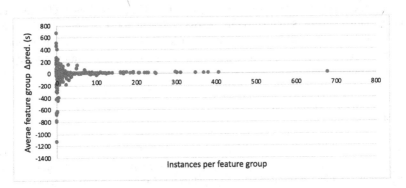

Fig. 9. With more instances per feature group, the average difference between actual and predicted response time converges to near zero.

6 Conclusions

As computational demands for resources in AmI environments increase in scale and complexity, a return to computing at the edge of the cloud is (somewhat ironically) seen by the community as the next forward step in context awareness [12]. The necessity of localized scalability and masking of uneven conditioning were foreseen in 2001 by [13], precisely to address the challenges of response time, battery life, bandwidth saving and data safety and privacy that edge computing aims to address.

Our exploration of real-world notifications is just the 2nd paper in literature (besides [10]) to address a body of notifications from all apps that a user has enabled on their device. In contrast with previous research, we have attempted to reduce the feature set for our classifier and prediction algorithms as much as possible. This approach results in lower storage, computational complexity, increased privacy for users and therefore better performance and power saving, if the classifiers and regressors are ran locally on the user device, as well as bandwidth saving if the data is uploaded for cloud processing. We demonstrate that "brute forcing" features into predictive models doesn't necessarily equate to better results, as we achieve very good outcomes in terms of both predicting the level of attentiveness and the actual response time to notifications, with just three synthesized features from a small number of raw data features (that can be discarded). The natural next step would be to explore the performance of our model in the wild, assessing its performance with unseen data and using it to drive intelligent notification deferment and modality choice policies. It would also be good to investigate gender aspects with a larger group of users, since in the current study, the group sizes are too small to provide adequate power for anything other than very large effects.

Our users were a homogeneous group and this places some limits on the generalizability of our findings beyond such users. However, this limitation also indicates that might be little need for personalized modelling in homogeneous user groups, which can overcome the "starting user" problem by partially sharing data between peers (e.g. groups of friends, relatives or the local community): in a sense, how we respond to notifications is, partly, a result of what others around us are doing. In future work we aim to examine privacy-preserving architectures for sharing such context and behaviour with new users transitioning across different local or regional cultures at different scales (e.g. tourists in new countries, or locals visiting a restaurant for the first time), in order to help devices automatically adapt their notification management support for users.

References

1. Okoshi, T., Tsubouchi, K., Taji, M., Ichikawa, T., Tokuda, H.: Attention and engagement-awareness in the wild: a large-scale study with adaptive notifications. In: 2017 IEEE International Conference on Pervasive Computing and Communications (PerCom), pp. 100–110 (2017)
2. Mehrotra, A., Pejovic, V., Vermeulen, J., Hendley, R., Musolesi, M.: My phone and me: understanding people's receptivity to mobile notifications. In: Proceedings of the 2016 CHI Conference on Human Factors in Computing Systems, pp. 1021–1032. ACM, New York (2016)
3. Anderson, C., Hübener, I., Seipp, A.-K., Ohly, S., David, K., Pejovic, V.: A survey of attention management systems in ubiquitous computing environments. arXiv:1806.06771 [cs] (2018)
4. Pielot, M., Cardoso, B., Katevas, K., Serrà, J., Matic, A., Oliver, N.: Beyond interruptibility: predicting opportune moments to engage mobile phone users. Proc. ACM Interact. Mob. Wearable Ubiquitous Technol. 1, 91:1–91:25 (2017)
5. Turner, L.D., Allen, S.M., Whitaker, R.M.: Reachable but not receptive: enhancing smartphone interruptibility prediction by modelling the extent of user engagement with notifications. Pervasive Mob. Comput. 40, 480–494 (2017)
6. Pielot, M., de Oliveira, R., Kwak, H., Oliver, N.: Didn't you see my message?: predicting attentiveness to mobile instant messages. In: Proceedings of the SIGCHI Conference on Human Factors in Computing Systems, pp. 3319–3328. ACM, New York (2014)
7. Poppinga, B., Heuten, W., Boll, S.: Sensor-based identification of opportune moments for triggering notifications. IEEE Pervasive Comput. 13, 22–29 (2014)
8. Okoshi, T., Ramos, J., Nozaki, H., Nakazawa, J., Dey, A.K., Tokuda, H.: Attelia: reducing user's cognitive load due to interruptive notifications on smart phones. In: 2015 IEEE International Conference on Pervasive Computing and Communications (PerCom), pp. 96–104 (2015)

 9. Turner, L.D., Allen, S.M., Whitaker, R.M.: Push or delay? Decomposing smartphone notification response behaviour. In: Salah, A.A., Kröse, B.J.A., Cook, D.J. (eds.) HBU 2015. LNCS, vol. 9277, pp. 69–83. Springer, Cham (2015). https://doi.org/10.1007/978-3-319-24195-1_6
10. Mehrotra, A., Musolesi, M., Hendley, R., Pejovic, V.: Designing content-driven intelligent notification mechanisms for mobile applications. In: Proceedings of the 2015 ACM International Joint Conference on Pervasive and Ubiquitous Computing, pp. 813–824. ACM, New York (2015)
11. Pielot, M., Church, K., de Oliveira, R.: An in-situ study of mobile phone notifications. In: Proceedings of the 16th International Conference on Human-computer Interaction with Mobile Devices & Services, pp. 233–242. ACM, New York (2014)
12. Shi, W., Cao, J., Zhang, Q., Li, Y., Xu, L.: Edge computing: vision and challenges. IEEE Internet Things J. 3, 637–646 (2016)
13. Satyanarayanan, M.: Pervasive computing: vision and challenges. IEEE Pers. Commun. 8, 10–17 (2001)

"Will the Last One Out, Please Turn off the Lights": Promoting Energy Awareness in Public Areas of Office Buildings

Joëlle Coutaz[1]([⊠]), Antonin Carlesso[2], Nicolas Bonnefond[2],
Raffaella Balzarini[2], Yann Laurillau[1], Nadine Mandran[1],
and James L. Crowley[2]

[1] Univ. Grenoble-Alpes, CNRS, Grenoble INP, LIG, 38000 Grenoble, France
{Joelle.Coutaz, Yann.Laurillau,
Nadine.Mandran}@univ-grenoble-alpes.fr
[2] Univ. Grenoble-Alpes, CNRS, Grenoble INP,
Inria, LIG 38000 Grenoble, France
{Antonin.Carlesso, Nicolas.Bonnefond,
Raffaella.Balzarini,
JamesL.Crowley}@univ-grenoble-alpes.fr

Abstract. Most previous research in sustainable HCI has focused on electricity consumption in domestic environments or private office spaces. Here, we address use of lighting in public areas of office buildings with the goal of understanding and measuring how calm technologies can inspire positive engagement by promoting awareness and competition. We have conducted a 15-month study with the design, deployment, and assessment of two complementary ambient apparatus (one centralized, one distributed) in an office building occupied by ICT start-up companies. Our results show that calm technology can be effective under specific conditions, resulting in a significant reduction of average electricity consumption. We also discovered that in the absence of automatic controls, approximately 25% of lighting consumption occurred during off-work hours.

Keywords: Eco-feedback · Ambient display · Calm technology
Energy consumption awareness · Persuasive technology · Sustainable HCI
Human-Building interaction · Office building

1 Introduction

Most research on energy consumption and lighting in office buildings has focused on the development of Building Management Systems (BMS) and energy efficient appliances, with focus on the use of electricity in the home [1, 4, 18, 23] or in private office spaces [5, 10, 14, 24]. In this paper, we address how awareness and competition can be harnessed to reduce consumption of lighting in shared public areas such as corridors and restrooms.

Collective control of lighting in shared public spaces requires occupants to shift from an individualistic selfish behavior, to a socially-conscious self-transcendent

A. Kameas and K. Stathis (Eds.): AmI 2018, LNCS 11249, pp. 20–36, 2018.
https://doi.org/10.1007/978-3-030-03062-9_2

behavior that includes concern for the well-being of others [12, 22]. Our goals in this research are to explore and understand how "calm" technologies can inspire such behavior, and to measure the impact of such technologies on occupants in terms of awareness and engagement. For this purpose, we have conducted a 15-month study involving three experimental conditions during which quantitative data have been recorded and compared to a baseline that covers the same period of the previous year. During this experiment, the occupants were not aware of the experiment.

A principal result is that a calm technology display can increase the awareness of electricity consumption in public areas, resulting in a significant reduction of average electricity consumption. We also discovered that during all the experiment, approximately 25% of lighting consumption occurred during off-work hours when the building was empty.

The article is organized as follows: we first review work from sustainable HCI as a background for persuasive technology and ambient awareness displays with particular attention to work on eco-feedback and design frameworks for the workplace. We then present the context of our study followed by a detailed description of the experimental process and the results. We close with a discussion of lessons learned and issues for future research.

2 Related Work

Sustainable HCI builds on research from a variety of domains [4], including "Ambient awareness" systems and "Persuasive technology" [17]. Ambient awareness systems employ calm technology to make users aware of the impact of their behavior. Persuasive systems draw on cognitive theories such as the Transtheoretical Model of Change [20] and Fogg's Behavioral Model [9] to invent ways to persuade users to behave in a sustainable way. In practice, there is a large overlap between ambient awareness displays and persuasive systems as exemplified by eco-feedback solutions and eco-visualization.

Eco-feedback solutions have often built on theories from environmental psychology [11]. For example, Schwartz's values theory predicts that the activation of self-transcendent intrinsic values is more effective and sustainable than self-enhancement extrinsic values [11, 15, 22]. As Weinstein has demonstrated in a controlled experiment, intrinsic aspirations and generosity can be activated by exposure to nature [25]. Nature inspired eco-visualization combined with informative art [6, 8, 21] has been used in the "7000 oaks and counting" project as a way to increase conservation behavior in a campus institutional building. However, to the best of our knowledge, this system has not been evaluated formally [13].

While many investigators have proposed designs for eco-visualization technologies in the home [1, 18, 23], few have explored the workplace. Notable exceptions include the "watts in it for me?" study [10], the Watt-lite display, and the EcOffices project. Over a three day-long workshop with a total of 65 participants from 5 universities, the "watts in it for me?" study produced a design framework that structures the problem space into 5 themes: visualisation, incentives, engagement, leadership, communication, and openness. Using this framework, the authors designed a layout for a display.

However, the design was not deployed or evaluated. The Watt-lite prototype was designed as a mediating object, projecting real time energy use on the floor to explore engagement and reflection with energy use [14]. The prototype was deployed four weeks in 8 factories. Preliminary results from that system show that social spaces are conducive for awareness. The EcOffices project has investigated the role of competition between workers for private office spaces [5].

Yun et al. [24] have demonstrated "an intelligent dashboard" that combines feedback on energy usage with online controls to remotely turn devices on and off and to set up automatic on/off controls at scheduled days and times. This system was evaluated with a 27 week-study with 4 groups of 20 participants (1 control group, and 3 groups provided with different levels of feedback and controls). Results showed that the addition of online controls improved savings. Unlike our study, this work was focused on office spaces, rather than public spaces in office buildings.

3 Context of the Study: A Real World Experimental Setting

3.1 The Office Building

This study was conducted in a three story 1200 m^2 building that serves as a living lab for research in smart object technologies, as well as a technology incubator and workplace for start-ups. The ground floor includes an open space with a cafeteria and a large entrance hall that provides access to 36 offices on the two upper floors. These upper floors have provided the arena for our experiments.

The two upper floors are well suited for conducting comparative experiments: they are very similar in terms of number of offices, and their public areas are identical with each floor having two hallways, two restrooms, and one meeting room. Similarly, the location and number of lights and switches are identical, and both floors have excellent natural lighting conditions during daylight hours.

3.2 The Occupants and the Financial Conditions

The offices are available to start-ups companies specialized in the development of Information and Technologies (ICT) with applications ranging from innovative cameras and sensors for medical applications, to novel solutions for networking and 3D graphics. The space is used by approximately 50 persons, including company founders, R&D engineers, hardware and software developers. Most occupants are highly qualified and work under tight time constraints. Rental conditions are based on the surface occupied with a rate per square meter that includes energy and water consumption. Thus, building occupants have no direct interest in reducing energy costs.

3.3 Data Recording

The building is a perpetual sensing device, instrumented with a BMS platform that continuously measures electricity consumption, temperature, and human presence in all areas of the building. This system records 1200 data values every ten minutes, including readings from 50 electric meters, 8 water meters, and 47 environmental controllers installed in each office. Data is automatically recorded for research purposes in a secure server. For ethical reasons, we have limited our data records and analysis to the electricity consumption of the public area of the first and second floors, excluding all data related to private spaces and presence detection.

Although the building is well instrumented, lighting in both public and private areas of the upper floors is manually controlled with mechanical light switches. Actions on light switches cannot be directly detected, and the occupants are fully responsible for switching these lights on and off.

4   The Research Process

Our five-phase study covered 15 months, starting early March 2017 and ending mid-May 2018. The first two phases served as preliminary field studies to inform the design of our eco-feedback techniques deployed in the next 3 phases. During this period, the building was occupied by the same 17 start-ups with some minor turnover of employees. Occupants were not made aware of the nature of our study. In the following, we describe the phases in more detail along with their justification and implications for the next phase.

4.1   Phase 0: Initial Field Inquiry

Experimental Conditions. The purpose of this phase was to collect occupants' view and attitude to energy savings related to both the workplace and their everyday life. Occupants were invited by email to fill in an online questionnaire. This questionnaire included 17 questions as well as entries for free expression, covering three topics: (1) Perception and control of comfort in the office as well as of lighting in the public areas of the building; (2) Usefulness and potential impact of real time visualization of the building consumption; and (3) Reward that would favor behavioral change.

The Results. We received 19 answers (63% male, 37% female) of which 90% had worked in the building for more than 6 months[1]. The principal results were:

- 70% of the respondents use public transportation, bicycle or car-pooling.
- The majority (15 out of 19) has observed that the lights are on for no reason in the public areas, and 12 of them claimed that they generally turn them off when not used. Interestingly, two respondents commented: "*It would be highly appreciated that the building does not stay lit up H24, typically on week-ends when no-one is at work*". "*Corridors and cafeteria are always on.*" On the other hand, almost no one had any idea of the electricity consumption of the building.
- To the question "Would you be in favor of a device that displays energy consumption of the building in real time (e.g. screen in the entrance hall, smartphone

---

[1] As the invitation was performed via a mailing list managed by the owner of the building, we do not know the exact number of occupants who received our message.

App, etc.)?" 15 occupants supported this idea whereas 3 out of 19 stated that they did not appreciate it, as: "*a screen in the entrance hall would consume too much just to show the consumption of the building*". 12 of them (63%) thought that this would have a positive impact on their own behavior, but the impact would be very unlikely on the other occupants.

- Reducing the carbon footprint is the primary incentive to behavioral change of the respondents whereas monetary reward (i.e. reducing rental cost) received only 7 favorable votes. One respondent commented: "*I am opposed to rewarding people for an action that should be evident for all.*" In addition, socializing was not considered to be an effective reward as no one selected the option "organizing a party with the occupants of the building" and 10 out of 19 voted for "not at all" and "very unlikely".

Conclusions and Implications for the Next Phase. The majority of the respondents showed clear concerns for sustainability. They observed that the lights are on uselessly, they felt responsible for turning the lights off in the public areas, they were not looking for monetary rewards, they tended to think that the "others are at-fault" [2], and that a screen display would be a waste just to show electricity consumption.

Our conclusions from Phase 0 were that the office environment of a technology incubator provides a challenging context for designing an apparatus that would encourage people to reduce lighting usage. Providing the occupants with real-time quantitative information is the obvious minimalist way to support awareness [10]. However, it was unclear whether typical visualization techniques were sufficient to promote curiosity and to maintain interest of busy people. Inspired by the principles of informative art [6, 8, 21], we hypothesized that "designing for the periphery" with the use of an additional layer of abstract expression to encourage moments of reflection, would be an appropriate option to address these issues. This became the focus for Phase 1.

4.2   Phase 1: Exposure to Abstract Representations

Design Rationale and Description. The goal of this phase was to collect occupants' reactions to abstract representations of quantitative data. Among the alternative forms of abstraction, particles have simple properties such as density, color, and size that can easily be used to display quantitative information. In addition, they can be animated in multiple ways to amplify the expression of a dynamic phenomenon.

We explored three particle-based representations: a "heart-beat" display where particles are blown away from a central point, a "smoke-stack" which combines particles (the smoke) with a picture of the office building, and a "snow-fall" display whose particles fall from the top of the screen (see Fig. 1). The smoke stack was rendered as augmenting an outside view of the building displayed with the surrounding mountains on a sunny day so that the occupants would be inspired to see their workplace as a collective space to be preserved.

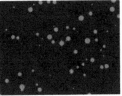

Fig. 1. The "heart-beat" (left). The "smoke-stack" (center). The snow-fall (right).

Experimental Conditions. The displays were presented on a large screen strategically located in the entrance hall adjacent to the cafeteria. The screen was visible from a distance to anyone passing through the hallway, as well as by people having lunch or taking coffee breaks. The occupants were not informed about the nature of the data represented, as the objective of this phase was to collect instantaneous reactions and personal emotional expressions. Occupants were invited to leave anonymous reactions to the displays on post-it notes.

Using a Wizard of Oz technique, the displays were selected serendipitously, with changes of color, size and density of the particles about six times per day. Comments on post-it notes were collected whenever the experimental condition had been modified. In addition, the wizard took notes about his own informal observations while discretely remaining in the area near the screen.

Qualitative Analysis. We collected 50 post-it notes over the six-week duration of Phase 1: 24 notes for the snow-fall display, 22 for the heart-beat, and 4 for the smoke-stack. Overall, the reactions can be grouped into five themes:

- Technology denial and/or concerns for the environment (5 post-its). For example, *"a screen that is of no use"*, *"a loss and waste of energy"*, *"a screen saver"* and, associated to the smoke-stack, *"pollution!!!"*
- Science-inspired imagination, mainly from the magnetic field (9 notes), typically related to the heart-beat: *"a magnetic nucleus"*, *"electrons orbiting an atom"*, *"Newton"*, *"a Tokamac (magnetic confinement)"*, *"particles in a coil"*.
- Nature-inspired imagination (9 notes) including animals (*"a jelly fish"*), plants (*"a dandelion"* and *"rose petals"*), or natural elements (mainly for the snow-fall" representation): *"snow"*, *"rain"*, *"cascades"* and the *"fountain of Versailles"*.
- Culture and leisure-inspired imagination (7 notes), typically, food experience related to the heart-beat (*"a 3D pop-corn machine"*, *"an apple dough-nut"*), cinema for the snow-fall (*"Star Wars"*, *"The Big Blue"*), and travel for the smoke-stack: *"a cruise ship"*, *"Costa cruise liners"*, *"Tintin in Tibet"*.
- Violent and destructive expressions, such as notes stating *"blood"* for the snow-fall display with fast falling large red particles.

In addition, 3 post-it notes, confirmed by the wizard's observations, indicate that occupants were influenced by an implicit culture of "IoT" and "experimental" ambience specific to the building. For example: *"A visual projection that depends on the number of persons in the building: the more people are present, the more dense is the visual*", or the "*animations evolve depending on the weather or the time of the day*". Interestingly, one post-it refers to the "*Roschach test*", a psychological test originally used to detect thought disorder by exposing subjects to specific inkblots, then used to identify a person's personality and emotional functioning. As for the wizard, he observed that "*people clap their hands hoping that the device will react*" or some of them "*look behind the screen to check the connections, trying to understand how the device works*".

Conclusions and Implications for the Next Phase. The key lessons for the design of incentive ambient apparatus drawn from this phase were: (1) The concept of animated particles as an abstract layer of information encourages reflection and is sufficiently rich to express a variety of phenomena while making it easy for people to understand the mapping between the properties of the particles and the information to be represented; (2) Under some conditions, particles may evoke violence and destructive feelings; (3) Interactivity is expected; and (4) For the apparatus to support "Sustainability through Design" (StD) [16], it must also be "Sustainable by Design" (SbD).

The requirement for both StD and SbD has led us to investigate two alternative approaches (1) A unique exemplar of a centralized ambient interactive apparatus located at a strategic place, useful and attractive enough to help offset "*the waste of energy*" criticized by a number of occupants; (2) A distributed sustainable incentive solution that would not consume any energy and located where the action is, that is, in this context of use, at the light switch level. These have been explored in phases 2 and 4.

4.3   Phases 2 and 3: Central Ambient Display and Friendly Competition

Phases 2 and 3 concerned the effectiveness of a central ambient display suggesting a friendly competition for energy savings. We have adapted Bartram's design dimensions [1] as a systematic framework for structuring our design questions: What are the appropriate data and motivational strategies to support positive engagement and various forms of knowledge (i.e. awareness, analytical, operational)? What attentional effort and interactivity are required from the occupants? When and where is data consumed? Table 1 summarizes the justification of our design choices.

Table 1. Design questions and justification of the design choices for the ambient display

Dimension	Design choice and justification
Data	Engineering measures aggregated at multiple temporal scales (current, hour, day, week) for supporting awareness of energy consumption, for provisioning actionable cues including self-monitoring
Attentional effort	Ambient display for low attention demand, at-a-glance sense making supported by the histo-trees
Interactivity	Passive interaction complemented with one single push-down action for accessing additional analytic knowledge on demand

(continued)

Table 1. (*continued*)

Dimension	Design choice and justification
Motivation and engagement to sustainability	Nature-inspired histo-trees metaphor to activate intrinsic motivation. Friendly competition based on social comparison between the two floors to reinforce positive behavior. Goal setting capability using last year consumption as an intra-floor norm. Visual positive appeal of the histo-trees and tangible data provided by the cairns board
Spatio-temporal context	Standalone always on apparatus as an integral part of the workplace at a strategic hot spot of the building (entrance hall and near the cafeteria)

Description. As shown in Fig. 2, the ambient apparatus included:

- A large wall-mounted antiglare screen placed at a carefully identified location in the building so that the apparatus is easily visible to passing persons.
- A soft padding push-button and a Cairns board, both built for this experiment by the research team.
- A mini-PC connected to the BMS for data acquisition, aggregation and rendering, as well as for logging the press and release events that resulted from the users' actions on the push-button.

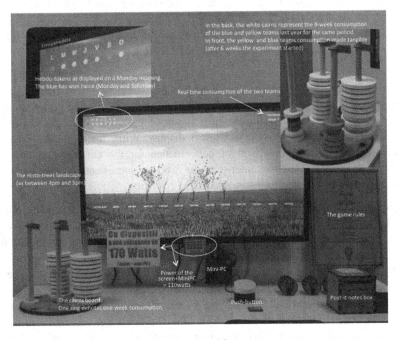

Fig. 2. The central ambient apparatus.

The computational system was completed with information printed on wooden panels: below the screen, the power of the apparatus (i.e. 170 watts) presented to inform occupants of energy consumption by the system; on the left hand side, the mapping used to translate raw electricity consumption into colored wooden discs (cairns board) with a radius inversely proportional to weekly consumption (an advanced computerized version of the same idea has been developed by Daniel et al. [3]). On the right end-side, the rules of the game "Challenge the switch" were displayed engraved in wood. The game presented each floor as a team represented by a color (yellow or blue). The winning team was the floor that used the least amount of electricity for each hour and each day.

The screen permanently displayed three types of information using three types of representation, chosen to communicate three different perspectives: utilitarian, nature-inspired, and symbolic:

- The utilitarian representation provided a real time display of the *current consumption* of the two floors expressed in watts. The engineering measure used (i.e. watts) was intended for ICT occupants who, according to the results from Phase 0, had no idea of the electricity consumption of the building.
- The nature-inspired expression presented a record of the last 13-h of consumption using *histo-trees*. A colored tree for the "winner of the hour" was displayed for each hour (from 8 am to 9 pm), along with a tree corresponding to the consumption during the previous night (i.e. the off duty hours from 9 pm to 8 am). The height and fullness of the trees were rendered in proportion to the virtue of the winning team. The branches of the trees swayed gently as if in a light breeze, creating a peaceful ambience. As the hours went by, the observers could get at-a-glance the overall trend of the day.
- Cumulative daily consumption for each team was rendered with tokens (*hebdo-tokens*), so that daily and weekly trends were visible.

A large push-button provided access to additional information about energy use: While the button remained pressed, a classic bar histogram was displayed so that the players could compare their electricity consumption with that of their competitors and possibly adjust their behavior for the next hours of the day. When the button was released, the screen returned to the histo-trees display. While the numerical histogram supported hourly-based comparison of performance for the current day, the cairns board was intended to support inter-team as well as intra-team comparisons on a weekly basis, using physicality as incentives to curiosity.

Experimental Conditions. As in previous phase, the ambient display was installed at a socializing spot, in the entrance hall and near the cafeteria. The functioning of the ambient device as well as the rules of the game were presented at a convivial "think drink" social event organized in the cafeteria, the evening before the experiment started. Of the 20 attendees, 3 occupants of the building participated in the social event.

During the nine-week trial of this Phase 2, the electricity consumption of the public area of the two floors was collected as well as the time-stamped events resulting from the press and release actions on the push-button. The event log was intended to trace the occupants' interest and involvement over time. As occupants were not aware they were involved in an experiment, the use of a camera and microphone to record emotions and attitude was excluded. Every Monday morning, colored discs of the appropriate size were added to the cairns for each team.

Qualitative Data Analysis. We conducted 21 semi-structured interviews, two to four weeks after the end of this phase, during the Phase 3-no-feedback period. Participants were recruited serendipitously near the cafeteria or the entrance hall of the building. All interviews – 15 to 20 min each, were audio-recorded and analyzed using the design choices of Table 1 as coding themes. Table 2 provides some examples of the occupants' reaction structured according to these themes where texts in italic denote suggestions for improvement.

Overall, the design of the ambient apparatus was well received by the occupants. In particular, the association of the pure utilitarian engineering measures with the positive visual appeal of the nature-inspired histo-trees worked well. The low-cost interactivity was appropriate. The social framing drawn from the friendly competition worked well "*at the beginning*". Although three persons indicated that the device "*belonged to the landscape*" or has become "*part of the every day life*", although they kept "*glancing at it once or twice a day at coffee breaks and lunch time*", four participants observed a decline of interest as "*the days became similar*".

All interviewees asserted that they had not modified their behavior after the end of this phase, as they "*never turn the light switches on*" and they "*switch the lights off in the hallway* [not that of the others, though] if they believe that they are "*the last one leaving the building*". Four occupants suggested transferring the responsibility to automation with timers and presence sensors. Although some of the occupants have noticed that, since Phase2, "*the corridors are always off*", it was unclear, at this point of the study, whether the ambient apparatus had activated or reinforced positive behavior.

Table 2. Verbatim as qualitative assessment of the ambient apparatus features.

Engineering measures
• Support for energy consumption awareness and understanding: "There was the current consumption for each floor in watts. It was interesting. It was useful." [P9, P13, P10] "I saw that corridors consumed 3000 watts, this is enormous, just for corridors!" [P5]
• Complementarity with the figurative representation: "to clearly see the numbers behind the trees" [P5]. "I tried to understand how the trees were generated. As a result, I looked at the data and I understood what was meant. It's good to have visibility on data." [P9]
• Missing measures for analytic knowledge: *"I would have liked to have a kind of a chart about a period that one could choose (week or month)...This is the kind of useful statistics depending on the weather conditions (sun, snow, rain)"* [P7]
• Missing measures for supporting the competition: *"It was difficult to assess which team was currently first within the current hour or within the current day. Thus, we did not know whether the situation was recoverable to win and make an effort to switch the lights off* [P17]

Attentional effort, at-a-glance sense making
"I would take a look every time I went by" [P5, P6, P9, P13,P12]. "One could check the evolution based on colors [of the trees] [P13]

(continued)

Table 2. (*continued*)

Interactivity – Use of the push down button and analytic knowledge

Affordance and self-monitoring: "There was a button, thus we felt compelled to press it to see what it did" [P1, P23]. "I pressed the button to check the tendency of the day at the building level" [P7, P5]

Motivation and engagement to sustainability through the Histo-trees

• Positive visual appeal and appropriate mapping with numerical data: "well done and fun" [P3, P21, P17, P11. "A good idea" [P18-19-20]. "This was good. I remember it. This means it left a mark" [P12]. I found this [the trees] rather nice, ... a playful indication" [P7]. "The less electricity is used, higher is the tree, otherwise a tree would not have been chosen" [P7, P10, P5]

• Potential for activating intrinsic motivation: " I appreciated the ecological aspect" [P10]. "It evokes nature... In addition, they [the trees] moved." [P13]

Motivation and engagement to sustainability: Friendly competition and social comparison

"Competing with the other floor has a nice feeling, *at the beginning*"[P7]. "*At the beginning*, it [the game] was interesting for the competition aspect" [P15]. We could also see which floor used the most energy." [P13] or "how we were doing" [P15-P16]. "Ah! We are first. Ah! We are good!" [P6]. "We are the best" [P11]

Motivation and engagement to sustainability: Cairns tangible data and social comparison

"This [the cairns] was to compare with the consumption last year. Thus, this was interesting." [P13]. "We have supposed that it was a physical version of histograms. We have compared with last year. We have consumed a lot less. Why?" [P15, P16]. "I think you added a ring at the end of every week to see the difference between the two floors" [P5]
Not noticed [P6]. Not understood [P11]. "I tried to move a disk to another pile but I did not know what I was doing. I was expected it to be computerized" [P8]. "I did not understand right away" [P9]

Spatio-temporal context

The location of the apparatus was appropriate except for 5 occupants who never go to the cafeteria: "I noticed it from the distance, but when I come in, I go straight to my office" or "*the device was not on our way so, ...*". On the other hand, for the other occupants "Typically, while coffee was getting ready, I went by the screen to check the situation" or "every lunch" or "coffee breaks" [P10, P12, P13, P6]

4.4   Phase 4: Augmented Sustainable Light Switches

Design Rationale and Description. The light switches of the building – white on white walls, are nearly invisible when illuminated with direct sunlight and very hard to see at dusk. There was obviously room for improving their perceivable affordance by turning them into gentle non-obtrusive reminders. Phase 4 sought to assess the effectiveness of drawing attention to the light switches. The hypothesis was that this approach should be more effective on reducing lighting reduction than that of Phase 2 as it is located where the action is. In addition, this approach is fully sustainable and easily reproducible.

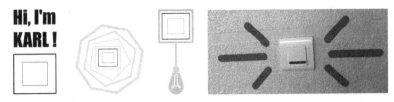

Fig. 3. Design options for light switch augmentation (from left to right): personification, waves propagating from the switch, hanging light bulb, glare of light.

Figure 3 shows several design options. The "glare of light" enhancement on the right was assessed as the most neutral and aesthetically appealing design by a number of our colleagues and was installed in the public areas accordingly.

Experimental Conditions. Reusing the concept of "yellow floor" and "blue floor", the light switches were enhanced with the corresponding colored stickers for each floor. The occupants were not informed that the experiment was still going on. In parallel, data about electricity consumption for each floor was recorded by the BMS.

5 Analysis of the Data Logged from Phases 2, 3, and 4

Raw data logs provided by the BMS over the 27 weeks of phases 2, 3, and 4 were preprocessed to check data quality and to produce data in a format appropriate for the analysis. This process has resulted in individual data files per floor and per phase, giving hourly and daily consumption. In addition, times of push and release of the push-button allowed for the analysis of occupants' interaction with the apparatus.

The occupants actively used the push-button in the first 4 weeks of Phase 2. Engagement decreased as time passed, partly due to Christmas and New Year vacation, as well as a decline of interest as reported by some occupants (cf. Sect. 4.3). As shown in Fig. 4, both for weekdays and weekends, the hourly consumptions average of the two floors were significantly lower in the three experimental conditions than for the base-line periods. In addition, these averages continued to decrease with time throughout Phases 2, 3, and 4. Interestingly, Floor 2, which was initially the highest consumer, became the most virtuous during the final phase. Meanwhile, weekend hourly consumption for the 1st floor overtook that of weekday. More generally, the chart of Fig. 4 also shows that the "weekend" columns denote higher consumption compared to workdays.

The decrease of hourly consumption across the three phases is consistent with the increase of daylight between mid-November and mid-May: while in Phase 2 as well as for half of Phase 3, people arrive before sunrise and leave after sunset. This changed during the second half of Phase 3 and Phase 4 as the days grew longer.

The seasonal effect can be alleviated using ratios as illustrated in Fig. 5. We observe that weekend consumption was as much as 36% of the total consumption (cf. Floor 1, phase 4). Figure 6 shows the distribution of consumption within workdays. Interestingly, off-work hours can represent up to 45% of workdays consumption

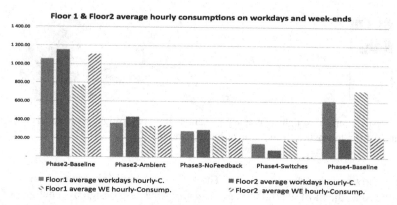

Floor 1 & Floor2 average hourly consumptions on workdays and week-ends

- Floor1 average workdays hourly-C.
- Floor1 average WE hourly-Consump.
- Floor2 average workdays hourly-C.
- Floor2 average WE hourly-Consump.

Fig. 4. Workdays VS weekends average hourly consumption for the 3 conditions and for the baselines used for phases 2 and 4 (i.e. the left-most and right-most group respectively).

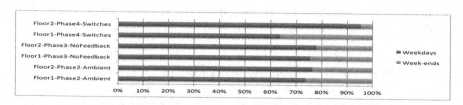

Fig. 5. Ratio (%) between workdays and weekends total consumption for the 3 conditions.

(cf. Floor 1, Phase 3). Going one step further, Fig. 7 shows in detail the number of times lights are left on in corridors and toilets during weekends and weekdays off-work hours. It shows that, for the 3 phases, the lights were left on in the corridors more often than in the toilets for Floor 1, whereas for Floor 2, this trend is reversed in Phase 4 where the corridors are generally switched off and the toilets become the main source of wasted consumption.

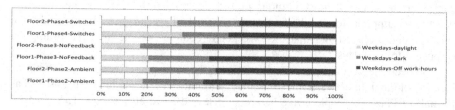

Fig. 6. Distribution of lighting consumption (%) within workdays.

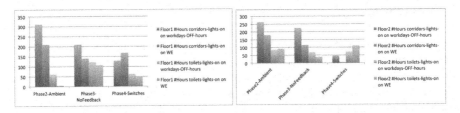

Fig. 7. Nb of hours lights are on uselessly in corridors & toilets – Floor 1(left), Floor 2 (right).

6   Discussion

Summary of the Findings. The data logs reveal a significant decrease in electricity consumption compared to the same period over the previous year of the experiment. One possible explanation is the evolution of the general socio-political context with an increase of concerns for sustainability. However, we believe that our experiments may also have played a role.

Interestingly, the number of hours that the lights are left on uselessly, for both weekends and night-time off-hours, decreased steadily over the 27-week trial. This measurement indicates that the apparatus has served as a seed for more positive behavior, contradicting interview statements by occupants that the ambient display did not influence their attitude towards sustainable behavior. The decrease of consumption from phases 2 to 3 is consistent with Cialdini's influence principles according to which humans tend to invent reasons to justify their actions "after the fact" [2].

We also note that the augmented light switches appear to be more effective than the ambient display. This is likely to occur because the augmented light switches provide actionable reminders in context. In Fogg's terms, they acted as facilitators that increase ability, thus lowering the action line threshold [9]. This is particularly clear for the occupants of the second floor who were initially the highest consumers. However, for this floor, the toilets, which are not on the way when leaving the building, became the principal source of useless consumption.

Limitations and Caveats. The order of the phase 2 and phase 4 trials may have affected the results in favor of the augmented light switch approach due to a possible increase in awareness. Nevertheless, the "augmented switch" idea is fully Sustainable-by-Design and so simple to implement that it provides a promising approach for future research.

The study was conducted in a relatively small building (36 offices) where it was not possible to control and identify the exact turnover of the employees. However, this limitation is counter-balanced by the real-world conditions of the experiment, as the occupants, who were unaware of their involvement in an experiment, were not tempted to act to please the researchers.

7 Conclusion

We have conducted a 15-month study on lighting consumption in the public spaces of a 36-office building occupied by ICT start-ups. This study included a 27 week-trial to assess the effectiveness of two complementary forms of ambient techniques (i.e. centralized VS distributed). Results appear to confirm previous work from environmental psychology or scattered in the literature related to eco-feedback technologies developed for the domestic environment. Unlike previous work on office workplaces, we have addressed consumption for lighting in shared public spaces of office buildings, and the 50 occupants of the trial were not aware they were involved in an experiment – i.e. they acted under no experimental constraint, were not given a task to perform, and where not generally observed when exposed to the two ambient apparatus.

The lessons and take-away messages from this study are three-fold

(1) The *"distributed-augmented switch-where the action is"* approach works as an effective facilitator. It is fully sustainable-by-design (SbD), cheap to produce and easily deployable. On the other hand, it does not mirror the current lighting consumption

(2) The *"centralized-friendly competition-ambient display"* approach is less SbD and more complex to deploy, but offers additional benefits provided that: (a) it is installed within a socializing space to favor engagement; (b) it supports glanceable sense-making to minimize attentional effort from busy people; (c) it combines engineering measures at multiple temporal scales (for provisioning actionable cues) with nature-based figurative aesthetic representations to activate intrinsic motivation and visual appeal; (d) it supports intra- and inter-social comparison as well as goal-setting to reinforce positive behavior; (e) it complements passive interaction with minimalist interaction techniques to access analytic knowledge on demand; (f) its behavior has to be consistent with that expected from the occupants (as one occupant remarked, *"I went by during Xmas vacation, and only one thing that was turned on was the screen. It breaks something! "*)

(3) Following Dourish's observation, scaling up the context should be considered as an important factor [7]. For example, in our case, maintenance, cleaning and supplies for the cafeteria and restrooms are provided by the local city government that owns the building. If these services are not sufficient, then as two occupants reported *"there is no point to make effort in conserving energy for these people* [the local government] *when there is no dish-soap."*

In addition, informing people – in a non-obtrusive but effective way, that *they are the last one to leave* is clearly key as this feature serves not only reducing electricity consumption in the public spaces but security as well (e.g. turning the intrusion detector security on/off during off-work hours as this is the case in the building of our study). This remains for future study.

Acknowledgement. This work was made possible with the support of the EquipEx Ami-Qual4Home ANR-11-EQPX-00 and the ANR-15-IDEX-02 as the cross-disciplinary project Eco-SESA. We thank the occupants of the building for their participation as well as Daniel Llerena, professor in experimental economy, for suggesting the friendly competition game approach, and

M. Yuiko, D. Shiffman, and R. Chao for their contribution to the particles and the tree available from the Processing web site [19].

References

1. Bartram, L.: Designing challenges and opportunities for eco-feedback in the home. In: Personal Visualization and Personal Visual Analytics July/August 2015, IEEE Computer Society, pp. 52–62 (2015)
2. Cialdini, R.: Influence: The Psychology of Persuasion (1984)
3. Daniel, M., Rivière, G., Couture, N.: Designing an expandable illuminated ring to build an actuated ring chart. In: Proceedings of 12th International Conference on Tangible, Embedded and Embodied Interactions (TEI 2018), pp. 140–147. ACM, Stockholm (2018)
4. DiSalvo, C., Sengers, P., Brynjarsdóttir, H.: Mapping the landscape of sustainable HCI. In: Proceedings of the SIGCHI Conference on Human Factors in Computing Systems, CHI 2010, pp. 1975–1984. ACM, Atlanta (2010)
5. Decorme, R., Zarli, A., Trousse, B., Senach, B.: Improving energy awareness and use in office buildings: the ICT-enables ECOFFICES challenge. In: Proceedings of International Conference on Computing in Civiland Building, ICCCBE 2012, Moscow, Russia (2012)
6. DiSalvo, C., Boehner, K., Knouf, N., Sengers, P.: Nourishing the ground for sustainable HCI: considerations from ecologically engaged art. In: Proceedings of the SIGCHI Conference on Human Factors in Computing Systems, CHI 2009, pp. 385–394. ACM, Boston (2009)
7. Dourish, P.: HCI and environmental sustainability: the politics of design and the design of politics. In: Proceedings of the 8th Conference on Designing Interactive Systems DIS 2010, pp. 1–10. ACM, Aarhus (2010)
8. Ferscha, A.: Informative art display metaphors. In: Stephanidis, C. (ed.) UAHCI 2007. LNCS, vol. 4555, pp. 82–92. Springer, Heidelberg (2007). https://doi.org/10.1007/978-3-540-73281-5_9
9. Fogg, B.J.: A behavior model for persuasive design. In: Proceedings of 4th International Conference on Persuasive technology, Persuasive 2009. ACM, Claremont (2009)
10. Foster, D., Lawson, S., Linehan, C., Wardman, J.: 'Watts in it for me': design implications for implementing effective energy interventions in organisations. In: Proceedings of the SIGCHI Conference on Human Factors in Computing Systems CHI 2012, pp. 2357–2366. ACM, Austin (2012)
11. Froehlich, J., Findlater, L., Landay, J.: The design of eco-feedback technology. In: Proceedings of the SIGCHI Conference on Human Factors in Computing Systems CHI 2010. ACM, Atlanta (2010)
12. Holmes, T., Blackmore, E., Hawkins, R.: The Common Cause Handbook: A Guide to Values and Frames, Public Interest Research Centre Ltd. (2011)
13. Holmes, T.: Eco-visualization: combining art and technology to reduce energy comsumption. In: Creativity and Cognition Conference 2007, pp. 153–162. ACM, Washington (2007)
14. Jönson, L., Broms, L., Katzeff, C.: Watt-Lite: energy statistics made tangible. In: Proceedings of DIS 2010, pp. 240–243. ACM, Aarhus (2010)
15. Knowles, B.: Re-imagining persuasion: designing for self-transcendence. In: Proceedings of the SIGCHI Conference on Human Factors in Computing Systems Extended Abstracts, CHI EA 2013, pp. 2713–2718. ACM, Paris (2013)

16. Mankoff, J., et al.: Environmental sustainability and interaction. In: Proceedings of the SIGCHI Conference on Human Factors in Computing Systems Extended Abstracts, CHI EA 2007, pp. 2121–2124. ACM, San José (2007)

17. Oinas-Kukkonen, H.: Harjumaa: persuasive systems design: key issues, process model, and system features. Commun. Assoc. Inf. Syst. **24**, 485–500 (2009)

18. Pierce, J., Paulos, E.: Beyond energy monitors: interaction, energy, and emerging energy systems. In: Proceedings of the SIGCHI Conference on Human Factors in Computing Systems CHI 2012, pp. 665–674. ACM, Austin (2012)

19. Processing home page. https://processing.org. Accessed 11 June 2018

20. Prochaska, J., DiClemente, C., Norcross, J.: In search of how people change: application to addictive behaviors. Am. Psychol. **47**(9), 1102–1114 (1992)

21. Redström, J., Skog, T., Hallnäs, L.: Informative art: using amplified artwork as information displays. In: Proceedings of Designing Augmented Reality Environments, DARE 2000, pp. 103–114. ACM, Elsinore (2000)

22. Schwartz, S.: Universals in the content and structure of values: theoretical advances and empirical tests in 20 countries. In: Advances in Experimental Social Psychology, vol. 25, pp. 1–65 (1992)

23. Yang, R., Newman, M.W., Forlizzi, J.: Making sustainability sustainable: challenges in the design of eco-interaction technologies. In: Proceedings of the SIGCHI Conference on Human Factors in Computing Systems, CHI 2014, pp. 216–117. ACM, Toronto (2014)

24. Yun, R., Aziz, A., Scupelli, P., Lasternas, B., Zhang, C., Loftness, V.: Beyond eco-feedback: adding online manual and automated controls to promote workplace sustainability. In: Proceedings of the SIGCHI Conference on Human Factors in Computing Systems, CHI 2015, pp. 1989–1992. ACM, Seoul (2015)

25. Weinstein, N., Przybylski, A., Ryan, R.: Can nature make us more caring? Effects of immersion in nature on intrinsic aspirations and generosity. Soc. Pers. Soc. Psychol. Bull. **35**(10), 1315–1329 (2009)

The UbiCARS Model-Driven Framework: Automating Development of Recommender Systems for Commerce

Christos Mettouris[1]([✉]), Achilleas Achilleos[2], Georgia Kapitsaki[1], and George A. Papadopoulos[1]

[1] Department of Computer Science, University of Cyprus, 2109 Nicosia, Cyprus
{mettour, gkapi, george}@cs.ucy.ac.cy
[2] Frederick University, 7 Y. Frederickou Str, 1036 Nicosia, Cyprus
com.aa@frederick.ac.cy

Abstract. Recommendations of products to customers are proved to boost sales, increase customer satisfaction and improve user experience, making recommender systems an important tool for retail businesses. With recent technological advancements in AmI and Ubiquitous Computing, the benefits of recommender systems can be enjoyed not only in e-commerce, but in the physical store scenario as well. However, developing effective context-aware recommender systems by non-expert practitioners is not an easy task due to the complexity of building the necessary data models and selecting and configuring recommendation algorithms. In this paper we apply the Model Driven Development paradigm on the physical commerce recommendation domain by defining a UbiCARS Domain Specific Modelling Language, a modelling editor and a system, that aim to reduce complexity, abstract the technical details and expedite the development and application of State-of-the-Art recommender systems in ubiquitous environments (physical retail stores), as well as to enable practitioners to utilize additional data resulting from ubiquitous user-product interaction in the recommendation process to improve recommendation accuracy.

Keywords: Ubiquitous product recommendation
Intelligent recommendations in physical stores · UbiCARS · Modelling

1 Introduction

As customers nowadays have the option to select from a huge variety of high quality products at competitive prices, retailers are in need to provide better service to win the trust of customers and achieve a sustainable customer relationship. Information systems can play a significant role in "sensing" what customers like and the sales trend. When information systems are not used and thus information cannot be acquired immediately, customer demands cannot be met in real time, risking losing customers' interest in shopping [1]. As [1] notes, with the change of market patterns and customer demand, it is particularly necessary for the retail industry to provide a pleasing, safe and convenient shopping environment, with consideration for customers.

© Springer Nature Switzerland AG 2018
A. Kameas and K. Stathis (Eds.): AmI 2018, LNCS 11249, pp. 37–53, 2018.
https://doi.org/10.1007/978-3-030-03062-9_3

Ambient intelligence (AmI) and ubiquitous computing characterize intelligent, pervasive and unobtrusive computer systems embedded into human environments, tailored to the individual's context-aware needs [2]. While AmI facilitates users to smoothly interact with the environment by means of intuitive interfaces embedded in objects, still the information generated by these interactions is not fully utilized. Another important aspect of AmI is *intelligence* by means of machine learning, agent-based software, and robotics [3]. This paper proposes the application of AmI concepts for the exploitation of generated user-product interaction information in physical stores, as well as the usage of State-of-the-Art intelligent recommendation techniques in physical and electronic environments for commerce.

Recommender systems (RSs) have been the answer to the information overload modern life consumers experience for more than two decades. RSs are essentially software tools able to discover the necessary knowledge about users in order to offer personalized recommendations to them. It is proved that, in e-commerce settings, recommendations of products to customers boost sales [4, 5], increase customer satisfaction [4] and improve user experience [6]. Therefore, not only customers benefit from recommender systems, but on-line retail stores as well [5].

While e-commerce sales grow exponentially[1], physical shopping is still the main shopping mode in comparison to e-commerce. Recent technological developments in AmI and ubiquitous computing though suggest that the success of RSs in the virtual world can be replicated in the real world, i.e., in physical retail settings. There already is a trend towards personalisation in the physical retail market and RSs with ubiquitous computing can be the means to make it more sophisticated and effective [5].

While RSs for e-commerce use information about user interaction on items online such as product ratings and purchase history to compute personalized recommendations of products to users, in ubiquitous settings other context-aware methods are applied to track user interest on products, such as tracking customers' in-store shopping path or the customers' staying time in the product area [12, 17]. The aim is to recommend to users similar products or other related things such as brand stores in a shopping mall or provide reviews and ratings on a product. However, to the best of our knowledge, none of the works in the literature uses a combination of user-item interaction data from both the physical scenario and the online scenario with the aim to enhance the recommendation accuracy in both settings. This constitutes the first contribution of this work.

Although open source recommendation frameworks are available (e.g. EasyRec, LensKit, LibRec[2]) for retail businesses to use as recommendation engines in building their own RS applications, it is nevertheless difficult for practitioners (software engineers, e-store developers) that are non RS experts to achieve such a task [7, 8]. These frameworks do not offer an abstraction from the technical details concerning the embedding of recommendations to an e-store, requiring from practitioners to work on code level. Moreover, and more importantly, they do not deal with the ubiquitous recommendation scenario to track user-item interaction at the physical store. Especially, since research has proven that Machine Learning (ML) algorithms are the most

---

[1] https://www.statista.com/statistics/379046/worldwide-retail-e-commerce-sales/.

[2] easyrec.org/, lenskit.org/, www.librec.net.

efficient in providing recommendations, it is even more difficult for non RS experts to utilize such algorithms in real applications because of their high complexity, especially in physical stores where Ambient Intelligence is required. In addition, due to the substantial number of ML algorithms and their variations proposed in the literature, a clear classification scheme for them does not exist [9], making it even more difficult for practitioners to select the ML algorithm that best fits their needs when developing a RS. Even researchers may find it challenging to track how ML algorithms in RSs are used [9]. Further, proof that expertise in recommendation technologies is needed to effectively implement RSs in retail businesses, is that many companies (vendors) exist that offer commercial proprietary RSs[3]. Such companies develop and deploy RSs in their business clients' websites or e-stores, aiming to increase their sales [10].

In this paper, we apply the Model Driven Development (MDD) paradigm on the physical commerce recommendation domain and propose a novel UbiCARS (Ubiquitous Context-Aware Recommender Systems) MDD Framework that aims: (i) to reduce complexity, abstract the technical details and expedite the development and application of State-of-the-Art context-aware RS in ubiquitous environments (physical retail stores) by practitioners that are not recommender system experts (first contribution of this work), and (ii) to enable these practitioners to track ubiquitous user-product interaction in the physical store and use this information in the recommendation process, together with user-product interaction data from the online scenario, a combination which is expected to further improve recommendation accuracy (second contribution of this work). A new graphical Domain Specific Modelling Language (DSML) for UbiCARS is proposed that drives model-based design and dynamic configuration of such systems for physical and online commerce, as well as system integration with pre-existing e-stores. To the best of our knowledge, a DSML for UbiCARS does not exist.

The paper is organized as follows: Sect. 2 provides the research background and related work. Section 3 discusses the proposed UbiCARS methodology, while the UbiCARS framework architecture is described in Sect. 4. In Sect. 5, we demonstrate the modelling process using the proposed UbiCARS MDD framework and discuss a use-case. The paper completes with conclusions and future work in Sect. 6. In the remainder of the paper we will refer to practitioners as *users* of the system and customers as *end-users*.

2 Background

2.1 Recommendation Methods for E-Commerce

Collaborative filtering (CF) constitutes the most adopted method for RS since is relies on user's *behaviour history*, such as previous transactions or ratings of items [11]. It is also independent of any domain. The most efficient CF approaches are the Model based

---

[3] Google Cloud Machine Learning (ML), SLI Systems Recommender, Azure ML, Amazon Machine Learning, SuggestGrid, Yusp.

that utilize intelligent Machine Learning techniques such as Matrix Factorization. In e-commerce settings, CF is preferable since it relies only on user behaviour and, therefore, explicit profiles for users and/or products are not needed [6]. Hence, users can receive recommendations without firstly being asked to complete a profile, a task users normally do not like. RSs for e-commerce use *explicit user feedback on products* such as product ratings by users to elicit and model user preferences and offer personalized recommendations of products users would enjoy [6, 12]. In case explicit feedback is not available, RSs use *implicit user feedback on products* by *tracking user behaviour* such as user transaction data (purchase history), clickstream data, click-through rate (CTR) and browser history information [13–16]. Problems with explicit techniques are that they require cognitive effort from users, and they interrupt their task at hand as they have to stop and rate items. A comparison between implicit and explicit feedback [13] found that: (i) the more time users spend on a content indicates that the more they like that content; (ii) more user visits on a content mean the user is interested in it; (iii) multiple user accesses to the same content shows user interest in that content. Yahoo proposed using dwell time on content items on the Yahoo home page as an implicit technique to measure how likely a content item is relevant to a particular user, and reported good results [16].

2.2 Recommender Systems in Physical Retail Stores

Research has been conducted on using the knowledge obtained from e-commerce RSs to offer recommendations to customers while being in physical business locations like a shopping mall or a grocery store. The authors in [12] suggest offering recommendations based (among other) on customers' *staying time* in each shopping mall area to recommend which shops customers should visit next. According to the authors, staying time at each selling area is considered as an important piece of information on user preferences in purchasing of goods. Evaluation of their RS performance against real sales data showed that, not only sales history, but also the customers' shopping path data make a RS highly accurate. In [17], a mobile RS for indoor shopping is proposed that uses indoor mobile positioning by using received signal patterns of mobile phones to recommend brand stores to users in a shopping mall. The proposed RS records users' past activities and context, among other the time spent in each store during every shopping process. In [18] a RS that recommends shops in a mall is described. To detect customers' location, RFID devices and related infrastructure have been deployed in a large-scale shopping mall. The work in [5] describes a scenario where the customer is recommended with products in store via a store-owned device called personal shopping assistant (PSA). The recommendations are based on the items that are currently in the cart, on customers' location, and on their purchase history. In [19], a RS for shopping is proposed that estimates user preferences on items based on their physical distance from the items, whether a user picks up an item or scans an object using a RFID reader device. Pfeiffer et al. [20] present a RS that uses eye-tracking to (implicitly) elicit preference information in a minimally intrusive manner in order to reduce users' effort: glasses are used as a more ubiquitous and personal object than smartphones.

2.3   Related Work on CARS Modelling

Context-Aware Recommender Systems - CARSs utilize the context in the recommendation process [11], making it more accurate, but also turning it into a complex (in comparison to un-contextual RSs) multidimensional problem: user × items × context → ratings. In our prior work [21] we have defined the novel concept of UbiCARSs as recommender applications that facilitate users on site through recommendations by using context-aware intelligent recommendation algorithms that operate on multidimensional datasets. In this paper, the concept of UbiCARS is used for enabling the computation of context-aware recommendations on context-aware datasets from both the physical store and the e-store scenario.

A number of works in the literature propose using modelling or other software engineering techniques to tackle RS complexity. A recommendation framework for assisting developers build CARSs and hybrid RSs is Hybreed [8]. Hybreed incorporates a set of standard recommendation algorithms and provides templates for combining them into hybrids with a significantly reduced amount of effort. In [22], we have proposed a context modelling system and learning tool to guide developers through the process of CARS context modelling. In [9], the authors investigate how ML algorithms in RSs are studied and used, as well as trends in ML algorithm research and development. In [23], the authors deal with the problem of web developers needing assistance, by means of proper methods and tools, for dealing with complexity issues in adopting recommendation techniques in their web applications. They explicitly mention the lack of model-driven methodologies for the specification of RS algorithmic and interface elements. The authors use UML to model an un-contextual RS algorithm. However, by modelling the recommendation algorithm itself, the complexity an algorithm can have to be able to be used in the proposed model-driven process is somewhat limited, in the sense that too complex recommendation algorithms will be difficult to be modelled. In [7] a user modelling framework for CARS is proposed to serve as a tool for developers and researchers to build data models for CARS. A CARS model schema and UML class description is provided.

Although the above works have similarities with our work, our proposal differs in five important aspects: (i) it defines a novel Domain Specific Modelling Language for UbiCARS (UbiCARS DSML), (ii) it focuses on the ubiquitous scenario of UbiCARS aiming to enhance product recommendation accuracy in physical commerce, (iii) it supports complex algorithms and data models from the State-of-the-Art of RS literature, (iv) it is easily extendable and (v) it is directly integrable with existing e-stores.

3   UbiCARS Framework

Model-driven Development aims at the abstract representation of the knowledge and activities of a particular application domain, as well as in automation. Application models are defined at an abstracted level and, using automated transformations or interpretations, they are converted into applications, eliminating or minimizing the need to write code. In this paper, we apply the Model-Driven Development paradigm on the physical commerce recommendation domain and propose the *UbiCARS MDD framework.* We define the *UbiCARS app* and *CARS system* as follows: UbiCARS app is a mobile application that: (i) enables tracking of end-user interaction with products on-location; (ii) displays product recommendations to end-user on-location. CARS is a server-side system (including the recommendation engine) that: (i) enables tracking of end-user interaction with products on-line; (ii) computes context-aware recommendations; (iii) displays product recommendations to end-users through the e-store.

3.1   UbiCARS Methodology

The proposed UbiCARS MDD framework defines a DSML for UbiCARSs for commerce and a corresponding graphical modelling editor. Via the editor, practitioners can use the DSML to drive model-based design and dynamic configuration of UbiCARS in commerce settings, as well as system integration with pre-existing e-stores. In Fig. 1 the multi-layered software architecture of the framework is presented. The UbiCARS DSML acts on the Modelling layer via an editor for practitioners to design their UbiCARS commerce applications. The DSML is cross-platform, meaning that any platform specific implementation details are abstracted from the designers.

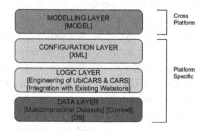

Fig. 1. Multi-layered software architecture.

When UbiCARS design is completed, the framework generates configuration files in eXtensible Markup Language (XML) for the Configuration layer, where a Parser extracts all user defined information and passes it to the logic layer that undertakes the engineering of UbiCARS. The Logic layer builds the necessary data models and database (DB) tables, whereas it also implements the system configurations indicated by the Configuration layer, including system integration with pre-existing e-stores. It also configures the system for the execution of the UbiCARS app. The Data layer prepares the necessary context-aware user-product interaction datasets to be fed to the CARS system. To use the MDD framework to build UbiCARS, a practitioner only needs to use the DSML editor to design the UbiCARS model. Then, automatically, the UbiCARS app and CARS system are configured and deployed.

3.2   Enhancing Recommendation Accuracy

Assuming a retail business with an e-commerce website and physical showrooms with products, our solution proposes that a UbiCARS app is used together with a CARS that operates on the e-store to enhance the overall recommendation efficiency (in [15], it is shown that users' diverse implicit feedback data can be used to improve recommendation accuracy). User's implicit feedback data acquired within the physical store complement user's explicit and implicit feedback data in the online scenario to enhance end-user preferences modelling and improve the overall recommendations for that user. In addition to e-commerce methods for tracking user behaviour (user purchase history, clickstream data and browser history information), we enable tracking of user's ubiquitous behaviour in real-time while in-store, aiming to acquire the ubiquitous user-item interaction (Fig. 2). Specifically, similarly to the dwell time used in online settings as user implicit feedback [14, 16], we propose utilizing the *"staying time in front of a product"* and *"scanning NFC tag of a product"*.

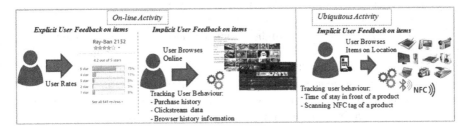

Fig. 2. Modelling user preferences.

A UbiCARS Scenario: RSs are most helpful in large shops with many product categories where the customer base is likely to be very heterogeneous [5]. We consider an electronics store with a large variety of electronic devices and peripherals that each requires a level of knowledge from customers in order to purchase the best suited product for their needs and preferences. The store showroom is equipped with Bluetooth beacons placed on products to track end-user interaction with products via a UbiCARS mobile app. While visiting a showroom, the user is not sure whether the products she is currently looking at are the best for her to purchase in terms of meeting her preferences. The store showroom cannot possibly host all the products that are offered online. End-user needs assistance to narrow down her options to a product or a selection of products that are most suitable for her. At this point the end-user can use recommendations of products.

Nicolas is a regular user of the Public e-store; he has purchased a few products in the past and also rated some of them online. When Nicolas uses the Public e-store, he likes the personalized product recommendations the website offers. Most of the times, the recommended products match his preferences so he checks them out. Nicolas is now at a Public physical store showroom browsing the products. He is quite interested in technology products and especially likes high end laptops. Public includes in its showroom only a small portion of the products that are offered in total by the store. Nicolas approaches a laptop on a shelf that he finds interesting. He reads a few specs from the small label on the laptop; he would like to know more information on its features, as well as receive product recommendations. Nicolas opens the Public UbiCARS app on his smartphone. The app receives signals from the Bluetooth beacons and sends related info to the server which (i) identifies the product Nicolas is in front of and (ii) computes Nicolas "staying time in front of the product". The Public UbiCARS app recommends to Nicolas three products which he checks out: the two are located in the same showroom, while the third can only be found online, so the app suggests purchasing it online. Nicolas finds it easy and playful to receive recommendations in store so he repeats the process for more products.

For Nicolas the e-store has recorded a number of ratings on products (explicit feedback) and has tracked his online interaction with products: browser history and online purchase history (implicit feedback). From such data, datasets are compiled to be used in the recommendation process (Fig. 3). Browsing history refers to the number of clicks on the product's name or icon in webpages where many products are listed or recommended, as well as the number of accesses in the product's webpage, while purchase history refers to number of purchases of the corresponding product.

The UbiCARS app contributes to the recommendation process by sensing the time (in seconds) Nicolas has stayed in front of a product (e.g. left dataset in Fig. 4). After Nicolas visit to the store, the UbiCARS app dataset will be available to the CARS for use in the next recommendation computation, in addition to those in Fig. 3. Recommendations for Nicolas the next time he will visit one of the Public physical stores or the Public e-store can be more accurate, since more relevant information will be used during their computation.

```
userid,itemid,rating,Day,Time   userid,itemid,AccessedOnline,Day,Time   userid,itemid,purchasedOnline,Day,Time
1,15,4,Weekday,Evening          1,24,1,Weekend,Morning                  1,24,1,Weekday,Afternoon
1,24,5,Weekend,Late_night       1,26,1,Weekday,Evening                  1,28,1,Weekday,Afternoon
1,25,2,Weekday,Morning          1,25,1,Weekday,Evening                  1,15,1,Weekend,Afternoon
```

Fig. 3. Datasets: ratings; browsing history; purchased history.

```
userid,itemid,StayedInFrontOf,Day,Time    userid,itemid,StayedInFrontOf,Day,Time,context
1,25,231,Weekday,Afternoon                13,25,231,Weekday,Afternoon,ElectronicsSection:Laptops
1,26,38,Weekday,Afternoon                 2,26,38,Weekday,Afternoon,ElectronicsSection:Consumables
1,22,178,Weekday,Afternoon                1,22,178,Weekday,Afternoon,ElectronicsSection:AppleProducts
```

Fig. 4. User's staying time in front of a product datasets.

3.3   The UbiCARS DSML

We have implemented the UbiCARS DSML to offer the highest possible level of abstraction from technical details for the ubiquitous product recommendation domain, as well as to simplify usage and instantiation by practitioners. The DSML was designed as an Ecore metamodel in Sirius[4], an open-source Eclipse project which allows leveraging the Eclipse Modelling technologies (EMF, GMF) to create custom graphical modelling workbenches. Figure 5 presents part of the Modelling Language (due to space limitations the full metamodel is referenced[5]).

---

[4] http://www.eclipse.org/sirius/.

[5] https://drive.google.com/file/d/1Dk7XgdCLusH0_AL7Aw-n8_FMupGI7KZY/view?usp=sharing.

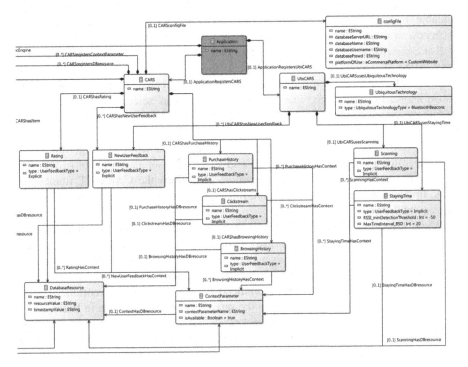

Fig. 5. The proposed UbiCARS DSML.

The `Application` element is the core element that represents a product recommendation system consisting of a `CARS` system and a `UbiCARS` app. `CARS` defines the user `Ratings` on products as an explicit user feedback element, and the `PurchaseHistory`, `ClickStream` and `BrowsingHistory` as those representing the user implicit feedback on products. A `CARS` can instantiate zero or one of these elements, while a number of custom `NewUserFeedback` elements can be defined by the user which can be explicit or implicit (default value is explicit).

In the physical commerce (ubiquitous) scenario, a `UbiCARS` app uses two implicit user feedback elements, the `StayingTime` element representing the staying time in front of products and the `Scanning` element representing the scanning of NFC tags of products. `UbiCARS` has zero or one of these elements, as well as a number of custom explicit or implicit `NewUserFeedback` elements to be defined by the user if needed.

Each of the aforementioned elements uses a `DatabaseResource` and may use a `ContextParameter`. A `DatabaseResource` specifies information about the database resource, where the respective information will be stored and retrieved from (timestamp may be also used as contextual information about time, defining thus the exact time the user interaction on the product took place). A `ContextParameter` captures the context of end-users while interacting with products. For instance, user location in terms of GPS coordinates or any custom defined attributes, such as "store electronics section" or "basement", can be defined. Context is assigned with a Boolean `isAvailable` to denote whether the corresponding context sensing mechanism is available or needs to be developed. A `ContextParameter` uses a `DatabaseResource` to denote where the corresponding context will be/is already stored.

`RecommendationEngine` (See footnote 5) computes the recommendations. The CARSKIT recommendation framework (Sect. 4) is the default engine in the metamodel; however, other recommendation frameworks can be used. The engine uses a `RecommendationAlgorithm` which the user can select from the available algorithms offered by the selected engine. Provided that the user has selected CARS-KIT to be the recommendation engine, the default algorithm used is context-aware matrix factorization `CAMF_CU`, while two more recommendation algorithms are available in the metamodel: `CAMF_ICS` and `CPTF` (Tensor Factorization) [24]. The metamodel can be easily extended with more algorithms the CARSKIT framework offers. In addition to algorithm selection, related algorithmic configuration parameters can also be defined.

While `RecommendationStorage` defines the place where computed recommendations are stored, `RecommendationPresentation` denotes the `platformOfPresentation` of the recommendations to end-users – whether it is through the e-store (via a Webpage) or through a smartphone screen (via UbiCARS app); the `visualizationFormat` of the recommendations – whether the recommendations will appear as a main or minor object in the screen, or as a widget (e.g. in Wordpress); and whether explanation of recommendations will be enabled. Recommendation explanations contribute to system transparency and trust, e.g. Amazon.com uses *"Customers Who Bought This Item Also Bought"*. Although providing accurate explanations when complex algorithms are used is a difficult task, a practitioner can provide a simplistic, generic version of explanations, such as *"These products are suggested to you based on your previous transactions, product ratings and interaction with products in our showroom"*. topN denotes the number of recommendations to be presented (e.g. top-5). It is used by algorithms that solve the top-N recommendation problem, as opposed to those that solve the prediction problem.

UbiCARS Specific Elements. The ubiquitous technology to be used by the UbiCARS app is determined by the `UbiquitousTechnology` element. The two supported technologies are `BluetoothBeacons` and `NFCScanning`. Other technologies could be used as well such as Wi-Fi[6], or more innovative ones used for indoor positioning such as *smart floors* [25] (although some investment will be required).

Bluetooth beacons enable other Bluetooth devices in close proximity to perform actions, indoor positioning among other. Depending on beacon type, their range may vary from 7 m to a few hundreds of meters[7]. Smartphone software can find its relative location to a Bluetooth Beacon in a retail store - retail stores already use beacons for mobile commerce as beacons can create a more engaging in-store experience for customers. Beacons have also been used for providing users with recommendations[8]. An important point is that during indoor positioning, location tracking is done by the smartphone software and not by the Bluetooth beacon, ensuring thus user privacy.

---

[6] lifehacker.com/how-retail-stores-track-you-using-your-smartphone-and-827512308.

[7] estimote.com/products/.

[8] www.huffingtonpost.com/kenny-kline/how-bluetooth-beacons-wil_b_8982720.html.

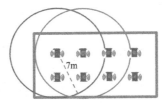

Fig. 6. Signal overlapping example: bluetooth beacons placed on products in a showroom.

Since products in showrooms are usually positioned relatively close to each other, by placing a Bluetooth beacon on each one of them, overlapping of signal coverage occurs (Fig. 6). Hence, customer's staying time in front of a product is calculated by using the Received Signal Strength Indicator (RSSI) of a Bluetooth enabled client (end-user smartphone) when Bluetooth beacons on products in the proximity are being sensed. No user action is needed other than installing the app and running it. The RSSI acts as a distance indicator between the device and the beacon, as devices closer to beacons register higher RSSI values. Devices scan for beacons continuously, taking about 10–15 s between two successive scanning cycles. For each end-user, based on traces of sensed beacons and corresponding received RSSIs in the available space/showroom (see Fig. 4), the system calculates an approximation of the distance from the end-user's device to each Beacon and is thus able to identify the products the user has been staying in front of and for how long. Through the RSSI_minDetectionThreshold parameter of the StayingTime element, practitioners can specify the minimum RSSI value that needs to be sensed by the end-user's device for the end-user to be considered that she is close enough to the product and therefore, she "has stayed in front of it". After lab experimentation where we have received RSSI values from −30 (corresponding approximately to 2 m) down to −120 (corresponding to approximately 8 m), we have specified the default value for the RSSI_minDetectionThreshold to be −50. Note that sensing RSSI values depends on the sensors used and room specifics, and is also sensitive to obstacles: therefore, experimentation and adjustments will be needed in each specific use case scenario. The MaxTimeInterval_BSD parameter specifies the maximum time interval between successive detections of an end-user in front of a product in order for these detections to be considered in the same "staying time session" in front of that product. Default value is 20, meaning that successive detections of an end-user device in front of a product beacon when less than 20 s apply between each detection result in the system adding the total time and attributing it to the same session.

Using the above default values, the staying time reasoning algorithm functions as follows (Fig. 7): when a device senses the same beacon for more than once and each successive sensing has a time difference of less than 20 s with the previous one, and furthermore at all times the RSSI value is higher than −50, then the system adds the corresponding time difference between the first and the last sensing and assigns the sum as the staying time of the end-user for that product. The above algorithm ensures that, in case an end-user passes by a product and walks away, no staying time will be assigned to her for the corresponding product.

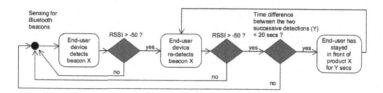

Fig. 7. Staying time reasoning algorithm.

Users can be motivated to scan an NFC tag of a product to find out more information on that product, visit its webpage, be recommended of similar products and read reviews [1, 5, 12, 18–20]. NFC technology requires the user to hold the mobile device in a 5 cm range from the product for an average of 3.3 s for detecting the product [20]. User's staying time in front of a product is a truly implicit user feedback since it happens without requiring user's active participation and without interfering with user's task (user's consent needs to be granted at a prior stage). Having users scan NFC tags of products, however, needs user participation, similar to user ratings, whereas it also interrupts users from their task. When a scan occurs, we can be certain that the user has shown some interest on the product, but not that she actually likes it. The same applies for staying in front of a product: the user may as well be looking at something else other than the product in front of her. Nevertheless, implicit feedback is important and can replace explicit techniques where the latter cannot be used.

4   UbiCARS Framework Architecture

The UbiCARS MDD Framework enriches an existing e-store with context-aware recommendations. The framework architecture is shown in Fig. 8. The online store frontend (client side) tracks user behaviour through the browser software and/or 3rd party software running on the browser. Server side tracking of user behaviour is

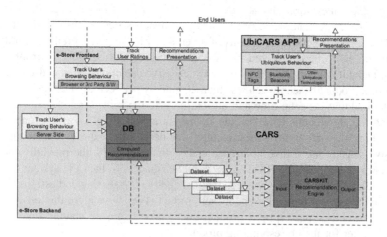

Fig. 8. Framework architecture.

accomplished by analysing server log files. *CARSKIT* [24] is an open-source Context-aware Recommendation Engine that offers State-of-the-Art recommendation algorithms. CARSKIT has been selected among other recommendation frameworks due to the many efficient recommendation algorithms it offers, its ease of use, and the flexibility with which it can be fine-tuned to work with multidimensional datasets.

System implementation considers two of the most well-known, open source e-commerce platforms, WordPress WooCommerce[9] and Drupal Commerce[10]. Practitioners may specify their platform of choice in the model to drive system configuration (`platformOfUse` of `configFile` element). The system provides code snippets and functional modules that can be installed in the corresponding platform and provide the following functionality: retrieve explicit user feedback in terms of end-user ratings on products, retrieve implicit user feedback in terms of end-user purchase history and browsing history (product webpages accessed) on the website, as well as display computed recommendations accordingly, as specified in the model. Integration with the UbiCARS mobile app is provided. Custom e-store configuration is also considered. Note that the cold start problem[11] also applies here. In this sense, after system configuration, the CARS system is not able to produce recommendations until customers have interacted with the electronic and physical stores. In case customer interaction pre-exists in a platform before system configuration, the system integrates and uses it, if relevant. For instance, in case customers have already rated products in WooCommerce before the system takes effect, the latter will consider the data during configuration and use it during the recommendation process.

5   UbiCARS Instance Model and Demonstrator

The UbiCARS MDD framework provides practitioners with a toolset to model, dynamically generate and configure a UbiCARS app and a CARS, as these were described in Sect. 3. The toolset is comprised of a DSML along with its modelling editor. Figure 9 shows the editor, its toolbox and a part of a model.

Through the properties view (right part of Fig. 9), information can be added/edited about the selected element. The model displayed in Fig. 9 defines the `Public Ubi-CARS` app that uses `BluetoothBeacons` and a `STAYING TIME` element that will track customer-product interaction in the physical store and engineer it into a dataset for the CARS to use in the recommendation process. The `Staying Time Context` adds `Indoor Location` as a contextual element to each customer-product interaction (e.g. the store department this interaction takes place). The right part of Fig. 4 shows a snippet of a resulting dataset for staying time with context. Note that datasets where implicit user feedback data (here the `StayedInFronfOf`) are not scaled as numbers from 1 to 5, need to be normalized before used in the recommendation engine, e.g. the

---

[9] https://wordpress.org/plugins/woocommerce/installation/.

[10] https://drupalcommerce.org/.

[11] Cold start is an inherent problem of RSs: to be able to produce meaningful recommendations, end-user interaction with products first needs to take place.

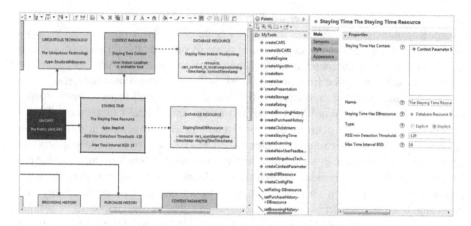

Fig. 9. The UbiCARS instance model & modelling editor.

number of seconds can be scaled from 1 to 5 indicating 5 levels: 1 corresponding to minimum staying time and 5 to maximum (these scales need to be defined by the practitioner depending on the use case scenario). The UbiCARS app provided is extendable and configurable. The system configures it to the level of communicating with Bluetooth beacons to determine the product ID and access the DB to store the data. A similar functionality is defined for scanning NFC tags. Next, context-aware multidimensional datasets are compiled by the system and used by the CARS.

For testing purposes we have designed and applied a number of models. Due to space limitations, a model example is referenced[12]. We have set up one example for each e-store platform (WooCommerce and Drupal Commerce), in which we have included electronic products, as these can be found in a real e-store. The datasets used and displayed in this work are produced via interaction of lab personnel with the e-stores. This interaction meant to simulate regular user activity on an e-store, such as browsing products, purchasing products and rating them. To simulate a physical store showroom, we have used a similar layout to the one in Fig. 6 to represent a mobile smartphone showroom. The products were Bluetooth enabled Android and IoS smartphones "for sale", eliminating thus, in this case the need for Bluetooth beacons. Beacons are expected to be more accurate than smartphones, however, when Bluetooth is embedded in the products for sale, budget (for beacons) can be saved.

Utilizing the data from online and physical end-user interaction with products, the system was able to produce 7 datasets: ratings, purchasing history, browsing history, staying time, NFC scanning (when models specify NFC instead of Bluetooth beacons), and two datasets for custom user feedback, one explicit and one implicit. Regarding custom end-user interaction, practitioners may specify the feedback data according to their needs, but the scoring scale still needs to be a number from 1 to 5. For instance, such feedback could be the amount of times a customer has walked passed a product: while the acquired end-user feedback can be a large number, e.g. 112, the dataset needs

---

[12] https://drive.google.com/file/d/13mXmGcCeImbpJ5G0oxP4Yj1z1bZiviyd/view?usp=sharing.

```
userid,itemid,userFeedback,Day,Time,context          userid,itemid,userFeedback,Day,Time,context
5,25,112,Weekday,Afternoon,ElectronicsSection:AppleProducts   5,25,4,Weekday,Afternoon,ElectronicsSection:AppleProducts
```

Fig. 10. Dataset of customers walking passed a product.

to be normalized as shown in Fig. 10. With the generated datasets and the automatically configured e-store, the system was able to compute recommendations and display them to end-users. However, due to the limited data available in comparison with real store data, cold start problems were experienced (Sect. 4).

6 Conclusions and Future Work

In this paper, we have presented our work on an MDD approach toward the development of UbiCARS applications for physical commerce. The approach provides a number of facilitators in the development of recommendations for commerce, aiming for faster development time, enhancement of recommendations accuracy and utilization of more efficient context-aware recommendation algorithms in relevance to existing works. While problems exist when using implicit user feedback on products [6], it is nevertheless important and can replace or complement explicit feedback techniques. In this work we have proposed using additional user-product interaction data from the physical store scenario to improve recommendation accuracy: users are expected to be more satisfied by the recommended products.

As future work, similarly to the evaluation process in [8], we plan to engage practitioners to use the UbiCARS MDD framework. Developers that have worked with e-stores will be asked to use the UbiCARS DSML and editor to integrate State-of-the-Art context-aware recommendations into their e-stores. We plan to use performance metrics, i.e. *task success* (how well was the task completed), *time-on-task* (time needed) [8], Lines-Of-Code (LOC) metric to measure effort, and SUS to measure system usability. As opposed to [8] where a stand-alone evaluation without competitors was conducted, we aim to compare our results with other frameworks by having users conduct the same tasks with other open-source recommendation frameworks. We also intend to study privacy aspects of collecting and utilizing user data, as well as mechanisms to inform users and consider their preferences.

References

1. Chen, C.-C., Huang, T.-C., Park, J.J., Yen, N.Y.: Real-time smartphone sensing and recommendations towards context-awareness shopping. Multimed. Syst. **21**(1), 61–72 (2015)
2. Bick, M., Kummer, T.F.: Ambient intelligence and ubiquitous computing. In: Adelsberger, H.H., Kinshuk, Pawlowski, J.M., Sampson, D.G. (eds.) Handbook on Information Technologies for Education and Training. Springer, Heidelberg (2008). https://doi.org/10.1007/978-3-540-74155-8_5
3. Cook, D.J., Augusto, J.C., Jakkula, V.R.: Ambient intelligence: technologies, applications, and opportunities. Pervasive Mob. Comput. **5**, 277–298 (2009)

4. Ricci, F., Rokach, L., Shapira, B., Kantor, P.B.: Recommender Systems Handbook, 1st edn. Springer-, New York (2010)
5. Walter, F.E., Battiston, S., Yildirim, M., Schweitzer, F.: Moving recommender systems from online commerce to retail stores. Inf. Syst. E-Bus Manag. **10**, 367–393 (2012)
6. Hu, Y., Koren, Y., Volinsky, C.: Collaborative filtering for implicit feedback datasets. In: Proceedings of the 8th IEEE International Conference on Data Mining, pp. 263–272 (2008)
7. Inzunza, S., Juárez-Ramírez, R., Jiménez, S.: User modeling framework for context-aware recommender systems. In: Rocha, Á., Correia, A.M., Adeli, H., Reis, L.P., Costanzo, S. (eds.) WorldCIST 2017. AISC, vol. 569, pp. 899–908. Springer, Cham (2017). https://doi.org/10.1007/978-3-319-56535-4_88
8. Hussein, T., Linder, T., Gaulke, W., Ziegler, J.: Hybreed: a software framework for developing context-aware hybrid recommender systems. User Model. User-Adap. Inter. **24**(1–2), 121–174 (2014)
9. Portugal, I., Alencar, P., Cowan, D.: The use of machine learning algorithms in recommender systems: a systematic review. Expert Syst. Appl. **97**, 205–227 (2018)
10. Aldrich, S.E.: Recommender systems in commercial use. AI Mag. **32**(3), 28–34 (2011)
11. Adomavicius, G., Sankaranarayanan, R., Sen, S., Tuzhilin, A.: Incorporating contextual information in recommender systems using a multidimensional approach. ACM Trans. Inf. Syst. (TOIS) **23**, 103–145 (2005)
12. So, W.T., Yada, K.: A framework of recommendation system based on in-store behavior. In: Proceedings of the 4th Multidisciplinary International Social Networks Conference, New York, NY, USA, pp. 33:1–33:4 (2017)
13. Núñez-Valdéz, E.R., Lovelle, J.M.C., Martínez, O.S., García-Díaz, V., de Pablos, P.O., Marín, C.E.M.: Implicit feedback techniques on recommender systems applied to electronic books. Comput. Hum. Behav. **28**(4), 1186–1193 (2012)
14. Peska, L.: Using the context of user feedback in recommender systems. In: Proceedings of the 11th Doctoral Workshop on Mathematical and Engineering Methods in Computer Science, MEMICS 2016, pp. 1–12 (2016)
15. Yang, B., Lee, S., Park, S., Lee, S.: Exploiting various implicit feedback for collaborative filtering. In: Proceedings of the 21st International Conference Companion on World Wide Web, WWW 2012 Companion, ACM, New York, NY, USA, pp. 639–640 (2012)
16. Yi, X., Hong, L., Zhong, E., Liu, N.N., Rajan, S.: Beyond clicks: dwell time for personalization. In: Proceedings of the 8th ACM Conference on Recommender Systems, RecSys 2014, pp. 113–120. ACM, New York (2014)
17. Fang, B., Liao, S., Xu, K., Cheng, H., Zhu, C., Chen, H.: A novel mobile recommender system for indoor shopping. Expert Syst. Appl. **39**(15), 11992–12000 (2012)
18. Jie, C., Dong, W., Canquan, L.: Recommendation system technologies of intelligent large-scale shopping mall. In: Proceedings of 2nd International Conference on Computer Science and Network Technology, Changchun, pp. 1058–1062 (2012)
19. Kawashima, H., Matsushita, T., Satake, S., Imai, M., Shinagawa, Y., Anzai, Y.: PORSCHE: a physical objects recommender system for cell phone users. In: Proceedings of 2nd International Workshop on Personalized Context Modeling and Management for UbiComp applications, California, USA (2006)
20. Pfeiffer, J., Pfeiffer, T., Meißner, M.: Towards attentive in-store recommender systems. In: Iyer, L.S., Power, D.J. (eds.) Reshaping Society through Analytics, Collaboration, and Decision Support. AIS, vol. 18, pp. 161–173. Springer, Cham (2015). https://doi.org/10.1007/978-3-319-11575-7_11
21. Mettouris, C., Papadopoulos, G.A: Ubiquitous recommender systems. Computing **96**(3), 223–257 (2014)

22. Mettouris, C., Papadopoulos, G.A.: CARS context modelling. In: Proceedings of the 9th International Conference on Knowledge, Information and Creativity Support Systems, KICSS 2014, pp. 60–71 (2014)

23. Rojas, G., Domínguez, F., Salvatori, S.: Recommender systems on the web: a model-driven approach. In: Di Noia, T., Buccafurri, F. (eds.) EC-Web 2009. LNCS, vol. 5692, pp. 252–263. Springer, Heidelberg (2009). https://doi.org/10.1007/978-3-642-03964-5_24

24. Zheng, Y., Mobasher, B., Burke, R.: CARSKit: a Java-based context-aware recommendation engine. In: 2015 IEEE International Conference on Data Mining Workshop (ICDMW), pp. 1668–1671 (2015)

25. Fu, B., Kirchbuchner, F., von Wilmsdorff, J., Grosse-Puppendahl, T., Braun, A., Kuijper, A.: Indoor localization based on passive electric field sensing. In: Braun, A., Wichert, R., Maña, A. (eds.) AmI 2017. LNCS, vol. 10217, pp. 64–79. Springer, Cham (2017). https://doi.org/10.1007/978-3-319-56997-0_5

A Workflow for Continuous Performance Testing in Smart Buildings

Elena Markoska[(⊠)] and Sanja Lazarova-Molnar

Mærsk Mc-Kinney Møller Institute,
University of Southern Denmark, Odense, Denmark
{elma, slmo}@mmmi.sdu.dk

Abstract. Continuous commissioning can be implemented through performance testing which analyses a building's behavior using a set of software-based tests. In this paper, we present a workflow for performance testing in smart buildings, including buildings that lack historical data. The difficulty in assessing behaviors of new buildings is in the lack of historical data to calibrate models that describe future behaviors. The proposed workflow uses a combination of country regulations, data driven, and white box models, to assess the building in various stages after its handover. We validate the workflow by comparing the results from the different models with the observed behavior of a case study building in Denmark. We examine the change in percentage of passed and failed performance tests, based on different thresholds delivered by the models. The results show an increased number of passed performance test for data driven models, and demonstrate the assessment of performance using the proposed workflow, from the beginning of the building's usage.

Keywords: Performance testing · Energy data modeling · Smart buildings
Thresholds for building commissioning

1 Introduction

Buildings partake with a fraction of approximately 40% in the world's overall energy consumption. This number can be reduced by roughly 15–30% by addressing relevant fault detection and diagnostics issues in a timely manner [1].

Practice shows us that often buildings have shortcomings at the time of handover, which are often discovered only at later stages in the building's lifecycle. Performance Tests/Performance Testing (PTs/PTing) is a means to continuously assess the behavior of the building. If a building's behavior is assessed from the very first day of handover, issues in performance can be detected immediately, thus enabling the prompt remedy of the underperformance, yielding energy savings.

PTing is conducted using an adaptable framework that can be applied to a wide variety of building types. A library of PTs provides a comprehensive set of examination for all buildings' subsystems [2]. A PT is a comparison between the observed and the expected behavior of the building. The observed behavior is obtained through calculations based on data acquired from metering and sensors. Many methods simulate the expected behavior of a building. Studies [3] show that black box or gray box models

© Springer Nature Switzerland AG 2018
A. Kameas and K. Stathis (Eds.): AmI 2018, LNCS 11249, pp. 54–59, 2018.
https://doi.org/10.1007/978-3-030-03062-9_4

are more suited for real-time PTing, with sufficiently low errors. However, they require historical data to be trained, which new buildings do not have [4].

Often countries have a set of regulations that determine rules regarding the occupant comfort and the expected energy usage for buildings. Buildings may be classified based on their energy consumption and are expected to perform as specified by their respective building class. This paper uses a smart building in Denmark as a case study, and thus refers to the Danish regulations for building energy consumption.

In this paper, we propose a workflow for real-time PTing in new buildings which do not yet have any historical data, and perform an evaluation of the changes in results from PTs when using different thresholds.

2   Background

The concept of continuous commissioning is a well-known practice, with established benefits. The initial investment in instrumentation in most cases has been returned within a 3 year interval, establishing the practice prudent for energy savings [5].

We use PTs as a general approach to continuous commissioning, applicable to various subsystems within a unified framework. This framework could be applied to different buildings with minimal human effort, regardless of their type. PTs are in essence software programs which provide a comparison between observed and expected behavior of a subsystem in the building, for a certain time interval. Based on this, the results are time series of pass/fail values. The detailed setup of this framework is given in [6].

The expected behavior, referred to as 'threshold', may be acquired through various techniques. In modelling of building energy data, the two most prominent approaches are physical and data driven models. Physical (white box) models, take into account physical properties of the building. Physics-based equations are applied, with as few assumptions as possible. These models require historical data to calibrate the simulation output of the expected behavior. Data driven models are trained based on collected historical data, by using a technique that is able to learn the patterns of the time series input. These models are also known as gray- or black box models.

Different techniques can be used in regards to both types of models. Karatasou et al. in [7] focus on energy forecasting based on Artificial Neural Network (ANN). Li et al. in [8] compare ANN and a hybrid neuro-fuzzy system. Building regulations often state the preferred building energy consumption. In Denmark, the BE10 tool [9] provides a threshold. The workflow proposed in this paper solves the problem of data unavailability in the early stages. The framework that this workflow is implemented in is capable of automatic instantiation of PTs based on a metadata model.

3   Performance Testing in Newly Constructed Buildings

The workflow for PTing in newly constructed buildings is graphically presented in Fig. 1. The horizontal line represents a timeline of the building's lifecycle. Each of the vertical dashed lines separates the different sections of the building's timeline.

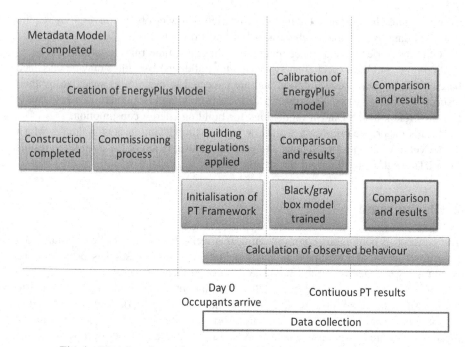

Fig. 1. Workflow for performance testing in newly constructed buildings

When construction is completed, all building components are installed and all setup configuration is known. The detailed knowledge of the installed components in the building allows for the creation of a white box model. The metadata needed for the development of the model prior to calibration, is metadata that is known when construction is completed. This model might be created in other stages of the building lifecycle, and it may be used for retrofitting. However, its existence is neither required nor necessary for PTing or for any other aspect of building operation.

As PTs require historical data to calculate the observed behavior, the Framework can be initialized once occupants arrive, and data collection begins. The first PTs can be executed when there is sufficient data accumulated. For occupant comfort PTs, real time assessment can be done without the need for any amount of prior data.

As we move further down the horizontal timeline, more data is acquired, thus enabling the training or calibration of additional models. This way, if there already exists an EnergyPlus model, it can be calibrated so that it represents the observed behavior of the building, as previously it had been impossible to calibrate it.

Additionally, this same data can be used to train gray box or black box models. While in our experiments we have chosen to work with ARIMA, the usage of different techniques for time series forecasting is not discouraged.

Once there is available forecast or simulation from either of the models, a comparison between the observed and the expected behavior could be performed, essentially yielding an outcome of a PT with a pass/fail Boolean value.

4   Validation of Workflow Through Examination of PT Results

This section elaborates the method for validating the proposed workflow, and provides a discussion of the results from the validation. The case study building used, is a new energy efficient university campus building, of 8500 m^2. It is well equipped with electricity meters that measure the energy consumption from lighting, ventilation units, and heating. Every room is instrumented with CO_2, temperature, etc.

The Danish Building Research Institute provides an energy performance modelling and simulation tool, Be10 [9], as the official energy tool for Danish buildings certification based on government regulations. The BE10 modelling tool provides a monthly value for expected energy consumption, and is delivered during handover.

As a white box model, we use EnergyPlus as it is a free and validated tool [10]. The model has been calibrated based on historical data, weather data, and occupancy schedules. The simulations span a time period from October 2016 to May 2017.

The ARIMA model is a type of statistical models which analyze and forecast time series data. We used an implementation of the ARIMA models from the Python-based library scikit-learn [11], with p, d, and q parameters with values 2, 1, 0 respectively.

4.1   Comparison Between Thresholds for Results from PTing

All executed PTs span the time interval between February – March 2017. Based on the collected data from the case study building, we have been able to execute a number of PTs to assess the observed behavior of the building. These PTs have been chosen based on the availability of simulations from the models. Table 1 shows the number of passed and failed PTs for the variables available from all models.

The evaluation of the observed behavior occurs by checking if it is lower or equal than the threshold. This kind of evaluation is applicable to PTs that evaluate electricity consumption, and CO_2 concentration. For PTs regarding temperature, a range is derived from the simulation by increasing and decreasing the modelled value by 2 °C. If the temperature is within this range, the PT passes. In most cases, the ARIMA model has the highest amount of passed PTs. The difference in the number of passed PTs reflects the accuracy of the prediction, as ARIMA forecasts have been shown to be most accurate in comparison to the other two, using standard statistical errors [3].

Failed PTs may be cause for concern or not. To evaluate this, focusing on the distance between the observed value and the threshold may evaluate whether the PT is close to passing, or a more significant deviation is occurring. An error can be deliberately introduced to eliminate situations of false alarm. Based on an analysis of this distance, it is possible to create a categorization of PTs according to the severity of the deviation. This enables filtering among failed PTs according to their priority.

An additional examination given the implemented models is to evaluate the amount of data that is required to train or calibrate the models. In the case of BE10, no calibration or training is necessary considering the fact that only initial static parameters are required to produce the model. However, different amounts of training and calibration data can affect the accuracy of the output of the models. To evaluate at

Table 1. Number of passed and failed PTs

Performance Tests (%)	BE10		EnergyPlus		ARIMA	
	Passed	Failed	Passed	Failed	Passed	Failed
Overall electricity consumption (kWh)	22.4	77.6	43.7	56.3	52.1	47.9
Ventilation electricity consumption Unit 1	22.4	77.6	39.8	60.2	49.5	50.5
Unit 2 (kWh)	22.4	77.6	36	64	52.9	47.1
Unit 3 (kWh)	16.2	83.8	8.9	91.1	72.6	27.4
Unit 4 (kWh)	14.9	85.1	10.9	89.1	63.9	36.1
CO_2 (ppm) Test room 1	N/A	N/A	43	57	53.3	46.7
Test room 2	N/A	N/A	91.6	8.4	61	39
Test room 3	N/A	N/A	95.1	4.9	60.8	39.2
Test room 4	N/A	N/A	63	37	59.7	40.3
Temperature (°C) Test room 1	N/A	N/A	38.8	61.2	100	0
Test room 2	N/A	N/A	41.9	58.1	100	0
Test room 3	N/A	N/A	43.6	56.4	100	0
Test room 4	N/A	N/A	35.5	64.5	100	0
Lighting energy (kWh)	5.4	94.6	33.5	66.5	59.7	40.3

which point specifically it's possible to transition from BE10 to EnergyPlus or ARIMA. As with most forecasts and simulations, it's necessary to determine how high an error is acceptable in the output of the models. Specifying the desired accuracy of the model would help determine the length of the training interval.

4.2   Discussion and Future Work

Quality of training data, size of time interval for training and calibration, and coverage of all subsystems by each model, in every stage of the building's lifecycle, must be considered. The historical data must represent the correct behavior of the building, i.e. when there are no faults and underperformance occurring. This data can be acquired in several ways. A building manager can select periods of data which are not representative of faulty behavior, and mark them as representative of correct behavior. Alternatively, examining operational data sheets from manufacturers for each component. These operational data sheets contain information regarding the expected behavior of a component under closed system testing. By mapping them to the observed behavior, we can determine a subset of data representative of correct behavior. Furthermore, the smaller the training interval, the greater the error of the forecast will be. Similar conclusions apply to calibrating a white box model.

5   Conclusion

We presented a workflow for real time PTing for new buildings that don't have historical data. The presented workflow uses building regulations, white-, and black/gray box modelling, in a unified approach to tackle PTing in newly constructed buildings.

The workflow has been tested on a case study building in Denmark. Danish regulations have been considered using a BE10 model. Using the operational data, an EnergyPlus model has been developed, and an ARIMA model has been trained.

The results from the study of the workflow show a varying percentage of passed and failed PTs when using different thresholds, with ARIMA proving to be more sensitive than the other models. As issues with applicability of PTing generally arise from lack of models and/or lack of collected operational building data, we are confident that the proposed workflow enables newly constructed building to be tested for their performance from the moment they start having occupants.

References

1. Katipamula, S., Brambley, M.R.: Methods for fault detection, diagnostics, and prognostics for building systems—a review, part I. Hvac&R Res. **11**, 3–25 (2005)
2. Markoska, E., Johansen, A., Lazarova-Molnar, S.: A framework for fully automated performance testing for smart buildings. In: Yang, X.S., Sherratt, S., Dey, N., Joshi, A. (eds.) Third International Congress on Information and Communication Technology. AISC, vol. 797, pp. 235–243. Springer, Singapore (2019). https://doi.org/10.1007/978-981-13-1165-9_21
3. Markoska, E., Lazarova-Molnar, S.: Comparative evaluation of threshold modelling for smart buildings' performance testing. In: The 9th International Green and Sustainable Computing Conference. IEEE (Submitted)
4. Li, X., Wen, J.: Review of building energy modeling for control and operation. Renew. Sustain. Energy Rev. **37**, 517–537 (2014)
5. Claridge, D.E., et al.: Is commissioning once enough? Energy Eng. **101**, 7–19 (2004)
6. Markoska, E., Lazarova-Molnar, S.: Towards smart buildings performance testing as a service. In: The International Workshop on Smart Cities Systems Engineering (2018)
7. Karatasou, S., Santamouris, M., Geros, V.: Modeling and predicting building's energy use with artificial neural networks: methods and results. Energy Build. **38**, 949–958 (2006)
8. Li, K., Su, H., Chu, J.: Forecasting building energy consumption using neural networks and hybrid neuro-fuzzy system: a comparative study. Energy Build. **43**, 2893–2899 (2011)
9. SBI: The Danish Building Research Institute - BE10 SBI tool, May. https://sbi.dk/beregningsprogrammet/Pages/Aendringer-til-tidligere-versioner-af-Be15-og-Be10.aspx#s=BE10
10. Crawley, D.B., Pedersen, C.O., Lawrie, L.K., Winkelmann, F.C.: EnergyPlus: energy simulation program. ASHRAE J. **42**, 49 (2000)
11. Pedregosa, F., et al.: Scikit-learn: machine learning in Python. J. Mach. Learn. Res. **12**, 2825–2830 (2011)

Sensor Networks and AI

Advancing Early Forest Fire Detection Utilizing Smart Wireless Sensor Networks

Peshal Pokhrel and Hamdy Soliman[(⊠)]

New Mexico Institute of Mining and Technology, Socorro, NM 87801, USA
peshal.pokhrel@student.nmt.edu, hss@nmt.edu

Abstract. Forests are an important part of the ecosystem and play a crucial role in preserving and maintaining the global environment. Forest fires around the world cost billions of dollars and priceless human lives. Earlier detection of forest fires might mitigate their threat. In this paper, a smart forest fire detection system which combines Wireless Sensor network (WSN) and Artificial Neural Network (ANN) technologies (henceforth SWSN) is proposed. A small scale experimental emulation of controlled fire is carried out with a deployed SWSN collecting data for many simulated scenarios, including the crucial fire-about-to-start scenario. The sensed data are used to train different models of ANNs, while measuring scenario detection success rates. Obtained experimental results are very promising and set the model in a competitive placement among peer-related work, which encourages the utilization of a SWSN approach in a range of other civil and military applications.

Keywords: Machine learning · Neural network
Wireless sensor network · Forest fire · Classification · Clustering
Permutation

1 Introduction

Recently, forest fires are increasing around the world and in the US, with severe consequences for property, wildlife, air quality (greenhouse effect), and human life. Nature causes about 10% of US forest fires via lightning and thermal activity, with the aid of dry plant matter; whereas the remaining 90% are caused by human activity, such as cigarettes, fireworks, power-line arcs, and campfires [3]. About 600,000 acres of trees are burned on average, every year. With the expectation of significant increase, in 2015, 10,000,000 acres of forest were burned in the US alone [14]. The more significant losses include property, possessions, injury, and loss of life for both civilians and firefighters. Hence, extensive research has been done on early forest fire detection. Our research goal is to design a Smart Asynchronous Event Detection Wireless Sensor Network (SAED-WSN) with the aid of Artificial Neural Network (ANN) modeling. Although our paper focuses on forest-fire applications, the SAED-WSN is very amenable for other applications such as environmental monitoring, smart home, security, health care, quality

© Springer Nature Switzerland AG 2018
A. Kameas and K. Stathis (Eds.): AmI 2018, LNCS 11249, pp. 63–73, 2018.
https://doi.org/10.1007/978-3-030-03062-9_5

control, volcanic eruption, cyber security, landslide detection, intrusion detection, body area networks, IoT, and much more. In this paper, the SAED-WSN (hereafter called SWSN) has one or more powerful base stations connecting the sensor device nodes (MOTEs). The number of MOTEs in our SWSN is proportional to the application field area. The SWSN MOTEs are deployed in a specific area to sense/collect specified fire related physical readings from the environment (temperature, sound, light, smoke, etc.) and send the sensed data to a sinknode (base station). An IRIS XM2110 sensor MOTE [1] was used for our small-scale forest fire emulation experiment. In this paper, different data encoding strategies, to train a variety of ANN models, are presented. The objective is to have the SWSN system accurately achieve the detection of forest fires at their earliest stage, along with other vital relevant scenarios. The paper is organized as follows. In Sect. 2, related research on forest fire is introduced. Section 3 describes the SWSN architecture. Section 4 covers the utilization of different data preprocessing techniques such as standardization and interpolation. Section 5 depicts our small scale SWSN field experiment and the sensed data collection process. In Sect. 6, we present and analyze the results of our experiment with different data encoding and ANN modeling strategies. Concluding remarks are presented in Sect. 7.

2 Related Research

Many other researchers are experimenting to detect forest fire as early as possible. Traditionally, forest fires were detected visually such as with guard towers located at the highest point of the forest supplemented by an Osborne fire finder to detect its location. Unfortunately, these techniques are inefficient in case of fog or bad weather (for more old solutions refer to [18]). In addition, satellite Moderate Resolution Imaging (MODIS) monitoring [17] is commonly used to detect forest fire. The satellite imagery MODIS has many barriers such as time of the day, weather conditions, and cloud cover. Afzaal et al. [4] proposed a sensor network that detects temperature and keeps robots in the field. This method is very expensive in comparison to a SWSN. Kai et al. [7] proposed a system that detects fire using only smoke detectors and camera/video analysis, which is costly and has limitations. Son et al. [17] proposed a forest fire surveillance system that uses a web application to analyze data collected from the forest. They proposed the use of sensors to detect heat and smoke alone. Soliman et al. [16] and Anamika et al. [8] proposed similar forest fire models. The former detects simple fire/no-fire scenarios; the latter detects three scenarios: Normal, Critical, and Fire, using a very limited ANN training set of only 42 data points. None of the stated WSNs provided a precise signaling of the significant scenario fire-about-to-start, preemptive enough for early first responder activity, when every second counts. Scenarios such as fire increasing/decreasing, lightening/thunder, and other criticalities were not explored. Anand et al. proposed a similar forest fire detection model using temperature, humidity and smoke using FFNN (Feed Forward Neural Networks) like perceptron but had only 70% accuracy [6].

3   SWSN Architecture

For the smart component of the architecture, MATLAB and Waikato Environment for Knowledge Analysis (WEKA) for the ANN modeling were utilized. A set of IRIS XM2110 MOTEs [1], each with 500 m of transmission range, 250 Kbps data rate, 128 KB of flash memory, and ZigBee network protocol (mesh routing), was used in our experiment. The IRIS board is capable of sensing light, temperature, and sound. The MIB520 USB gateway [2], manufactured by MEMSIC, is used to program the IRIS motes. It is connected to a PC in the field, in order to collect sensed, raw data as the SWSN *sync node*. Every sensor node aggregates raw sensed data, then tags and forwards them to the *sync node* for smart ANN processing. We utilize one of the most popular data mining tools in the machine-learning field, WEKA 4.9. It provides various important encoding strategies and ANN training algorithms.

4   Our Approach

In our experiment, sensed data are handled in two phases, namely *collection* and *processing*. For data, IRIS sensors are placed within range of each other for better communication, since IRISs function as external packets routers too. Moreover, the use of IRISs in our SWSN helps in lowering power consumption at longer communication range. The MOTE's sensed raw data are aggregated and formatted into packets, each containing the following fields: arrival time, sending node number, and the three physical readings of temperature, light, and sound. Hence, sensed Data from the 12 sensors are aggregated as *Information* in one record. Then, the recorded *information* is tagged *spatially* (location, i.e., sensor ID) and *temporally* (i.e., timestamp) to become *Knowledge*. An ANN processes the collected *sync node knowledge*. ANN is an information processing paradigm inspired by the human brain's method of processing textitinformation [10]. Two prominent ANN capabilities for *classification* and *generalization* are applied to the collected *knowledge*. Utilizing the ANN, the *knowledge* is then categorized into classes (one per each trained scenario), allowing for useful variations of the class.

ANN has a massive number of highly interconnected simple processing elements, called neurons, connected via synaptic weights which can be trained to solve certain problems with its *soft computing* capabilities. ANNs excel over traditional mathematical model in some specific applications where *classification* or *association* and *generalization* are the main project goals, e.g. pattern/speech recognition, image processing, data classification (our experiment), etc. Two major learning approaches in the training of ANN are the *un/supervised* models. The training of ANN models involves the adjustment of connectivity strength between the neurons, based on the target application, mimicking learning in biological systems, which involve adjustments to synaptic weights between biological neurons. Through the data collection from fire experimentation in the field, different important scenarios were mimicked (e.g. thunder, lightning, rain, fire, no-fire, and the most important one: "fire about to start"), and the training vectors labeled accordingly. Hence, the ANN models will learn through the *training* phase about the above scenarios, in order to detect them during the *operating* mode, at our SWSN field of deployment (forest).

Many techniques were used to convert/preprocess the raw sensed data through different encoding strategies for varied data types, namely *feature-scaling* and *interpolation*. The physical data readings (temperature, light, sound), within the knowledge records, are raw numeric values with differing units and values; hence, differing ranges. In the ANN training vectors (knowledge records), the data fields with the highest range will dominate the Euclidean distance in the vector-similarity check process, a key factor in the ANN training phase. To overcome this problem the *feature-scaling* mechanism is utilized [15]. It has two methods: *Rescaling* and *Standardization*. In this experiment, *Standardization* was used, whereas *Rescaling* went unexplored. *Standardization* is done via subtracting the mean and dividing by the standard deviation, for each feature (temperature, light, and sound).

The purpose of using *Standardization* on the sensed raw data features is to take advantage of the standard normal distribution, i.e. each vector component/field value is centered around zero, which gives a standard deviation of 1. The next step is the utilization of the *Interpolation* technique [11], which fills any missing sensed data readings due to networking effects, e.g. collision, routing problems, etc. Moreover, the lack of consistent data arrival to the *sync node* may lead to missing some of the sensed data (training vectors fields), which if severe enough, might render the training process of the ANNs ineffective. *Interpolation* is inevitable, and varies based on dynamics of data arrival to the *sync node*. The *least squares* regression line mechanism [13] was the chosen interpolation scheme for the standardized data, using the last four readings adjacent to the missed data. The interpolation of the data [11] is shown in Figs. 1 and 2, where the spaces in Fig. 1 are filled properly, as shown in Fig. 2. The interpolated data are then encoded into *spatial vectors* (SV) (the aggregated processed readings, i.e. sound, temperature, and light from all sensors), one per MOTE sensing unit time. Then, a sequence of N of the SVs are averaged into average temporal vectors (ATV). Hence, each of the ATV fields is the average of N SV corresponding fields (in our experiment N = 20, but not fixed). There are two advantages of using the ATVs in the training process over training directly with SVs. First is the capture of some environmental dynamics, since one ATV will encode some history of the environmental changes via a sequence of N SVs averaged over a period of N time units. The second advantage of ATV is less required storage space versus using SV to train ANN (memory capacity may limit the direct storage of a large number of SVs). Note that N varies between different scenarios, e.g. N for "intensive fire" is higher than for "fire-about-to-start", which may lead to an *overfitting* problem. To overcome such an issue, the SMOTE [9] algorithm is employed. With SMOTE, starting with only 900 ATV vectors, 26301 ATVs were synthesized, with 2391 ATV *training* vectors per scenario. To test our SWSN model, we used 15 ATVs per each scenario. Table 1 contains some raw data from the experiment to show the nature of the collected data. Table 2 displays data after using all the preprocessing techniques.

Table 1. Sample data before preprocessing

Light	Temperature	Sound	Node Id
1000	530	486	10
1000	542	493	15
1003	538	493	1

Table 2. Sample data after preprocessing

Light	Temperature	Sound	Node Id
0.483132	−1.350479	−0.053467	11
0.184565	−1.543044	0.361287	15
0.24629	−1.408305	0.4322589	2

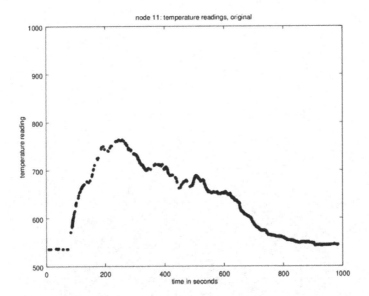

Fig. 1. Before interpolation with missing data

5   Experiment

The SWSN testing experiment has 15 IRIS XM2110 wireless sensors MOTEs. The sensors were placed as shown in Fig. 3. The elliptical experimental firebed is about 2 m long and 1.5 m wide. The fifteen sensors were arranged around the firebed. During the experiment, three sensors were consumed by fire, yet they yielded very valuable data related to dying sensors. Figure 3 is a snapshot of the firebed after the experiment. The dot-circled sensors are active, whereas solid-circles indicate damaged sensors. The purpose of the experiment was to collect actual physical readings from the field, instead of stochastically generating them. A forest fire environment was emulated, i.e. via pounding on a metal

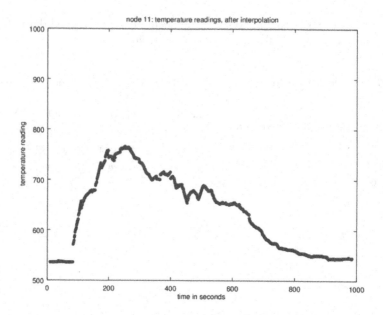

Fig. 2. After interpolation with missing data

Fig. 3. Experimented Firebed after performing the experiment

plate (simulating **thunder**), using a flashlight (mimicking **lighting**), and a fan (generating **wind**). Although 25 sq. ft. is very small compared to the actual size of a forest, without loss of generality it represents a cell in a hierarchy of clustered WSNs that can easily expand to an actual deployment of a full scale SWSN in much larger terrain of forest. The experimentally sensed reading intensities are relatively weak; hence they were scaled to reflect the much higher levels that would be found in nature. *Base case* scenario data (before any fire or other actions) are collected for 10 min, and an additional 10 min for the fire and associated action scenario. Different fire intensity scenarios were emulated by varying accelerant in the experimental course. The entire experiment was video recorded for later scenarios labeling and association of their stamped time. Based on the actual timeline and human monitoring the collected data was applied with different scenarios. Such scheme resulted in labeling 11 different classes/scenarios, after watching the video recordings of the experiment.

Before using the collected data, to encode SVs and ATVs, for training the ANN classifiers, raw data preprocessing techniques were employed, i.e. *feature scaling*, and *interpolation*. Different ANN models were trained to compare results, using two separate sets of ATVs *training* vectors namely "training" and "testing" sets.

6   Results

Different WEKA ANN models (namely LVQ1 and LVQ3) are used, utilizing the ATV vector encoding approach, to compare their accuracies. The LVQ (Learning Vector Quantization) training approach consists of two steps. First step is an unsupervised learning method which is used for input data clustering/subclassing. Second step is the supervised learning phase, with the aid of well known labeled vectors which is used to refine the position of the cluster/subclass learned centroids. This provides better classification and accuracy and minimizes the number of misclassification cases [5]. Hence, LVQ is also called a *semi-supervised* learning ANN. Figure 4 is an example of LVQ architecture, in which preprocessed input vectors are divided into six initial guessed clusters/subclasses. The second linear LVQ learning step of its algorithm applies supervised learning via some well known labeled vectors that belong to known scenarios, which combine the resulting clusters (subclasses) into final classes (desired output learned scenarios). For example in Fig. 4 the first two clusters are in Class 1 and the rest of the clusters are in Class 2 [5].

Optimized learning rate algorithms LVQ 1 & 3 were used, as the accuracy in LVQ algorithms seemed more suited for this problem than other ANN models. For every classifier, we used the *cross validation* technique where input ATVs are split in N folds [12]. Where $(N-1)$ is used for "training" and 1 fold is used for "testing". Hence, We used *Cross validation* of 10 for all the encoding techniques, which indicates the data are folded in 10 halves, and 9 folds are used to train the system and one fold is used to test the system. Fifteen data points were manually chosen for each of the 11 scenarios for testing (a total of $15 \times 11 = 165$). The 11 emulated desired scenarios/classes are listed below:

Model Scenarios/Classes: (monitored via the camera)

- Thundering
- Extensive fire

- Fire decreasing
- Fire increasing
- Fire about to start
- Fire with thunder
- Fire with thunder/lightning
- Intensive fire
- Lightning
- No Fire (base case)
- Rain started and fire stopped (raining over fire).

Different LVQ classifiers were studied using two different types of datasets (a cross validation data set and testing data set) whose accuracy was tested in WEKA

From Tables 3 and 4, it is apparent that both testing data and cross validation give very promising results. When using the primitive SV without averaging, the

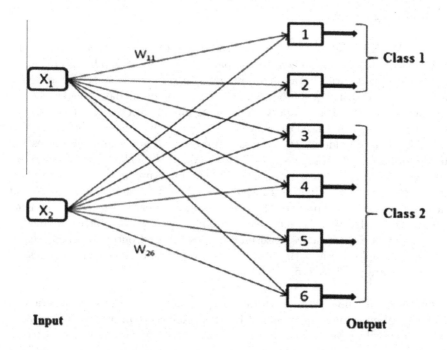

Fig. 4. LVQ network structure [5]

Table 3. Classifier using cross validation

Classifier	Results
LVQ 1	84.05262
LVQ 3	84.3694

Table 4. Classifier with testing data

Classifier	Results
LVQ 1	81.8182
LVQ 3	81.8182

Table 5. Classifier with testing data

Scenarios	Accuracy
No fire	96.3
Lightening	93.9
Thundering	85.8
Fire about to Start	**89.1**
Extensive fire	83.4
Intensive fire	83.4
Fire increasing	86.4
Fire decreasing	72.4
Fire with thundering	82.3
Fire with thundering and lightening	86.71
Rain started, and fire stopped	75.3

obtained accuracy was only around 40%. However, using the ATVs to capture some of the fire's environment "dynamics" through the process of averaging SVs, was superior to the direct use of SV only. The ATV approach almost doubled the SWSN accuracy for the crucial scenario *fire-about-to-start*, to almost 90%. Table 5 shows each of the 11 individual scenario accuracies in the SWSN. Another important scenario is lightning (prominently associated with forest fire), which was detected with 94% accuracy.

```
=== Confusion Matrix ===

    a    b    c    d    e    f    g    h    i    j    k   <-- classified as
 1913    0    0    0    0    0    0    0   66   42  370 |   a = No_fire
    0 1674  316  108  127   55   45   15   51    0    0 |   b = Lightening
    0   63 1912  121  295    0    0    0    0    0    0 |   c = Thundering
    0    0    0 2391    0    0    0    0    0    0    0 |   d = fire_about_to_started
    0    0    0    0 2391    0    0    0    0    0    0 |   e = Extensive_fire
    0    0    0   61   52 2039   78  161    0    0    0 |   f = Intensive_fire
    0    0    0    0    0  113 1899  377    0    2    0 |   g = fire_increasing
    0    0    0    0    0  175   64 2152    0    0    0 |   h = Fire_decreesing
  124    0    0    0    0   42   88  143 1434  251  309 |   i = fire_with_thundering
    0    0    0    0    0   20   23  124  191 1912  121 |   j = fire_with_thundering_lightening
    0    0    0    0    0    0    0    0    0    0 2391 |   k = rain_started_and_fire_stopped
```

Fig. 5. Confusion matrix of LVQ1 for cross validation of 10

The WEKA confusion matrices (shown in Figs. 5 and 6) give a better estimate of the results of the LVQ 1 & 3 classification models, including in/correct classification. They also show the data distribution in every predicted class/scenario, for better projection of the results.

```
=== Confusion Matrix ===

    a    b    c    d    e    f    g    h    i    j    k   <-- classified as
 1913    0    0    0    0    0    0    0    0    0  478 |   a = No_fire
    0 1674  478  234    5    0    0    0    0    0    0 |   b = Lightening
    0    0 1912  479    0    0    0    0    0    0    0 |   c = Thundering
    0    0    0 2391    0    0    0    0    0    0    0 |   d = fire_about_to_started
    0    0    0    0 2391    0    0    0    0    0    0 |   e = Extensive_fire
    0    0    0   44   48 2109  190    0    0    0    0 |   f = Intensive_fire
    0    0    0    0    0   53 1911  427    0    0    0 |   g = fire_increasing
    0    0    0    0    0    0  239 2152    0    0    0 |   h = Fire_decreesing
    0    0    0    0    0    0    0    0 1434  743  214 |   i = fire_with_thundering
    0    0    0    0    0    0    0    0  256 1912  223 |   j = fire_with_thundering_lightening
    0    0    0    0    0    0    0    0    0    0 2391 |   k = rain_started_and_fire_stopped
```

Fig. 6. Confusion matrix of LVQ3 for cross validation of 10

7   Conclusions

Although, forest fires cannot be totally prevented, our SWSN early detection system may be able to alleviate the problem, via a combination of WSN and machine learning technologies (ANN). This paper presents a promising approach for the early detection of forest fires in real time. Pre-data processing was a challenge and required the aid of some prominent ANN data standardization techniques, in addition to the averaging of spatial vectors (SVs), to capture the dynamics of critical scenarios with *about-to-start* semantics, e.g. fire, lightning, rain, etc. The experimental results are very encouraging, yet we are aware of the challenges of deploying a SWSN model into actual forest terrain. Our SWSN design might be a cell in a larger topology for full scale deployment in the forest. One important facet of our work is studying the effect of different encoding strategies (spatial versus temporal data vectorization) on the success of different ANN classifier training. Future work will aim at system robustness, energy consumption, and security. We are currently researching a different approach to capture the true dynamics of *about-to-happen* scenarios, allowing for higher accuracy and more preemptive warning time prior to event occurrence. Moreover, we plan to utilize the design philosophy of our scheme to build a generic early asynchronous event detection system for much wider civil and military applications, e.g. Wireless Body Area Networks (WBAN), computing environments Intrusion Detection, IoT, Tsunami, Earthquake, Volcanic Activity, Border Intrusion, etc.

References

1. Iris homepage. http://www.memsic.com/userfiles/files/Datasheets/WSN/IRIS_Datasheet.pdf
2. Mib520 usb interface board. http://www.openautomation.net/page/productos/id/31/title/MIB520-USB-Gateway
3. National park service: Wildfire causes and evaluations. In: Wildland Fire - Learning in Depth (2016). https://www.nps.gov/articles/wildfire-causes-and-evaluations.htm
4. Afzaal, H., Zafar, N.A.: Robot-based forest fire detection and extinguishing model. In: 2016 2nd International Conference on Robotics and Artificial Intelligence (ICRAI), pp. 112–117 (2016). https://doi.org/10.1109/ICRAI.2016.7791238

5. Amezcua, P.M.J.: A new neural network model based on the LVQ algorithm for multi-class classification of arrhythmias. Inf. Sci. **279**, 483–497 (2014). https://doi.org/10.1016/j.ins.2014.04.003

6. Anand, S., Manjari, R.K.K.: FPGA implementation of artificial neural network for forest fire detection in wireless sensor network. In: 2017 2nd International Conference on Computing and Communications Technologies (ICCCT), pp. 265–270 (2017). https://doi.org/10.1109/ICCCT2.2017.7972284

7. Cai, M., Lu, X., Wu, X., Feng, Y.: Intelligent video analysis-based forest fires smoke detection algorithms. In: 2016 12th International Conference on Natural Computation, Fuzzy Systems and Knowledge Discovery (ICNC-FSKD), pp. 1504–1508 (2016). https://doi.org/10.1109/FSKD.2016.7603399

8. Chauhan, A., Semwal, S., Chawhan, R.: Artificial neural network-based forest fire detection system using wireless sensor network. In: 2013 Annual IEEE India Conference (INDICON), pp. 1–6 (2013). https://doi.org/10.1109/INDCON.2013.6725913

9. Chawla, N.V., Bowyer, K.W., Hall, L.O., Kegelmeyer, W.P.: SMOTE: synthetic minority over-sampling technique. J. Artif. Int. Res. **16**(1), 321–357 (2002). http://dl.acm.org/citation.cfm?id=1622407.1622416

10. Christos Stergiou, D.S.: Neural Networks, vol. 4 (2005). UK

11. Davis, P.J.: Interpolation and Approximation. Dover Publications, Mineola (2014)

12. Kohavi, R.: A study of cross-validation and bootstrap for accuracy estimation and model selection **14** (2001)

13. Miller, S.J.: The method of least squares (2006)

14. NIFC: 2015 statistics and summary. In: Wildland Fire Summaries (2016). https://www.predictiveservices.nifc.gov

15. Raschka, S.: Python Machine Learning. Packt Publishing, Birmingham (2015)

16. Soliman, H., Sudan, K., Mishra, A.: A smart forest-fire early detection sensory system: another approach of utilizing wireless sensor and neural networks. In: SENSORS 2010, pp. 1900–1904. IEEE (2010). https://doi.org/10.1109/ICSENS.2010.5690033

17. Son, B., Her, Y.S.: A design and implementation of forest-fires surveillance system based on wireless sensor networks for South Korea mountains **6** (2005)

18. Zhang J-H, Y.F.M.: Detection, emission estimation and risk prediction of forest fires in china using satellite sensors and simulation models in the past three decades-an overview. Int. J. Environ. Res. Public Health, 112–117 (2011). https://doi.org/10.3390/ijerph8083156

Online Guest Detection in a Smart Home Using Pervasive Sensors and Probabilistic Reasoning

Jennifer Renoux[✉], Uwe Köckemann, and Amy Loutfi

Center for Applied Autonomous Sensor Systems, Örebro University, Örebro, Sweden
{jennifer.renoux,uwe.kockemann,amy.loutfi}@oru.se

Abstract. Smart home environments equipped with distributed sensor networks are capable of helping people by providing services related to health, emergency detection or daily routine management. A backbone to these systems relies often on the system's ability to track and detect activities performed by the users in their home. Despite the continuous progress in the area of activity recognition in smart homes, many systems make a strong underlying assumption that the number of occupants in the home at any given moment of time is always known. Estimating the number of persons in a Smart Home at each time step remains a challenge nowadays. Indeed, unlike most (crowd) counting solution which are based on computer vision techniques, the sensors considered in a Smart Home are often very simple and do not offer individually a good overview of the situation. The data gathered needs therefore to be fused in order to infer useful information. This paper aims at addressing this challenge and presents a probabilistic approach able to estimate the number of persons in the environment at each time step. This approach works in two steps: first, an estimate of the number of persons present in the environment is done using a Constraint Satisfaction Problem solver, based on the topology of the sensor network and the sensor activation pattern at this time point. Then, a Hidden Markov Model refines this estimate by considering the uncertainty related to the sensors. Using both simulated and real data, our method has been tested and validated on two smart homes of different sizes and configuration and demonstrates the ability to accurately estimate the number of inhabitants.

1 Introduction

Ambient Assisted Living (AAL) technologies provide services such as health control, emergency detection systems or activity monitoring [17]. Recent advancements in areas such as pervasive sensing, robotics and human-machine

---

This work and the authors are supported by the distributed environment Ecare@Home (Swedish Knowledge Foundation 2015–2019) and the MoveCare project (European Commission H2020 framework program for research and innovation, ID 732158).

© Springer Nature Switzerland AG 2018
A. Kameas and K. Stathis (Eds.): AmI 2018, LNCS 11249, pp. 74–89, 2018.
https://doi.org/10.1007/978-3-030-03062-9_6

interaction bring these systems closer to real applications. Activity and context recognition are two very important aspects of these systems as they enable to act depending on the constantly evolving situation. In the case of multi-person activity recognition, group activity recognition has been attracting an important amount of work recently [4, 8]. However, these systems are computer vision based technique and are hardly usable in Smart Homes where the presence of cameras is not desirable. To our knowledge, all existing not vision based context and activity recognition techniques have been designed or trained for an assumed number of occupants in the home (usually one or two) and cannot handle other numbers of persons [3].

However, real-life situations in our homes usually involve visits from other persons, especially in the domain of AAL where the users considered are often living alone or with their partner, and are regularly visited by caregivers or guests. These unexpected visits, if undetected and unaccounted for, might degrade or even impede the possibility for such systems to make correct inference about alarms, activities of daily living and more.

The ability to detect the presence of guests and estimate the number of persons in the environment at a given time is of paramount importance for the development of AAL systems and their adaptation to real-life scenarios. The contribution of this work is a framework capable of estimating the number of occupants in a Smart Home using pervasive binary sensors. This framework combines a Constraint satisfaction Problem (CSP) Solver with a Hidden Markov Model (HMM) to handle uncertainty and recover from wrong estimations.

The paper is presented as follows. First, we present a brief summary of existing work about person counting in various environments. Then Sect. 3 presents the developed model. The evaluation protocol and the results are presented in Sect. 4. Finally, Sect. 5 will discuss the capabilities and limitations of our approach.

2   Related Work

While commercial solutions for person counting are said to exist, they use various sets sensors, such as thermal imagers or break beam sensors [14] which suffer from a number of shortcomings. In addition to their costs, these solutions have the major disadvantage of not being robust to occlusion and are unable to recover from a false detection. They are therefore efficient only if one wishes to estimate a crowd or a stream of persons passing but, indeed of little use in a smart home where the counting needs to be more precise and robust. Other systems that allow people tracking and counting use vision-based sensors [11, 15]. While these systems are efficient and reliable, the use of cameras makes them unsuitable for smart some environments for obvious privacy reasons. Finally, wearables such as RFID readers can be used to identify and track occupants of a Smart Home (e.g. in [16], but they require the user to carry the device with them and are therefore not usable to detect persons who are only visiting and do not carry such a device.

Pervasive sensing is becoming more efficient and affordable thanks to the rapid development of small low-cost sensors. This paradigm is already used in various of Ambient Intelligence applications [2,9] and offers an ideal setup for an unobtrusive method of counting people in the environment. However, even though these applications require to know the number of occupants in the environment, they usually avoid this problem by assuming a fixed number of occupants and consequently, very little research is available where pervasive sensing is used for person counting. Some recent work focused on estimating the number of pedestrians in environments using binary sensors and Monte-Carlo methods [6], but these are again hardly usable in Smart Home situation due to various assumption about the topology of the environment. Recently, [13] proposed a system using probabilistic reasoning to perform counting in Smart Home, but the assumptions made by the authors (total independence of the sensors) greatly limits its usability.

Counting the number of persons in a environment with unobtrusive environmental sensors under realistic hypotheses remains an open research question. In the next sections, we will be presenting our model aiming at addressing this issue while reducing the number of hypotheses considered.

3   The Model

We describe the input to our system as observations of *Features of Interest (FoI)*. A FoI for person counting is the representation of a real-world element that is monitored and indicates the presence of a person. A basic example of such a FoI is *couch occupancy* which could be observed by a pressure sensor. In the same way the FoI *room presence* could be measured by a motion sensor. More complex FoIs can be considered, such as actions on objects (e.g., a door that is being opened or closed). We assume that each FoI is in one of two different states, representing whether they are currently *active* or *idle*. To each FoI is associated an interval $[min, max]$, called the *arity* of the FoI, representing how many persons minimum (resp. maximum) can activate this FoI at once. For instance, a motion sensor will be associated with the interval $[1, \infty]$ as it is activated if one persons enter its range and the activation remains the same whatever number of persons are present. A pressure sensor on a couch however could be associated with the interval $[1, 3]$ as one person at least needs to sit on the couch for the sensor to be activated but a maximum of 3 persons can sit together on the couch. By using FoIs instead of the actual sensor, we make it possible to represent different granularity of detection. It is possible for instance to estimate the number of persons sitting on a couch by analyzing the raw value given by the pressure sensor and thresholding it differently. This sensor could then be represented by several FoIs, each associated to a different threshold. We call *activation line* the set of all states for all FoIs in the environment at a given point in time.

We represent possible overlaps of FoIs in an undirected graph, called *Co-activation Graph (CG)*. Each node in the CG represents a FoI and two nodes are connected if a single person can activate both FoIs at the same time. A simple example would be a pressure sensor on a couch and a motion sensor in the room containing the couch. A single person could activate both FoIs by sitting on couch and being detected by the motion sensor.

Finally, we assume that the environment has only one *entry point* from which a single person can enter or exit at a given time point, and that this entry point is monitored and therefore associated to a FoI. We also assume that the maximum number of persons that can be in the environment at once is bounded. We denote this number Ω.

Figure 1 illustrates the overall approach. The environment and sensors need to be modeled to create the co-activation graph required by the CSP solver (see below). The CSP solver also receives the current activation line representing the state of all FoIs. Using this input, the CSP produces an estimate of the number of people in the environment for each time point. The Probabilistic Reasoner then uses these estimates as observations to generate a state sequence, in which each state contains the number of persons present in the environment at the associated time point. The reasoner uses a sliding window over the observations sequence in order to perform the counting online. We now describe this approach in detail over the next few sections.

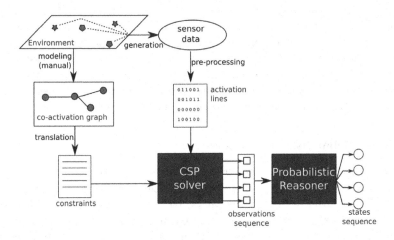

Fig. 1. Overall diagram of our person counting system

3.1   The Constraint Satisfaction Problem

Constraint Satisfaction Problems (CSPs) [5] are modeled by providing a set of variables X, a set of domains $D[x]$ for each $x \in X$, and a set of constraints C that specify allowed (or disallowed) relations between different variables. A solution to a CSP is an assignment for each variable in X that satisfies all constraints in C.

To get an estimate of the number of people in an environment we create a CSP in the following way. Let $P = \{1, \ldots, \Omega\}$ represent a set of persons. We create one variable $x \in X$ for each FoI with $D[x] = 2^P$. An assignment of a variable x is the set of persons observed by a specific FoI. Further, as input for each FoI x we assume to know $\alpha_x \in \{True, False\}$ (i.e., the activation line), as well as $\min_x \in \{1, \ldots, \Omega\}$ and $\max_x \in \{1, \ldots, \Omega\}$ (the minimum and maximum number of persons indicated by the FoI). For each pair of FoIs x_1 and x_2 we use $CG(x_1, x_2) \in \{True, False\}$ indicating whether or not two FoIs have an edge in the co-activation graph.

Given this information we impose the following constraints:

$$\forall x \in X : \neg \alpha_x \Leftrightarrow |x| = 0 \tag{1}$$

$$\forall x \in X : \alpha_x \Leftrightarrow \min_x \leq |x| \leq \max_x \tag{2}$$

$$\forall x_1, x_2 \in x : x_1 \cap x_2 = \emptyset \vee CG(x_1, x_2) \tag{3}$$

Constraint 1 states that if FoI x is not activated it does not observe any person. Constraint 2 states that if FoI x is activated it observers any number of persons between the minimum and maximum allowed for this FoI. Finally, Constraint 3 states that two FoIs can only observe the same person when they are neighbors in the co-activation graph.

To solve this problem we modeled it in the constraint processing language MiniZinc[1] and used the default solver that comes with the MiniZinc software. We chose constraint processing to solve this sub-problem as it is easy to model and we can rely on existing solvers to create solutions relatively fast. While we do not use minimization in order compute solutions fast enough, we assume that solutions to the CSP are close the minimal number of persons in the environment. The reason for this is that the constraints above are much easier to satisfy when each FoI x is assigned the smallest possible number of persons.

3.2   The Probabilistic Reasoner

The role of the probabilistic reasoner is to take a sequence of outputs produced by the CSP solver and refine them by considering *aleatory* uncertainty and *epistemic* uncertainty. Aleatory uncertainty is caused by randomness and variability in the system, in our case possible false sensor measures. Epistemic uncertainty is due to a lack of knowledge, in our case overlapping FoIs which can produce the same activation line for different numbers of persons within their range. To deal with both types of uncertainty, we need a reasoning model capable of:

- capturing and using a priori knowledge about the environment such as its dynamic, the relations between the environment state and the observed output,
- reasoning sequentially over series of inputs.

Hidden Markov Models (HMM) are a very well studied class of Bayesian reasoning models capable of capturing such information. A HMM is made of

---

[1] http://www.minizinc.org/.

hidden states that can generate observations. A transition matrix explicits the dynamic of the model, which respects the Markov Property, i.e., that the state at time t only depends on the state at time $t - 1$. Finally, an emission matrix defines the probability with which a given state can generate a given observation. HMMs have been successfully used in various applications involving sequential reasoning, especially in speech and handwriting recognition [7,10]. A complete overview of HMMs can be found in [12].

In our framework, the variable being modeled in the HMM is the number of persons in the environment. Mathematically, our person counting HMM is described as follows:

- $S = \{s_0, \ldots, s_m\}$ is the set of states, with $\forall s_i = [\omega_i, \alpha_i]$ with $\omega_i \in [0, \Omega]$ being the number of persons in the environment and $\alpha_i \in \{True, False\}$ is the state of the entry point. By construction, there is $|S| = (\Omega + 1) * 2$ states in the state space.
- $V = \{v_0, \ldots, v_n\}$ is the observation alphabet, with $\forall v_i = [\delta_i, \alpha_i]$ with $\delta_i \in [0, \Omega]$ being the estimate given by the CSP solver and $\alpha_i \in \{True, False\}$ being the same state of the entry point. By construction, there are $|V| = (\Omega + 1) * 2$ elements in the observation alphabet.
- $Q = q_1, \ldots, q_T$ is a fixed sequence of T states
- $O = o_1, \ldots, o_T$ is a fixed sequence of T observations
- $\pi = [\pi_i], \pi_i = P(q_1 = s_i)$ is the initial probability array. Without prior information, π is a uniform distribution.
- $A = [a_{ij}], a_{ij} = P(q_t = s_j | q_{t-1} = s_i)$ is the transition matrix, storing the probability of state s_j following s_i.
- $B = [b_i(k)], b_i(k) = P(o_t = v_k | q_t = s_i)$ is the observation matrix, storing the probability that observation v_k is produced from state s_i.

Note that the states in our HMM do not only include hidden variables but also part of the observation. The reason for this design choice is due to the fact that considering the state of the entry point as part of the observation enables us to model the dynamic of the system with a finer granularity than considering only the result of the CSP. Indeed, this FoI has the specificity to announce when somebody is likely to have entered or to left the environment. However, by considering this FoI in the observation, our system looses its Markovian property as the state at time t depends on both the state and the observation at time $t - 1$. By integrating the FoI in the state as well, we can restore the Markovian property.

The transition matrix is defined based on static, likely and unlikely transitions. Static transitions are simply transitions from s_i to s_i. Definition 1 gives the likely transitions for normal case, i.e. $\omega_i \neq 0$ and $\omega_i \neq \Omega$ (Eq. 4), and for the border cases (Eq. 5).

Definition 1 (Likely transition). *A transition between $s_i = [\omega_i, \alpha_i]$ and $s_j = [\omega_j, \alpha_j]$ is considered likely if and only if for $0 < \omega_i < \Omega$:*

$$
\begin{cases}
\begin{aligned}
& \omega_j = \omega_i \ and \ \alpha_j = True \\
or \ & \omega_j = \omega_i + 1 \ and \ \alpha_j = True
\end{aligned} \quad for \ \alpha_i = False \\[1.5em]
\begin{aligned}
& \omega_j = \omega_i \ and \ \alpha_j = False \\
or \ & \omega_j = \omega_i - 1 \ and \ \alpha_j = False
\end{aligned} \quad for \ \alpha_i = True
\end{cases}
\tag{4}
$$

The following transitions are also considered likely:

$$
\begin{aligned}
s_i &= [0, False] \text{ to } s_j = [1, True] \\
s_i &= [0, True] \text{ to } s_j = [0, False] \\
s_i &= [0, True] \text{ to } s_j = [1, True] \\
s_i &= [\Omega, False] \text{ to } s_j = [\Omega, False] \\
s_i &= [\Omega, True] \text{ to } s_j = [\Omega - 1, True]
\end{aligned}
\tag{5}
$$

The intuition behind this modeling is that if the entry point becomes activated ($\alpha_i = False$ and $\alpha_j = True$), it is likely that either someone already in the environment activated it or someone just entered the environment. On the opposite, if the entry point was activated and is now idle ($\alpha_i = True$ and $\alpha_j = False$), it is likely that either someone stayed in the environment but left the FoI's range or someone just left the environment. By construction there is then 2 likely transitions for the normal cases and 1 or 2 for the special cases.

All transitions that are neither static nor likely are considered unlikely. From the previous definition, we can derive the transition probabilities for static and likely transitions. All static transitions have a probability $a_{ii} = p_{static}$. The probabilities of likely transitions are computed as follows for the special cases:

$$
\begin{aligned}
a_{ij} &= p_{likely} \text{ for } & s_i &= [0,0] \text{ and } s_j = [1,1] \\
a_{ij} &= \tfrac{p_{likely}}{2} \text{ for } & s_i &= [0,1] \text{ and } s_j = [0,0] \\
a_{ij} &= \tfrac{p_{likely}}{2} \text{ for } & s_i &= [0,1] \text{ and } s_j = [1,1] \\
a_{ij} &= p_{likely} \text{ for } & s_i &= [\Omega,0] \text{ and } s_j = [\Omega,1] \\
a_{ij} &= p_{likely} \text{ for } s_i &= [\Omega,1] \text{ and } s_j = [\Omega - 1, 0]
\end{aligned}
\tag{6}
$$

For the normal cases:

$$
a_{ij} = \tfrac{p_{likely}}{2}
\tag{7}
$$

The probabilities for the unlikely transitions can be easily derived from Eqs. 6 and 7 :

$$
a_{ij} = \frac{p_{unlikely}}{|S|^2 - (n_{i,likely} + 1)}
\tag{8}
$$

where $n_{i,likely}$ is the number of likely transitions from state s_i.

The emission matrix is defined similarly by considering impossible, correct, probable and unprobable emissions. It also uses the fact that, as discussed previously, the CSP is more likely to underestimate the number of persons in the environment rather than overestimate it. Given this knowledge and considering a state $s_i = [\omega_i, \alpha_i]$ and an observation $v_k = [\delta_k, \alpha_k]$, we know that:

– the emission of v_k in state s_i is impossible by construction iff $\alpha_i \neq \alpha_k$,
– the emission of v_k by s_i is correct iff $\omega_i = \delta_i$ and $\alpha_i = \alpha_k$,
– the emission of v_k while in s_i is probable iff $\omega_i > \delta_k$ and $\alpha_i = \alpha_k$,
– the emission of v_k while in s_i is unprobable iff $\omega_i < \delta_k$ and $\alpha_i = \alpha_k$.

From this it is possible to derive the emission probabilities:

$$
\begin{aligned}
b_i(k) &= p_{correct} & \text{for } \delta_k = \omega_i \\
b_i(k) &= \frac{p_{probable}}{\omega_i} & \text{for } \delta_k < \omega_i \\
b_i(k) &= \frac{p_{unprobable}}{\Omega - \delta_k} & \text{for } \delta_k > \omega_i
\end{aligned}
\tag{9}
$$

4 Evaluation

4.1 Evaluation Design

To evaluate our system, we used simulated and real datasets. Simulated data was necessary for two reasons. First available datasets only consider one or two occupants while it is important to evaluate the performance of our system on larger number of occupants. Second, available datasets have limitations in the size of the environment they consider (usually small) and its coverage (usually partial), while we wished to evaluate the difference in the performance of our system depending on the size and the coverage. For these reasons, we use three different configurations:

1. ARAS: small environment, partial coverage, reproducing the House A from [1], presented on Fig. 2a. Tests have been performed on simulated and real data for this environment.
2. ARAS-FC: small environment, full coverage, modified from ARAS by adding motion sensors in each room to create a full coverage, presented on Fig. 2a. Due to the lack of available dataset for this environment (the ARAS dataset considering only partial coverage), tests have been performed on simulated data only.
3. House 2: large environment, full coverage, presented on Fig. 2b. This environment has been chosen to study the different in performance between a small and a large environment. Due to the lack of available dataset for this environment, tests have been performed on simulated data only.

For the three environment, one FoI has been created for each sensor present.

The real dataset used for the ARAS environment is the dataset provided in [1], which consists of 30 days of data with one activation line per second, i.e. 86400 activation lines per day. The first 3 days of data have been used to learn the parameters of the system while the 27 remaining days have been used to evaluate the system.

Data were simulated using a pseudo-random walk in a Markov Chain. A node in the Markov Chain represents a possible Feature of Interest. One node represents the outside of the apartment. Two nodes are connected if the user can access the ending FoI from the starting FoI without activating any other

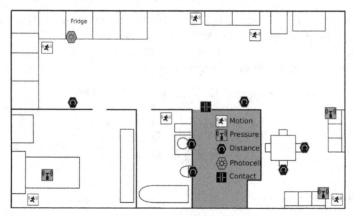

(a) Map of ARAS (without motion sensors) and ARAS-FC environments. ARAS-FC is the full-coverage version of ARAS, in which motion sensors have been added in each rooms. Figure modified from [1].

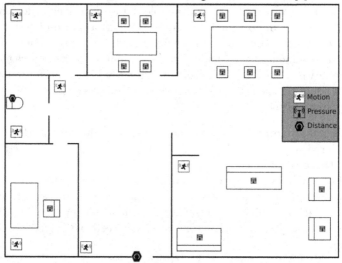

(b) Map of the House 2 environment with sensors

Fig. 2. Map of test environments with sensors

FoI. The transitions probabilities were decided arbitrarily to represent plausible transitions. Each node is also associated with a maximum number of persons that can be present on this node at the same time. Multi-agent pseudo random walks are performed over the Markov Chain to generate datasets: at each time step, all the agents randomly select an accessible node with available space and move to this location. Data simulated this way is obviously not realistic, i.e., the agents are going to perform a sequence of movements without following any specific activity plan, changing location and therefore activated node much more often than a real person would. However, despite this lack of realism, simulating data this way allowed us to obtain relatively large datasets quickly on various number of persons. A total of 1000 activation lines have been generated and used to learn the parameters of the HMMs and 10000 have been used to evaluate the system, distributed in 10 runs of 1000 lines.

For each environment we optimized 9 different HMMs, one per maximum number of persons allowed ranging from 2 to 10. Due to a lack of space, only the results for the HMMs created with 4, 6, 8 and 10 persons maximum (referred respectively as HMM-4, HMM-6, HMM-8 and HMM-10) will be presented in this paper. The other HMMs showed similar trends. The optimization of the HMM has been done by learning the transition and the observation matrices. The learning of the transition matrix (resp. observation matrix) has been performed by calculating the frequency of likely and unlikely transitions (resp. correct, probable and unprobable emissions). For tests using simulated data, the learning has been performed over 1000 activation lines, different from the ones used for testing. For tests using real data, the learning has been performed over 3 days of data, i.e. 3×86400 activation lines and the been performed over the 27 remaining days.

In order to assess the usefulness of the HMM, we perform each experiment using only the CSP or the combination CSP+HMM. This step has been done to ensure that the HMM was indeed useful and that the CSP alone was not enough to achieve acceptable prediction. Finally, preliminary experiments not presented in this paper for lack of space showed that the size of the sliding window, when 10 or above, do not impact significantly the results of the prediction. Therefore, these experiments have been conducted with a sliding window of size 10.

4.2   Results

Simulated Data. Figure 3 presents the accuracy obtained for the ARAS and ARAS-FC environments. Accuracy is defined as the proportion of exact matches between the predicted and actual number.

Figure 4 presents the average distance between the predicted number of persons and the actual number of persons for the different ARAS environment. Note that the distance has been only computed when the prediction was incorrect. From the experiments, we observed first of all that the accuracy of the system in the ARAS-FC environment is much better than the one in ARAS with an improvement of 46% on average. This highlights the importance of choosing and positioning properly the sensors when performing counting with pervasive sensors. The second point to be noted is that, as expected, the system with HMM is performing better than the system without HMM with an average improvement of 38% for ARAS and 17% for ARAS-FC. Third, we noticed that the performance of the system decreases slightly when the HMM is optimized for a higher maximum number of persons. Finally, we noticed that the accuracy of the system is globally good for 0 to 3 persons (99% to 68% accuracy on average for ARAS-FC) but decrease dramatically for 4 persons and more. (45% to close to 0% on average). Our hypothesis to explain this difference is twofold:

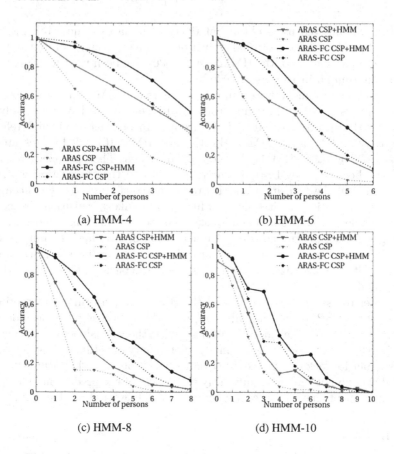

(a) HMM-4

(b) HMM-6

(c) HMM-8

(d) HMM-10

Fig. 3. Accuracy obtained on ARAS and ARAS-FC environments

1. The size of the environment (rather small) makes it impossible to discriminate between persons after a certain number. Indeed, the number of FoIs that a person can activate and have a finite arity is rather small and therefore limits the possibility of detection. This hypothesis will be enforced by our experiments in the House 2.

2. the behavior of the simulated agents are very erratic and they change location during the simulation more often and with less coherence than real agents, which creates more difficult situations for the reasoner. Indeed, HMMs in general are used and capable of recognizing patterns and changes in these patterns by making use of sequences of observations. In our case, there is no pattern not make use of and the changes in the environment are very erratic, making it more difficult to predict. We could hypothesize that a real agent would follow more consistent patterns that the Markov Chains we used for simulated data failed to capture. More experiments either with real or more accurate simulated data would be needed to test this hypothesis.

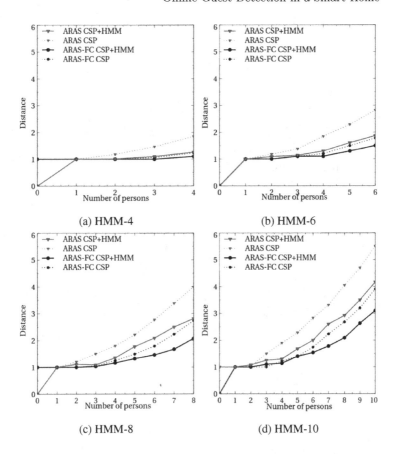

Fig. 4. Distance obtained on ARAS and ARAS-FC environments

However, it is interesting to note that despite the drop in accuracy, the distance between the predicted number of persons and the actual one remains low in the case of ARAS-FC CSP+HMM.

Figure 5 presents the detection accuracy obtained for the Home 2, with and without the HMM and for various maximum number of persons. As before, we noticed that in this environment the system is performing better with HMM than without (improvement of 19%). We also noticed that the overall detection accuracy is much better in Home 2 than in ARAS-FC for larger number of persons, which tends to confirm the hypothesis that the size of the environment (and more specifically the number of FoIs associated to finite arity) affects the performance of our system.

Figure 6 presents the average distance between the predicted number of persons and the actual number of persons, restricted to the cases where the prediction was incorrect. Once again, we notice that despite the drop in the accuracy, the distance between predicted and actual number of persons remains rather low, even for large number of persons.

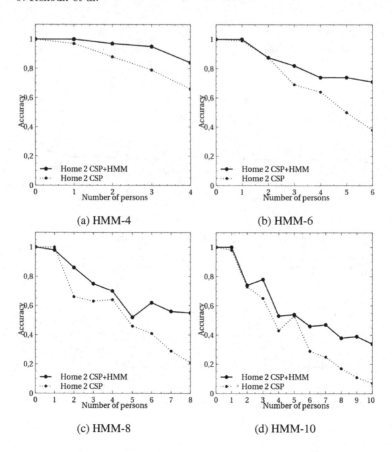

(a) HMM-4　　　　　　　　　　(b) HMM-6

(c) HMM-8　　　　　　　　　　(d) HMM-10

Fig. 5. Accuracy obtained on the House 2 environment

Real Data. Tests on real data have been performed on the ARAS environment using both HMM-4 and HMM-10 in order to compare the results. With both HMM-4 and HMM-10, our system reached an overall detection accuracy of 80% (against 83% for HMM-4 and 76% for HMM-10 with simulated data). The differences between the results obtained with simulated and real data are not significant enough to enable us to confirm or contradict our hypothesis that real data are easier to reason upon than simulated data. More experiments, especially with higher number of persons, are required but the lack of such data currently makes it impossible to do so. However, the high percentage of accurate detection with real data is by itself a promising result regarding the ability of our system to detect accurately the number of persons in the environment with real data. This result, once more, needs to be confirmed with other datasets considering different number of persons.

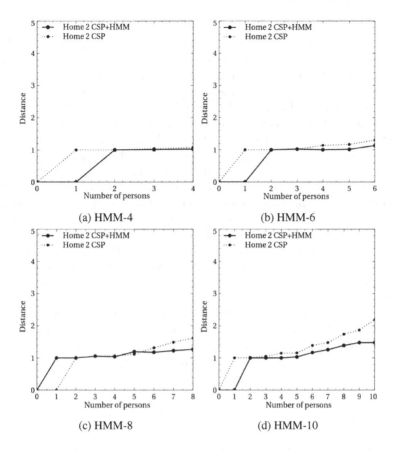

(a) HMM-4   (b) HMM-6

(c) HMM-8   (d) HMM-10

Fig. 6. Distance obtained on the House 2 environment

5 Discussion

We presented a system capable of counting the number of persons present in an environment using pervasive sensors and a combination of a CSP solver and a Hidden Markov Model. Our system is capable of performing online counting with an overall accuracy of 80% on both simulated and real data. These results have been achieved while learning the parameters of the HMM using very basic statistic computation.

Extensive experiments enabled us to identify a set of factors that influence the result of this system. First of all, the coverage of the environment by the sensors is of high importance. For good results, the environment needs to be as fully covered by sensors as possible, meaning that the number of places in which a person can be located without being sensed by any sensor needs to be as small as possible. Then, the maximum number of persons allowed in the environment must be realistic enough to capture various situations but not too high to keep the detection accurate. Even with a higher maximum number of persons allowed than required, the system is still performing very well to discriminate between 0, 1, 2 or more occupants, making it reliable to detect guests in various E-Health and Ambient Assisted Living systems.

Our system is based on different assumptions that could be relaxed in future work. First of all, it assumes a single entry point in the environment. While this assumption holds for a lot of environments such as regular apartments, other environments such as houses might present additional entry points (e.g., a garage door, or a back-door to a garden). Our system needs to be adapted for these situations. Then, the second and most constraining hypothesis is the maximum number of persons considered. This assumption had been made to avoid dealing with infinite sets of possible states, which is a common difficulty in reasoning. However, this constrains the user to choose an appropriate maximum since it impacts the performances of our system. Relaxing this assumption while keeping a good detection accuracy is an important step to take.

Apart from relaxing these assumptions, we would like to investigate ways to increase the accuracy of the system. One possibility in this direction, could be to model the environment in a more fine-grained manner (e.g., per room instead of per home). There are several ways to attempt improving the counting performance when a large number of persons are involved, such as providing ground truth to the system or a more complex formulation of the HMM, especially considering likely and unlikely transitions. In addition Finally, it would of interest to establish a theoretical baseline of how well any counting system can perform with a given set of sensors.

References

1. Alemdar, H., Ertan, H., Incel, O.D., Ersoy, C.: ARAS human activity datasets in multiple homes with multiple residents. In: Proceedings of the 7th International Conference on Pervasive Computing Technologies for Healthcare, PervasiveHealth 2013, pp. 232–235. ICST (Institute for Computer Sciences, Social-Informatics and Telecommunications Engineering), ICST, Brussels, Belgium, Belgium (2013)
2. Alirezaie, M., et al.: An ontology-based context-aware system for smart homes: E-care@ home. Sensors **17**(7), 1586 (2017)
3. Benmansour, A., Bouchachia, A., Feham, M.: Multioccupant activity recognition in pervasive smart home environments. ACM Comput. Surv. (CSUR) **48**(3), 34 (2016)
4. Choi, W., Savarese, S.: A unified framework for multi-target tracking and collective activity recognition. In: Fitzgibbon, A., Lazebnik, S., Perona, P., Sato, Y., Schmid, C. (eds.) ECCV 2012. LNCS, vol. 7575, pp. 215–230. Springer, Heidelberg (2012). https://doi.org/10.1007/978-3-642-33765-9_16
5. Dechter, R.: Constraint Processing. Elsevier Morgan Kaufmann (2003)
6. Fujii, S., Taniguchi, Y., Hasegawa, G., Matsuoka, M.: Pedestrian counting with grid-based binary sensors based on Monte Carlo method. SpringerPlus **3**(1), 299 (2014)
7. Gales, M., Young, S., et al.: The application of hidden Markov models in speech recognition. Found. Trends® Signal Process. **1**(3), 195–304 (2008)

8. Ibrahim, M.S., Muralidharan, S., Deng, Z., Vahdat, A., Mori, G.: A hierarchical deep temporal model for group activity recognition. In: Proceedings of the IEEE Conference on Computer Vision and Pattern Recognition, pp. 1971–1980 (2016)

9. Noor, M.H.M., Salcic, Z., Kevin, I., Wang, K.: Ontology-based sensor fusion activity recognition. J. Ambient. Intell. Humanized Comput., 1–15 (2018)

10. Plötz, T., Fink, G.A.: Markov models for offline handwriting recognition: a survey. Int. J. Doc. Anal. Recognit. (IJDAR) **12**(4), 269 (Oct 2009)

11. Prathiba, G.T., Dhas, Y.P.: Literature survey for people counting and human detection. IOSR J. Eng. (IOSRJEN) **3**(1), 05–10 (2013)

12. Rabiner, L.R.: A tutorial on hidden markov models and selected applications in speech recognition. Proc. IEEE **77**(2), 257–286 (1989)

13. Renoux, J., Alirezaie, M., Karlsson, L., Köckemann, U., Pecora, F., Loutfi, A.: Context recognition in multiple occupants situations: detecting the number of agents in a smart home environment with simple sensors. In: Knowledge-Based Techniques for Problem Solving and Reasoning (KnowProS 2017) (2017)

14. Teixeira, T., Dublon, G., Savvides, A.: A survey of human-sensing: Methods for detecting presence, count, location, track, and identity. ACM Comput. Surv. **5**(1), 59–69 (2010)

15. Vera, P., Monjaraz, S., Salas, J.: Counting pedestrians with a zenithal arrangement of depth cameras. Mach. Vis. Appl. **27**(2), 303–315 (2016)

16. Wang, L., Gu, T., Tao, X., Chen, H., Lu, J.: Recognizing multi-user activities using wearable sensors in a smart home. Pervasive Mob. Comput. **7**(3), 287–298 (2011). https://doi.org/10.1016/j.pmcj.2010.11.008

17. Wilson, C., Hargreaves, T., Hauxwell-Baldwin, R.: Smart homes and their users: a systematic analysis and key challenges. Pers. Ubiquitous Comput. **19**(2), 463–476 (2015)

Eliminating the Ground Reference for Wireless Electric Field Sensing

Julian von Wilmsdorff[1,2](✉), Florian Kirchbuchner[1,2] (ID),
Andreas Braun[1,2] (ID), and Arjan Kuijper[1,2] (ID)

[1] Technische Universität Darmstadt, Karolinenplatz 5, 64289 Darmstadt, Germany
[2] Fraunhofer IGD, Fraunhoferstr. 5, 64283 Darmstadt, Germany
{julian.von.wilmsdorff,florian.kirchbuchner,andreas.braun,
arjan.kuijper}@igd.fraunhofer.de
http://www.tu-darmstadt.de
http://www.igd.fraunhofer.de

Abstract. Capacitive systems are getting more and more attention these days. But many systems today like smart-phone screens, laptops, and non-mechanical buttons use capacitive techniques to measure events within several centimeters of distance. The reason that battery-powered devices don't have high measurement ranges lies in the principle of capacitive measurement itself - the electrical ground is an inherent part of the measurement.

In this paper, we present a method for passive and wireless capacitive systems to eliminate the reference to ground. This bears a couple of advantages for mobile, battery-powered capacitive sensor designs in the field of ambient intelligence. We compare the detection range of normal passive capacitive systems with our new approach. The results show that our improvements result in a higher detection range and higher power efficiency.

Keywords: Capacitive sensor · Electric field sensing
Ground reference

1 Motivation and Related Work

The Internet of Things is growing fast. More and more IoT applications are developed every day. According to Kahn et al., two of the key challenges of the IoT are information privacy and to make network devices as energy efficient as possible [9]. But to accumulate more user information, many systems use sensor technologies that compromise the privacy of a user in various ways. With microphones and cameras, controlling a device can be achieved through voice commands and gestures. But these sensors are capable of delivering more information than just the needed control commands, like the identity of the users or the classification of their actions in the environment.

This is why the capacitive technology is a good fit for IoT applications. Their range is limited and it is harder, yet not impossible, to identify users. The most

© Springer Nature Switzerland AG 2018
A. Kameas and K. Stathis (Eds.): AmI 2018, LNCS 11249, pp. 90–99, 2018.
https://doi.org/10.1007/978-3-030-03062-9_7

popular capacitive technology to identify users are dedicated capacitive finger-print sensors. But, as shown by Holz et al. [7], even touchscreens can be used for this purpose. One could also use the impedance of a user to the environment, realized with a sweep over different AC frequencies, as shown by Harrison et al. [6]. However, most of these capacitive technologies that concern the privacy of users have a touch detection range. Even if capacitive systems are able to iden-tify users over a larger range, as shown by Grosse-Puppendahl et al. [4], they do not invade the privacy of a user as much as optical or acoustical systems because the identification of a user is depending on wearing the same footwear.

The privacy concerns of a user are important, but so is the electric power consumption of an IoT technology. Systems that require a lot of energy are bound to locations with power outlets and power lines to supply themselves. This argument is another reason why capacitive sensors are effective for modern IoT applications. They can be implemented with very low power requirements. An example of an ultra low power human body motion sensor was made by Cohn et al. [1]. They used static electric field sensing, which in this paper is called passive capacitive sensing, to implement a wearable device that uses 3.3 μW for measurement.

A typical value for the range of capacitive sensors are 0 to 50 cm [3]. There are some capacitive systems that scale up to 200 cm, as shown by Iqbal et al. [8]. But these systems use more complex circuits and multiple amplifier stages, which are not suited for low power and thus mobile applications. Mobile Applications are needed to make up for the limited range of these sensors. Scattering multiple small sensors gives us the same effective detection range, but without the needed calibration as for the long-range sensors [8].

A big drawback of mobile capacitive sensors is the missing ground reference. As explained later in Sect. 2.1, a ground reference is needed for capacitive mea-surement. The optimal ground reference is a wired connection to the ground, which contradicts the idea of a mobile use case. That is the reason why we, later on, present a possible setup for passive capacitive sensors, that don't need a ground reference.

2   The Physics of Electric Field Sensing

As already mentioned, there are active and passive capacitive systems. To get a better understanding of our solution, we will first briefly discuss both sensor principles.

2.1   "Classic" Active Capacitive Sensing

There are several active capacitive measurement so-called "modes". All active capacitive system have in common that they actively create an alternating electric field by charging and discharging conductive surfaces. For brevity and because the underlying physical principals are the same, we will only discuss loading-mode.

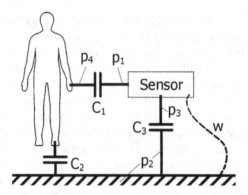

Fig. 1. Wireless systems do not have the direct connection (w) from the electrical ground potential (p_3) to the real ground potential (p_2).

Figure 1 illustrates the basic circuit of a loading-mode setup. The output of the sensor is the time that is needed to do a charging and discharging cycle of C_1 (since fully charging an ideal capacitor would take an infinite amount of time it will only be charged to a certain percentage). The current that charges the electrode (p_1) is constant, but the distance between the user and the electrodes varies. The capacitance of C_1 is derived by

$$C = \epsilon_0 \epsilon_r \frac{A}{d} \tag{1}$$

where C is the electrical capacitance of C_1. A is the area of the hand of the user or the area of the electrode (whichever is smaller) and d is the distance between them. ϵ_r is the permittivity of the material between user and electrode (for air, $\epsilon_r \approx 1$) and ϵ_0 is a constant value.

So, by measuring C_1, a capacitive sensor is able to approximate the distance of a user nearby.

2.2 Passive Electric Field Sensing

Passive electric field sensing is based on the same physical principals. The main difference between active electric field sensing and passive electric field sensing is that the passive technology doesn't actively charge and discharge the electrode. Passive electric field sensing measures the displacement current that is generated in the electrode by a statically charged, moving object.

A simple comparison for this effect is moving a charged rubber balloon along human hairs. The hair starts moving to the balloon. But in our case, the human hair is replaced by copper wires or copper plates. Since copper is conductive, it doesn't move towards the balloon, but the charged particles inside the copper (free electrons or electron holes) do. In other words - an electric current is created.

The principal setup for a passive electric field sensor is the same as shown in Fig. 1. But this time, the voltage from potential p_1 to potential p_3 is measured.

Since

$$Q = CU \tag{2}$$

where Q is the charge of C_1, C is the electrical capacitance and U is the voltage, we are able to measure C_1

Let us assume that, for simplicity's sake, the charge of C_1 is constant. This may only hold true for a short period of time. Sooner or later, the charge on C_1 will change due to triboelectric charging, which occurs naturally on every person through friction.

By measuring U we can now calculate C because Q is constant and thus again approximate the distance of a user d as shown in Sect. 2.1.

To put it simply, the current that flows from p_1 to p_3 indicates the distance of a user. Please note that a current only flows in closed circuits. In our case the closed circuit is build up by C_1, C_2 and C_3. That is why changing the capacitance of C_2 (the user lifts their feet) or C_3 (the sensor is moved) will have a similar effect as changing C_1 (the user moves towards/away from the sensor).

3   Proposed Solution

Instead of using operational amplifiers to detect user activities, we will use an instrumentation amplifier. Operational amplifiers for passive capacitive systems have been used in ambient assisted living before, as seen for example by Fu et al. [2] or in the Platypus system [4].

Instrumentation amplifiers in the domain of electric field sensing are currently used for ECGs [10]. Matthies et al. are showing an application for a type of ECG to evaluate facial expressions. But these use cases for activity classification with electric field sensing are bound to touch range.

With operational amplifiers, an often used setup for passive electric field sensors looks like shown in Fig. 4a. An example of this setup is given by Harland et al., which are using an equivalent setup to detect electrical human body activity [5]. But this setup has a dependency to the ground reference.

By using an Instrumentation Amplifier, which uses four inputs, we can effectively eliminate the need for a ground reference. Figure 4b shows a simplified circuit of an activity sensor. The output of the instrumentation amplifier can be derived as:

$$V_{out} = (V_{in1+} - V_{in1-}) - (V_{in2+} - V_{in2-}) \tag{3}$$

In our case, when the instrumentation amplifier is connected as shown in Fig. 4b, this results in:

$$V_{out} = (p_{ant1} - p_{Vss}) - (p_{ant2} - p_{Vss}) \tag{4}$$

where p_{ant1} and p_{ant2} are the electric potentials of the electrodes and p_{Vss} is the ground potential. Hence:

$$\Leftrightarrow V_{out} = p_{ant1} - p_{ant2} \tag{5}$$

Note that this formula is simplified since no amplification or other internal effects of the instrumentation amplifier, such as the reference voltage, for example, are modeled. As demonstrated, connecting the ground potential to both sides of the instrumentation amplifier will remove it effectively.

4   Comparison of Grounded and Not Grounded Sensors

We gathered data from the discussed two sensor types to compare them to each other. The hardware that was used as well as the experimental setups are discussed in the following.

4.1   Evaluation Design

To evaluate our solution we conducted the following experiments. We used a classic passive electric field sensor which is implemented with an operational amplifier to compare it to our solution with an instrumentation amplifier. We want to test the detection range of human activities. The experimental setup consists of different markings on the floor which are indicating different distances to the sensor. We evaluated four different sensor setups in our experiment to show that grounding is the key factor of electric field sensing technologies with operation-amplifiers. These setups were placed on a small table in front of the marks on the floor. Figure 2 illustrates the evaluation.

Fig. 2. Evaluating the range of the setups.

At the beginning of the test, the charge of the participating person will be normalized to eliminate outliers for more reliable results. These outliers can be caused by big accumulations of an electrical charge. Just by sitting in a chair for a longer period of time and constantly rubbing on the back of the seat can accumulate very high charges. This would lead to seemingly huge detection ranges of the sensors. To normalize the charge of a person, the person has to touch a grounded wire. This will drain most of the charge. But in a realistic scenario, a person will carry a certain charge. Therefore, the person has to walk a small distance to accumulate new charge, which is generated by the worn cloth and shoes rubbing to each other and rubbing on the floor.

A person is standing at the distance marker with the biggest distance (2,5 m) to the sensor setup. Then the person has to lift one foot after another, as high as the knee. This will simulate the electrical behavior of step. With this test design, the simulated steps will be more similar to one another because a person cannot vary this movement as much as a natural step.

Then, the person has to move forward 10 cm to the next mark on the floor and lift their feet again. This will be repeated until the sensor detects the moving person. Every sensor is rigged to a LED which indicates that an activity was detected.

This procedure is repeated for every of the four different sensor setups. The experiment was conducted with 16 different people. Every person had to activate every sensor setup two times. The setups are build up as follows:

1. For the first setup consists of an electric field sensor with an operation-amplifier. The sensor is hooked up to an external power supply with 3 V. Hence, the sensor posses a direct connection to ground through the power supply (see Fig. 3a).
2. The second setup consists of the same sensor as the first setup, but this time the sensor is powered by two batteries. The voltage of the two batteries is, as in the first setup, 3 V (see Fig. 3b).
3. The third setup is similar to the second one. The only difference is that, additionally to the battery pack, the sensor is connected to the negative supply cable of an external power supply. This means again that the sensor is grounded, but receives its power from the battery pack because the positive terminal of the power supply is not connected (see Fig. 3c).
4. The last setup evaluates an electric field sensor build with an instrumentation amplifier. The sensor is powered by a single 3 V coin cell and has no ground connection (see Fig. 3d).

The sensing electrodes of all setups have the same size. But because the last setup consists of an instrumentation amplifier that measures human activity in a differential way, the last setup has to have two electrodes.

4.2   Hardware

The basic circuits of the sensor with operation-amplifier are illustrated in Fig. 4a. Figure 4b shows our approach with instrumentation amplifier. A human activity will be detected if the sensor output is over approximately 60mV of $\frac{V_{cc}}{2}$. This functionality is realized with a simple comparator.

As indicated in Fig. 4a and b, both circuits have very a very high impedance connection to $\frac{V_{cc}}{2}$. This assembly group prevents long-lasting railing of the sensor output to V_{cc} and V_{ss} because it will slowly but steadily pull the sensor output to $\frac{V_{cc}}{2}$. Decreasing the resistance of R_{bias} will improve this behavior even further,

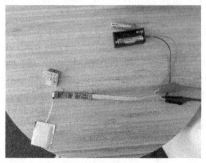

(a) Sensor with operation-amplifier and external power supply.

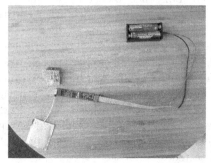

(b) Sensor with operation-amplifier powered by batteries.

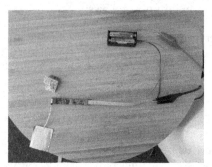

(c) Sensor with operation-amplifier powered by batteries and ground connection.

(d) Sensor with instrumentation amplifier.

Fig. 3. The different sensor setups.

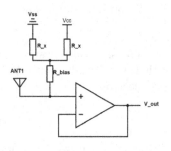

(a) Circuit of an electric field sensor including an operation-amplifier.

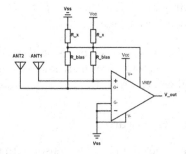

(b) Circuit of an electric field sensor constructed with an instrumentation amplifier.

Fig. 4. Comparison between the used sensors.

but at the cost of sensitivity. If R_{bias} is too low, no activities can be detected at all.

The power consumption for the measurement module with operation-amplifier is about $100\,\mu$W. For our approach with instrumentation amplifier, $40\,\mu$W are needed to power the measurement module.

4.3 Results

Figure 5 illustrates the data resulting from the experiments described in Sect. 4.1.

We can conclude that it makes little to no difference for a sensor to use a normal external power supply or batteries. The arithmetic mean value for a sensor built with an operation-amplifier a connected to a power supply is 65 cm, with batteries and a connection to ground 67 cm. The standard deviation of the sensors is high as the first and third quantiles of the box plot already suggests. They are 33 cm (with power supply) and 36 cm (with batteries and ground connection). The maximum detection range for both setups is 130 cm.

When connected only to a battery, with no connection to the ground, the sensor with operation-amplifier performs much worse. In average, a distance of 34 cm was measured, which is half of the sensors original performance when grounded, with a standard deviation of 23 cm.

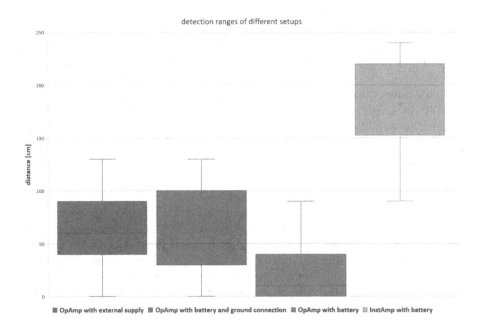

Fig. 5. Comparison of the different sensor setups. Indicated for each sensor are the minimum and maximum value, the first and third quantile and the median.

When an instrumentation amplifier is used, the average detection range is 182 cm, the standard deviation is 46 cm. This detection range is achieved without any connection to ground.

As already mentioned, the standard deviation of the detection ranges is high, which would indicate that the sensors are quite unreliable or the tests are not conclusive. But this high standard deviation is the result of a strong influence of the test persons. The worn clothes and more important the shoes of the persons have a high impact on the sensor performance.

So, we calculate for each person the differences between each setup and then we transfer the mean value of this differences per setup in the following confusion matrix Table 1.

Table 1. The mean average difference of the setups. All values in [cm].

	setup 3a	setup 3b	setup 3c	setup 3d
setup 3a	0	-42,3	0,3	119,4
setup 3b		0	42,6	161,6
setup 3c			0	119,0
setup 3d				0

The setups compared for every person are very conclusive; In 93% of the cases, setup 3a (external power supply) detects a user earlier than setup 3b (batteries). On average the advance is 42,3 cm as shown in Table 1. Our solution, setup 3d even detects every single person ahead of all other setups by more than a meter.

To conclude, the detection range of the sensors has a high average deviation. But still, the sensor ranges can be clearly ordered. battery-powered sensors based on operation-amplifiers have the smallest detection range, sensor setups that are grounded have medium detection ranges and sensors based on instrumentation amplifiers perform best.

5   Conclusion and Future Work

We first gave a short summary of the physical principles of active capacitive measurements and passive capacitive sensing. It was pointed out why the ground connection of these sensors plays an important role for the measurement circuits.

Then we presented our solution to this problem and it was shown that our approach to eliminate the ground reference for electric field sensors has big advantages over implementations with operation-amplifiers. The detection range of human activity nearly triples while the energy consumption is cut in half. Hence, when implemented with instrumentation amplifiers, electric field sensors are well suited for applications in ambient intelligence.

Our goal for future work is to transfer our solution to classic active capacitive systems. This is challenging because active capacitive systems rely on a slightly different measurement principle. To implement the idea of our approach with an active system, one would have to create an electric field between two electrodes. This way, the system would not be dependent on its ground connection. Since many active systems use the popular 555-timer to create an electric field, this idea is hard to implement because the 555-timer creates the needed high/low-pattern in respect to its ground.

References

1. Cohn, G., et al.: An ultra-low-power human body motion sensor using static electric field sensing. In: Proceedings of the 2012 ACM Conference on Ubiquitous Computing, pp. 99–102. UbiComp 2012, ACM, New York (2012). https://doi.org/10.1145/2370216.2370233

2. Fu, B., Kirchbuchner, F., von Wilmsdorff, J., Grosse-Puppendahl, T., Braun, A., Kuijper, A.: Indoor localization based on passive electric field sensing. In: Braun, A., Wichert, R., Maña, A. (eds.) AmI 2017. LNCS, vol. 10217, pp. 64–79. Springer, Cham (2017). https://doi.org/10.1007/978-3-319-56997-0_5

3. Grosse-Puppendahl, T., Berghoefer, Y., Braun, A., Wimmer, R., Kuijper, A.: Opencapsense: a rapid prototyping toolkit for pervasive interaction using capacitive sensing. In: IEEE International Conference on Pervasive Computing and Communications (PerCom) 2013, pp. 152–159. IEEE (2013). https://doi.org/10.1109/PerCom.2013.6526726

4. Grosse-Puppendahl, T., et al.: Platypus: indoor localization and identification through sensing of electric potential changes in human bodies. In: Proceedings of the 14th Annual International Conference on Mobile Systems, Applications, and Services, pp. 17–30. ACM (2016). https://doi.org/10.1145/2906388.2906402

5. Harland, C., Clark, T., Prance, R.: Electric potential probes-new directions in the remote sensing of the human body. Meas. Sci. Technol. **13**(2), 163 (2001). https://doi.org/10.1088/0957-0233/13/2/304

6. Harrison, C., Sato, M., Poupyrev, I.: Capacitive fingerprinting: exploring user differentiation by sensing electrical properties of the human body. In: Proceedings of the 25th Annual ACM Symposium on User Interface Software and Technology, pp. 537–544. ACM (2012). https://doi.org/10.1145/2380116.2380183

7. Holz, C., Buthpitiya, S., Knaust, M.: Bodyprint: biometric user identification on mobile devices using the capacitive touchscreen to scan body parts. In: Proceedings of the 33rd Annual ACM Conference on Human Factors in Computing Systems, pp. 3011–3014. ACM (2015). https://doi.org/10.1145/2702123.2702518

8. Iqbal, J., Lazarescu, M.T., Tariq, O.B., Lavagno, L.: Long range, high sensitivity, low noise capacitive sensor for tagless indoor human localization. In: 7th IEEE International Workshop on Advances in Sensors and Interfaces (IWASI) 2017, pp. 189–194. IEEE (2017). https://doi.org/10.1109/IWASI.2017.7974248

9. Khan, R., Khan, S.U., Zaheer, R., Khan, S.: Future internet: the internet of things architecture, possible applications and key challenges. In: 10th International Conference on Frontiers of Information Technology (FIT) 2012, pp. 257–260. IEEE (2012). https://doi.org/10.1109/FIT.2012.53

10. Wang, W.S., Wu, Z.C., Huang, H.Y., Luo, C.H.: Low-power instrumental amplifier for portable ecg. In: IEEE Circuits and Systems International Conference on Testing and Diagnosis, 2009. ICTD 2009, pp. 1–4. IEEE (2009). https://doi.org/10.1109/CAS-ICTD.2009.4960836

Deep Learning Approach for Estimating a Human Pose on a Mobile Device

Martin Moder and Michael Schellenbach[✉]

University of Applied Sciences, Bottrop, Germany
martin.moder@stud.hs-ruhrwest.de, michael.schellenbach@hs-ruhrwest.de

Abstract. Current deep convolutional neural networks (CNNs) approaches enable accurate marker-free estimation of body poses observed in an image. We think that this marker-free estimation approach develops all its potential in the field of pose estimation, if this is possible in real time and on a mobile device. In this work, we focus on the implementation of a modern CNN approach for the body pose estimation and a redesign of the CNN architecture, so that it can be applied on a mobile device. The results of our experiments show that even current smartphones can propagate our architecture in reasonable time.

Keywords: Pose estimation · Image analysis · Deep learning

1 Introduction and Motivation

The CNN enables a huge step forward in the field of computer vision, including articulated body pose estimation which creates the research branch of convolutional pose machine. The specific task of a convolutional pose machine that estimates an articulated body pose is to recover the current pose of an articulated body only from image-based observations. The challenge arises from the complexity of the articulated bodies, e.g. the human body has 244 degrees of freedom, and the influence of the environment. With the increasing accuracy of such image-based pose estimation systems, poses of a body, such as the body of a human, a hand, or a non-human creature, can be more and more reliably detected under real-world conditions. The further development of these systems is necessary because the current applications of these systems are increasingly in demand for many applications including such as marker-free motion capture (e.g. human-computer interfaces), physiotherapy, 3D animation, ergonomics studies, robot control, and visual surveillance.

Our idea for using this technology is the mobile recording and the mobile post processing analysis of the kinematic model of a subject, e.g. to assist an expert in the gait analysis. The system should be able to work locally without server connection, so that the result of a measurement is immediately available in each environment. In addition, the local computation can increase user privacy and can lowering data and server cost. This leads us to the question to what extent current convolutional human pose machine algorithms can be run on a

© Springer Nature Switzerland AG 2018
A. Kameas and K. Stathis (Eds.): AmI 2018, LNCS 11249, pp. 100–105, 2018.
https://doi.org/10.1007/978-3-030-03062-9_8

mobile device. For this purpose, we have studied current research in this area and implemented the part affinity fields detector of Cao et al. [1], because off the promising trade-off between detection performance and propagation runtime. With our implemented version of the part affinity fields detector we redesigned the CNN architecture for the resource-limited mobile application.

2   Brief Introduction to Part Affinity Fields Detector

The algorithm presented by Cao et al. [1] achieves state of the art results in terms of accuracy on the COCO [7] benchmark in the estimation of multi-person 2D poses. In addition, the method provides a problem-optimized post-processing step of filtering the trained CNN model output detections and assign them to full body pose in real-time for multiple persons in the image.

2.1   Overall Pipeline

In Fig. 1, the overall pipeline of the system is visualized, from the normalized color input image (see Fig. 1a) of the size $w \times h$ to the output image (see Fig. 1e) which contains 2D positions of the anatomical key points of all persons in the image. In between, first, the input image is propagated through a CNN so that a prediction can be made in the form of a set of 2D confidence maps S with the information content about the position of the body parts (see Fig. 1b) and a set of 2D part affinities fields (PAF) L that encodes the location and orientation of limbs[1] as vector fields (see Fig. 1c). The set $S = (S_1, S_2, ..., S_J)$ has J confidence maps, one per part, where $S_j \in R^{w \times h}, j \in \{1...J\}$. The set $L = (L_1, L_2, ..., L_c)$ has C vector fields, one per limb, where $L_c \in R^{w \times h \times 2}, c \in \{1...C\}$, each image location in L_c encodes a 2D vector.

The parsing step is basically a matching problem to create full body poses from the detections. This matching problem is significantly reduced in complexity by two assumptions. At first, the part connections are reduced to a minimum to obtain a spanning tree skeleton structure (e.g. see Fig. 1e) rather than using all connection between parts. Second, the tree structure is decomposed into a set of bipartite graphs, in which each graph connects all possible pairs of part detections of several persons which are adjacent in the tree structure (e.g. see Fig. 1d). Overall, this results in a bipartite assignment problem in which the associated PAF weights the possible connections candidates for each limb type independently, which can be solved by the Hungarian algorithm [6]. With all limb connection candidates, the connections can be assembled that share the same part detection candidates into full-body poses of multiple people.

2.2   CNN Architecture

Just like the CNN meta architecture for object detection [3], a "backbone" CNN analyzes the input image and generates an output tensor Cao et al. [1] use the

---

[1] Cao et al. reference to part pairs as limbs.

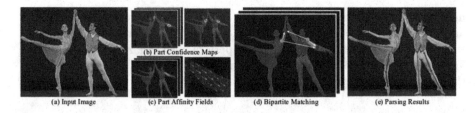

(a) Input Image   (b) Part Confidence Maps   (c) Part Affinity Fields   (d) Bipartite Matching   (e) Parsing Results

Fig. 1. Overall pipeline of multi-person pose estimation. The input image is propagated through a two-branch CNN, which creates two types of predictions. The body part detection confidence maps (b) and the part affinity fields (c) for part association. The PAFs are used as weighting so that pairs of parts can be created via a bipartite assignment of adjacent parts (d). Finally, with the pair of parts whole body poses are put together for each person (e).

VGG-19 [10] network as a "backbone" network, which is finetuned[2] during training and regulated. The tensor F is then propagated through a branched iterative CNN architecture, which in the first stage creates the prediction $L^1 = \phi^1(F)$ and $S^1 = \rho^1(S)$ simultaneously (see Fig. 2). In each subsequent stage, the previous result of the branches is first concatenated with F and used as input for the further prediction, $S^t = \rho^t(F, S^{t-1}, L^{t-1}), \forall t \geq 2$, $L^t = \rho^t(F, S^{t-1}, L^{t-1}), \forall t \geq 2$, where ρ^t and ϕ^t are the CNNs for inference at Stage t. This iterative architecture inspired by Wei et al. [12] refines the prediction iterative and indirectly enables large receptive fields.

3   Squeezing the CNN Model

Our overarching objective in this paper is to design a new CNN architecture that has few weights parameters and a less interference time while maintaining the same accuracy as the original architecture of Cao et al. [1]. To achieve this, we design three incremental reduction steps

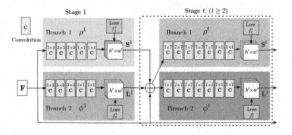

Fig. 2. CNN for iterative refinement of predictions.

and evaluate each of them. The first two steps modify the t-stage block CNN (see Fig. 2) and the last steps modifies in addition to the second step the "backbone" CNN. **Step A**: Replace the 7×7 from the t-stage block CNN filters with three 3×3 filters. This replacement preserves the required 7×7 receptive field and results in fewer weights parameters, less computation, and more nonlinearity. **Step B**: Replace 3×3 filter from step A with a 3×1 and 1×3 filters cascade.

---

[2] The weights of the net are already trained on a similar dataset and are adjusted for the new task or dataset.

Inspired by Iandola et al. [4], this substitution leads to further parameter reduction and an increase in nonlinearity with the same computational complexity.

Step C: Inspired by Wu et al. [13] a strongly minimized version of the VGG network is examined as a "backbone" CNN for the in step B modified t-stage block CNN Architecture, which leads to a considerable reduction of the parameters (see Table 2).

The replacement of the original 7×7 convolution filters results overall in a deeper network. In addition to the positive features mentioned above, the training is difficult because it comes to gradient vanishing. This negative effect is compensated by interposing a Batchnormalization [5] layer between each filter and a ResNet-inspired shortcut [11] (see Fig. 3) between filter operations. These actions have enabled the training of our new architectures.

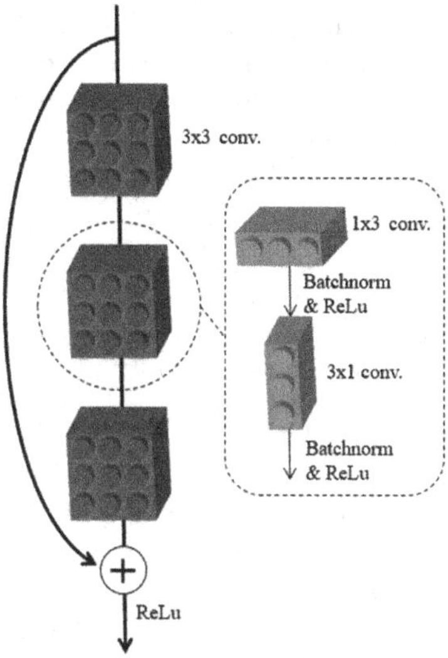

4   Results

To study the effect of the aforementioned reduction steps, a series of experiments

Fig. 3. Shortcut for convolution filters. On the left side this figure shows the replacement of the 7×7 filter with three 3×3 filters mentioned in step A. The right side shows the further modification mentioned in step B.

were performed on the COCO dataset, whereas experiment C includes finally all three reduction steps. The official COCO keypoint[3] evaluation [2] defines the object keypoint similarity (OKS) as main competition metric. The OKS plays the same role as the Intersection over Union (IoU) in object detection field. To characterizing the performance of a keypoint detector the OKS is thresholded for different accuracy categories and relative to the image object sizes to finally calculate the mean average precision (AP) [2] for all detection on the validation or test dataset. Table 1 summarizes the results of the COCO benchmark on the validation dataset for each experiment.

Cao et al. [1] argue that the running time of their system is mainly influenced by the CNN. Therefore, we focus in this work only on the runtime to calculate a pass through the CNN and assume that the duration of the parsing step does not have a high impact on the entire runtime. To analyze the runtime performance of our CNN architectures, we run the CNNs on different devices, see Table 2.

The original frame size is resized to 368×368 pixel for each picture during interference. With the smartphones and the tablet, a rise of the temperature and of the runtime are noticeable during the tests. Therefore, the test time for the smartphone and the tablet is set to one minute.

---

[3] Coordinates which point on the pose part.

Table 1. Results on the COCO 2016 keypoint challenge. $AP^{50 \; or \; 70}$ stands for the average precision over all detection which are only considered as true positive if the OKS is above 50 *or* 70. $AP^{[50,96]}$ stands for summarized average precision over the interval $[50, 96]$ as threshold. AP^L or AP^M stands for the average precision for relative to the size of the Image large or medium scale human poses. The evaluation and the training is done using a 368×368 resolution of the input Image. The last row shows the result of the original architecture, here a total of 6 stages are used, in all other experiments only 3 stages are used.

Experiment name	$AP^{[50,96]}$	AP^{50}	AP^{75}	AP^M	AP^L
A	43.5	68.3	44.4	36.5	54
B	42.8	70.3	43	40.9	46.2
C	35.8	61.8	35.4	27.1	48.4
Original	49	73.3	52	43.5	57

Table 2. Benchmark results for interference on several devices.

device	A	B	C	Original
iPhone 6s	894 ms	724 ms	443 ms	2440 ms
iPhone 7	750 ms	549 ms	415 ms	2430 ms
iPad 2016	5417 ms	5200 ms	2410 ms	Out of RAM
GTX 1080Ti	33.3 ms	33.3 ms	33.2 ms	53.4 ms
Intel - Core i7-8700K	548 ms	586 ms	330 ms	910 ms
Size	18M	15M	13M	53M

5   Discussion

The results in Table 2 demonstrate that the incremental reduction has a large impact on the runtime on mobile devices. We observe that in the smartphone category the iPhone 6s and the iPhone 7 are suitable with the architecture C for the analysis of short image sequences, since the temperature increase is noticeably smaller and the runtime much more stable.

The accuracy of detection decreases with each experiment (see Table 1), which is likely to correlate with the number of parameters and is probably reduced by a reduction in the number of detected parts. In addition, we noticed that the architectures estimate relatively large objects better than relatively small ones, leading us to the idea of using multiple scaling of the input image, as demonstrated by Redmon et al. [9] and Liu et al. [8].

In a next step we would like to investigate to what extent the reduction of the multi-pose estimation problem into a single-pose estimation changes the runtime and the accuracy. We would like to continue at this point and reduce the number of parts to be detected in an application-oriented manner, such as in the case of a gait analysis. We would like to implement the above-mentioned idea of a multi-scaled architecture and evaluate further backbone CNN candidates.

Furthermore, we would like to compare the estimation results with a tracking system results, in the real case of a gait analysis.

6 Conclusion

In this paper, we demonstrate a feasibility analysis of the Part Affinity Field Estimator on a mobile device and an iteratively scaling down of the original CNN architecture. Our experiments show that current smartphones can propagate our architecture limited in time by the heat development. We therefore think that with the current rapid development of AI algorithms and their use in smartphone technologies it is only a matter of time until the markerless pose estimation can be done efficiently on a mobile device over a larger period of time.

References

1. Cao, Z., Simon, T., Wei, S., Sheikh, Y.: Realtime Multi-Person 2D Pose Estimation using Part Affinity Fields. CoRR abs/1611.08050 (2016). http://arxiv.org/abs/1611.08050
2. COCO Consortium: COCO Keypoint Evaluation Metric. http://cocodataset.org/#keypoints-eval
3. Huang, J., et al.: Speed/Accuracy Trade-offs for Modern Convolutional Object Detectors. CoRR abs/1611.10012 (2016). http://arxiv.org/abs/1611.10012
4. Iandola, F.N., Moskewicz, M.W., Ashraf, K., Han, S., Dally, W.J., Keutzer, K.: SqueezeNet: AlexNet-Level Accuracy with 50x Fewer Parameters and ¡1MB Model Size. CoRR abs/1602.07360 (2016). http://arxiv.org/abs/1602.07360
5. Ioffe, S., Szegedy, C.: Batch Normalization: Accelerating Deep Network Training by Reducing Internal Covariate Shift. CoRR abs/1502.03167 (2015). http://arxiv.org/abs/1502.03167
6. Kuhn, H.W.: The Hungarian Method for the Assignment Problem. Naval Research Logistics Quarterly 2(1–2), pp. 83–97. https://doi.org/10.1002/nav.3800020109, https://onlinelibrary.wiley.com/doi/abs/10.1002/nav.3800020109
7. Lin, T., et al.: Microsoft COCO: Common Objects in Context. CoRR abs/1405.0312 (2014). http://arxiv.org/abs/1405.0312
8. Liu, W., et al.: SSD: Single Shot MultiBox Detector. CoRR abs/1512.02325 (2015). http://arxiv.org/abs/1512.02325
9. Redmon, J., Farhadi, A.: YOLOv3: An Incremental Improvement. CoRR abs/1804.02767 (2018). http://arxiv.org/abs/1804.02767
10. Simonyan, K., Zisserman, A.: Very Deep Convolutional Networks for Large-Scale Image Recognition. CoRR abs/1409.1556 (2014). http://arxiv.org/abs/1409.1556
11. Szegedy, C., Ioffe, S., Vanhoucke, V.: Inception-v4, Inception-ResNet and the Impact of Residual Connections on Learning. CoRR abs/1602.07261 (2016). http://arxiv.org/abs/1602.07261
12. Wei, S., Ramakrishna, V., Kanade, T., Sheikh, Y.: Convolutional Pose Machines. CoRR abs/1602.00134 (2016). http://arxiv.org/abs/1602.00134
13. Wu, B., Iandola, F.N., Jin, P.H., Keutzer, K.: SqueezeDet: Unified, Small, Low Power Fully Convolutional Neural Networks for Real-Time Object Detection for Autonomous Driving. CoRR abs/1612.01051 (2016). http://arxiv.org/abs/1612.01051

Toward a Smart City Using Tentacular AI

Atriya Sen[1]([envelope]), Selmer Bringsjord[1], Naveen Sundar Govindarajulu[1],
Paul Mayol[1], Rikhiya Ghosh[1], Biplav Srivastava[2], and Kartik Talamadupula[2]

[1] Rensselaer Polytechnic Institute (RPI), Troy, NY 12180, USA
{sena3,selmer,govinn,mayolp,ghoshr3}@rpi.edu
[2] IBM Research, Yorktown Heights, NY 10598, USA
{biplavs,krtalamad}@us.ibm.com

Abstract. The European Initiative on Smart Cities [2] is an effort
by the European Commission [4] to improve quality of life throughout
Europe, while progressing toward energy and climate objectives. Many
of its goals are relevant to and desirable in the world at large. We propose that it is essential that artificial agents in a Smart City have *theories of the minds* of its inhabitants. We describe a scenario in which
such theories are indispensable, and cannot be adequately and usefully
captured by current forms of ambient intelligence. Then, we show how
a new form of distributed, multi-agent artificial intelligence, *Tentacular AI*, which among other things entails a capacity for reasoning and
planning based in highly expressive cognitive calculi (logics), is able to
intelligently address this situation.

Keywords: Internet of Things · Artificial intelligence
Multi-agent systems

1 Introduction

It will be necessary for artificial agents in any smart city to predict and explain
the behavior of other people and agents. In order to do this, it is *necessary*
to have the ability to ascribe mental states to others and to reason about such
mental states. Artificial agents without the ability to understand 'common-sense
psychology' of this sort would be severely handicapped in their interactions with
humans. The best strategy for predicting and explaining actions might be to
analyze behavior in *intensional* terms, i.e., in terms of mental states such as
beliefs and desires.[1] As an example of this in the realm of Smart Cities, we
consider a scenario where an artificial agent embedded in a car decides and
predicts a parking spot, based on its beliefs about the intentions and actions of
other people parked in nearby spaces. Intelligent parking has been considered
before [6,15,16]. Yet our aim here is not to present an optimal or even excellent

---

[1] Note intensional states here denote cognitive states (including beliefs, knowledge,
desires, intentions etc.). Extensional states denote states of the world without taking
into account cognitive states. See [12,13] for more details.

© Springer Nature Switzerland AG 2018
A. Kameas and K. Stathis (Eds.): AmI 2018, LNCS 11249, pp. 106–112, 2018.
https://doi.org/10.1007/978-3-030-03062-9_9

solution to this particular problem, but merely to leverage it to illustrate the utility of our exceptionally general framework for cognitive IoT. Further, we do *not* consider here issues of morality, ethics, public policy, or governance, though these are linked inexorably to many domains. They will be discussed in a future publication.

We only make some brief comments about related work. There exists a standard *ontology*, the Semantic Sensor Network Ontology (SSN) [1], for reasoning about sensor data in the Internet and Web of Things. In a different domain, [5] makes an extensive comparison of ontologies based on SSN, and concludes that it is essential that temporal aspects of modeling be considered explicitly in ontological reasoning, a need which is not met by the state of the art. Our approach directly addresses this issue, our formalism being based upon an event calculus, as described in Sect. 2.1. Our approach is to be distinguished from *Cognitive Robotics* and general Cognitive Systems not only in that it is fundamentally *multi-agent*, but also in that cognitive aspects such as perception and attention are external to it. Instead, we restrict our attention to the "social" aspects of cognition, as necessitated in order to model and reason over deontic and epistemic modalities. Such models may be instantiated by automatically sensing and parsing human artifacts such as contracts, explicit consent, natural-language instructions, explicit goals, and so on.

2   Framework

2.1   The Deontic Cognitive Event Calculus

The **deontic cognitive event calculus** ($\mathcal{DCEC}$) is a sorted (i.e. typed) quantified modal logic (also known as sorted first-order modal logic) that includes the event calculus [14], a first-order calculus used for commonsense reasoning. $\mathcal{DCEC}$ belongs to the **cognitive calculi** family of logical calculi; it has a well-defined syntax and inference system; see Appendix A of [12] for a full description. The inference system is based on natural deduction [11], and includes all the introduction and elimination rules for first-order logic, as well as inference schemata for the modal operators and related structures.

Reasoning in $\mathcal{DCEC}$ is performed via a first-order modal logic theorem prover, ShadowProver, which uses a technique called **shadowing** to achieve speed of reasoning without sacrificing consistency in the system.

Planning in $\mathcal{DCEC}$ is handled by a STRIPS-style planner, Spectra, that builds upon ShadowProver. Unlike classical planners, Spectra can represent a state as any arbitrary formula, and not just as a set of propositional atoms. In addition, as Spectra is built upon ShadowProver, we can use any arbitrary modal formula, such as "John believes everyone has left the room" in its state built from the $\mathcal{DCEC}$. Spectra can also have arbitrary formulae as its goal, e.g., "No two blocks on the table should be of the same color." The planner can also use a knowledge-base of the world to work with far more complex formulae and definitions.

2.2   Tentacular AI

For a description of this developing AI technology, please see [3,8]. We have a set of agents $a_1, \ldots, a_n$. Each agent has an associated (implicit or explicit) contract that it should adhere to. Consider one particular agent τ. During the course of this agent's lifetime, the agent devises goals to achieve so that its contract is not violated. Some of these goals might require an agent to exercise some or all of the six attributes of Tentacular AI [3]. If some goal is not achievable on its own, τ can seek to recruit other agents by leveraging their resources, beliefs, obligations, etc.

3   Scenario

> Parking spaces in the downtown region of a large city are very scarce on a workday. A busy executive Alice will need to park near a certain office, where she is to attend a meeting. She cannot afford the time required to search for parking.

A sample course of reasoning may proceed as follows. **Learning:** The TAI agent in the executive's car consults her calendar. Using *anti-unification*, it determines a spot S where it *believes* she *intends* to park. **Sensing:** It *communicates* with the car parked at location S, and determines a time T when its owner is likely to return, based on his *communicated intention*. It also notes the current location of the owner. **Reasoning:** From the current location of the owner, it *infers* that he will probably not be able to return at time T. **Planning:** The TAI agent formulates a plan to circle the block *twice*, which should allow sufficient time for the owner of the parked car to return. There are two ways to circle the block; a car parked on the route A is likely to move out earlier than any car on the route B. The agent determines that the executive should take the route A first, and then route B. Finally, it checks that this plan does not violate any terms of the contract. In particular, it verifies that our executive does not *know* the location of the owner of the parked car.

3.1   Contract Parsing

In order to reason effectively, information and resources must be made available to the Tentacular AI agent by its users. An example is a contract, to be accepted by the user at the time of installation of the agent.[2] We cannot describe our natural language parsing technology here; for details we refer the reader to a previous work [7]. We simply report that the contract may be automatically parsed into a $\mathcal{DCEC}$ logical formalism, and show how a few contract points have been parsed into their corresponding formulae.

---

[2] TAI applications like this give rise to privacy concerns which could possibly be resolved by employing either **differential privacy** [9] or privacy based on **zero-knowledge proofs** [10].

The TAI agent will communicate with other TAI agents, and use information from them to determine and suggest plans of action.

$$\forall [x, y, info, t, poa], \bigwedge \left(\begin{array}{l} \mathsf{TAI\_agent}(x), \mathsf{TAI\_agent}(y), \mathsf{communicate}(x, y, info, t), \\ info \rightarrow \mathsf{deter}(x, poa, t), info \rightarrow \mathsf{suggest}(x, poa, t) \end{array} \right)$$

The TAI Agent will not communicate any information which may be used to identify or locate the owner of the car, to any other TAI agent or person.

$$\forall [x, y, z, owner, info, t],$$
$$\bigwedge \left(\begin{array}{l} \mathsf{TAI\_owner}(owner, y), \mathsf{TAI\_agent}(y), \\ \mathbf{K}(x, info, t) \rightarrow \mathbf{P} \left(\begin{array}{l} x, holds(id(owner, ID), t) \\ | holds(\mathsf{location}(owner, LOC), t), t \end{array} \right) \end{array} \right) \rightarrow \begin{array}{l} \neg \mathsf{communicate} \\ (y, z, info, t) \end{array}$$

The TAI agent may identify deviation from a previously determined plan, and suggest new goals toward which further planning may be directed.

$$\forall [x, poa1, poa2, t1, t2, t3, goal], t1 \le t2 \le t3,$$
$$\bigwedge \left(\begin{array}{l} \mathsf{TAI\_agent}(x), \mathbf{K}(x, poa1, t1), \\ \mathbf{P}(x, poa2, t2), poa1 \ne poa2 \end{array} \right) \rightarrow \bigwedge \left(\begin{array}{l} \mathsf{suggest}(x, goal, t2), \\ goal \rightarrow \mathsf{deter}(y, poa3, t3) \end{array} \right)$$

The owner of the TAI agent may receive (optional) notifications to share their specific location with other TAI agents, in situations when the location would otherwise not be disclosed.

$$\forall [x, owner, y, t],$$
$$\bigwedge \left(\begin{array}{l} \mathsf{TAI\_agent}(x), \mathsf{TAI\_agent}(y), \mathsf{TAI\_owner}(owner, x), \\ \neg \mathbf{K}(y, holds(\mathsf{location}(owner, LOC), t), t), \\ \mathbf{S}(x, owner, \diamond \mathbf{S}(owner, y, holds(\mathsf{location}(owner, LOC), t), t)) \end{array} \right)$$

3.2 Learning

In the situation above, some agent τ either in the environment or on one of Alice's personal devices needs to infer that Alice intends to park in this location. The agent τ, for instance, might have access to the following two pieces of information.

Past Information

$\mathbf{p}_1$: Bob had intended at t_1 to park at a spot x at time t_2 when he had a meeting at y at t_3; and x was the nearest parking location from y (with $t_{i+1} = t_i + 1$).

$$\mathbf{B} \left(\tau, \mathsf{now}, \left[\begin{array}{c} \mathbf{B}(bob, t_1, meeting(bob, y, t_3) \wedge nearestParking(x, y)) \\ \rightarrow \\ \mathbf{I}(bob, t_1, happens(action(park(bob, x)), t_2)) \end{array} \right] \right)$$

p$_2$: Similarly, Jim had intended to park at a spot u when he had a meeting at v and u was the nearest parking location from v.

$$\mathbf{B}\left(a, \text{now}, \begin{bmatrix} \mathbf{B}(jim, t_5, meeting(jim, v, t_7) \wedge nearestParking(u, v)) \\ \rightarrow \\ \mathbf{I}(jim, t_5, happens(action(park(jim, u)), t_6)) \end{bmatrix} \right)$$

From the above information and using I_{AU}, τ can infer the following:

$$\mathbf{B}\left(\tau, \text{now}, \forall \alpha, m, n, t \begin{bmatrix} \mathbf{B}(\alpha, t_i, meeting(\alpha, n, t_{i+2}) \wedge nearestParking(m, n)) \\ \rightarrow \\ \mathbf{I}(\alpha, t_i, happens(action(park(\alpha, m)), t_{i+1})) \end{bmatrix} \right)$$

Then using $I_{spec\mathbf{B}}$ and $I_{spec\mathbf{I}}$, τ can get the following formula, which states the agent believes that Alice will intend to park at q if she believes she has a meeting at r.

$$\mathbf{B}\left(\tau, \text{now}, \begin{bmatrix} \mathbf{B}(alice, t_i, meeting(alice, r, t_{i+2}) \wedge nearestParking(q, r)) \\ \rightarrow \\ \mathbf{I}(alice, t_i, happens(action(park(alice, m)), t_{i+1})) \end{bmatrix} \right)$$

3.3 Reasoning

The following formulae describe the communication between the car that is seeking parking and the car parked in the spot S desired by it. The reasoner is provided this information:

Reasoner Input

r$_1$: Car A perceives Car B saying that its owner won't return on time:

$$\mathbf{P}(car_A, \text{now}, \mathbf{S}(car_B, \neg holds(\text{location}(ownerB, S), t_{13}))) \tag{1}$$

r$_2$: If Car A believes that Car B believes that its owner won't return on time then Car A believes the same too:

$$\begin{aligned} &\mathbf{B}(car_A, \text{now}, \mathbf{S}(car_B, \neg holds(\text{location}(ownerB, S), t_{13}))) \\ &\rightarrow \mathbf{B}(car_A, \text{now}, \neg holds(\text{location}(ownerB, S), t_{13})) \end{aligned} \tag{2}$$

From these, Car A, seeking to park, may deduce that the owner of the parked car will not return in the time stipulated. This conclusion is a pre-requisite for the following planning step.

$$\mathbf{B}(car_A, \text{now}, \neg holds(\text{location}(ownerB, S), t_{13})) \tag{3}$$

3.4 Planning

In the final planning step, the TAI agent formulates a plan to circle the block *twice*, which should allow sufficient time for the owner of the parked car to return. For this particular problem, while a plain STRIPS-style planner can generate the required plan, we need $\mathcal{DCEC}$-based planning to ensure that private information is not leaked. It particular, the planner, Spectra, has to ensure that Alice, the owner of car_A, does not *know* the location of the owner of the parked car.

Acknowledgements. This research is made possible by joint support from RPI and IBM under the AIRC program; we are grateful for this support. Some of the research reported on herein has been enabled by support from ONR and AFOSR, and for this too we are grateful.

References

1. Semantic sensor network ontology (2017). https://www.w3.org/TR/vocab-ssn/. Accessed 7 July 2018
2. European initiative on smart cities (2018). https://setis.ec.europa.eu/set-plan-implementation/technology-roadmaps/european-initiative-smart-cities. Accessed 25 June 2018
3. Tentacular AI (2018). http://kryten.mm.rpi.edu/TAI/tai.html. Accessed 7 July 2018
4. The European Commission's Priorities (2018). https://ec.europa.eu/commission/index_en. Accessed 25 June 2018
5. Alirezaie, M., et al.: An ontology-based context-aware system for smart homes: E-care@ home. Sensors **17**(7), 1586 (2017)
6. Bessghaier, N., Zargayouna, M., Balbo, F.: Management of urban parking: an agent-based approach. In: Ramsay, A., Agre, G. (eds.) Artificial Intelligence: Methodology, Systems, and Applications, pp. 276–285. Springer, Heidelberg (2012)
7. Bringsjord, S., Licato, J., Govindarajulu, N., Ghosh, R., Sen, A.: Real robots that pass tests of self-consciousness. In: Proceedings of the 24th IEEE International Symposium on Robot and Human Interactive Communication (RO-MAN 2015), pp. 498–504. IEEE, New York (2015)
8. Bringsjord, S., Govindaralajulu, N.S., Sen, A., Peveler, M., Srivastava, B., Talamadupula, K.: Tentacular artificial intelligence, and the architecture thereof, introduced. In: To be Presented at the FAIM Workshop on Architectures and Evaluation for Generality, Autonomy & Progress in AI (2018)
9. Dwork, C.: Differential privacy: a survey of results. In: Agrawal, M., Du, D., Duan, Z., Li, A. (eds.) TAMC 2008. LNCS, vol. 4978, pp. 1–19. Springer, Heidelberg (2008). https://doi.org/10.1007/978-3-540-79228-4_1
10. Gehrke, J., Lui, E., Pass, R.: Towards privacy for social networks: a zero-knowledge based definition of privacy. In: Ishai, Y. (ed.) TCC 2011. LNCS, vol. 6597, pp. 432–449. Springer, Heidelberg (2011). https://doi.org/10.1007/978-3-642-19571-6_26
11. Gentzen, G.: Investigations into logical deduction. In: Szabo, M.E. (ed.) The Collected Papers of Gerhard Gentzen, pp. 68–131, North-Holland, Amsterdam, The Netherlands (1935). This is an English version of the well-known 1935 German version

12. Govindarajulu, N.S., Bringsjord, S.: On automating the doctrine of double effect. In: Sierra, C. (ed.) Proceedings of the Twenty-Sixth International Joint Conference on Artificial Intelligence, IJCAI-2017, pp. 4722–4730, Melbourne, Australia (2017). https://doi.org/10.24963/ijcai.2017/658, Preprint available at this URL. https://arxiv.org/abs/1703.08922

13. Govindarajulu, N.S., Bringsjord, S.: Strength factors: an uncertainty system for a quantified modal logic (2017). https://arxiv.org/abs/1705.10726, Presented at Workshop on Logical Foundations for Uncertainty and Machine Learning at IJCAI 2017, Melbourne, Australia

14. Kowalski, R., Sergot, M.: A logic-based calculus of events. New Gener. Comput. 4(1), 67–95 (1986)

15. Muñoz, A., Botía, J.A.: Developing an intelligent parking management application based on multi-agent systems and semantic web technologies. In: Graña Romay, M., Corchado, E., Garcia Sebastian, M.T. (eds.) Hybrid Artificial Intelligence Systems, pp. 64–72. Springer, Heidelberg (2010). https://doi.org/10.1007/978-3-642-13769-3_8

16. Sana, B., Riadh, H., Rafaa, M.: Intelligent parking management system by multi-agent approach: the case of urban area of Tunis. In: 2014 International Conference on Advanced Logistics and Transport (ICALT), pp. 65–71 (2014)

Activity and Situation Recognition

Surface Acoustic Arrays to Analyze Human Activities in Smart Environments

Biying Fu[1,2(✉)] ⓘ, Matthias Ruben Mettel[3], Florian Kirchbuchner[1,2] ⓘ,
Andreas Braun[1,2] ⓘ, and Arjan Kuijper[1,2] ⓘ

[1] Technische Universität Darmstadt, Karolinenplatz 5, 64289 Darmstadt, Germany
[2] Fraunhofer IGD, Fraunhoferstr. 5, 64283 Darmstadt, Germany
{biying.fu,florian.kirchbuchner,andreas.braun,
arjan.kuijper}@igd.fraunhofer.de
[3] Bartholomaestrasse 2, 65375 Oestrich-Winkel, Germany
matthias.mettel@gmail.com
http://www.tu-darmstadt.de
http://www.igd.fraunhofer.de

Abstract. Smart Environments should be able to understand a user's need without explicit interaction. In order to do that, one step is to build a system that is able to recognize and track some common activities of the user. This way, we can provide a system that provides various services for controlling installed appliances and offering help for every day activities. Applying these services in the users' environment should make his life more comfortable, easier, and safer. In this paper, we will introduce an embedded sensor system using surface acoustic arrays to analyze human activities in a smart environment. We divided basic activity groups ranging from walking, cupboard closing to falling, including their extended sub-activity groups. We expanded walking into walking barefoot, with shoes and with high heels and further extended closing cupboard with three cupboards locating on different positions. We further investigated the usage of single pickup or a combination of 4 pickups with their effect on the recognition precision. We achieved an overall precision of 97.23% with 10-fold cross validation using support vector machine (SVM) for all sub-activity group combined. Even using one pickup only, we can achieve an overall precision of more than 93%, but we can further increase the precision by using a combination of pickups up to 97.23%.

Keywords: Ubiquitous sensing · Human activity recognition
Acoustic sensing · Surface wave

1 Introduction

Smart living is an important part of current research. The key idea is to provide various services as the smart environment understand the needs of the inhabitants, using ubiquitous sensors. Applying these services can make the inhabitants feel more convenient and safer in their everyday life. To incorporate smart living

© Springer Nature Switzerland AG 2018
A. Kameas and K. Stathis (Eds.): AmI 2018, LNCS 11249, pp. 115–130, 2018.
https://doi.org/10.1007/978-3-030-03062-9_10

into our everyday life, an important feature is the tracking of users' daily activities. For example, the system has to detect when the user wants to cook for offering recipes, or if the user has fallen to call for help. Currently, various sensors like motion sensors, wearable tokens or smartphone built-in sensors (e.g., accelerometer, gyroscope) are used for tracking. The number of different sensors can lead to high costs of the complete system and high power consumption because more processing power is required to manage all sensors and analyze the context. Additionally, the nature of the used sensors leads to different problems. Wearable sensors like smart wristbands have the hassle that the users have to remember to wear these sensors. If they do not wear these sensors the system is ineffective and may not achieve its goal. Another solution is the use of cameras as shown by Mettel et al. [15]. It is easy to track various activities (e.g. walking, sitting and lying) with cameras. The disadvantage of this kind of sensors is the hardware limited detection range, privacy issues, and security issues. To improve the current state of smart living systems, it is necessary to find sensors that are not intrusive, removed from the user's awareness, and can track multiple activities with a high reliability. One solution is to use floor-based systems. It is installed under the floor covering, is invisible and there is no need for a direct line of sight which could be disturbed by objects.

In this paper, we present a novel concept for a floor-based sensing system using pickups installed in a living environment to identify different group of activities of daily life. The use of pickups has the advantage that only acoustic waves of the surface are recorded and any environmental sounds or speech will not be directly recognizable. The computation effort is rather low compared to image processing and doesn't suffer from the problem of occlusion. We start with a set of basic activity groups such as *walking, cupboard closing* and *falling*. We then further experimented with extended sub-activity groups. We verified the possibility of extending walking into three different classes, like *walking barefoot, walking with shoes* and *walking with high heels*. We further expand the closing of cupboards with three different cupboards locating at three different positions.

2   Related Work

Comparable floor-based sensor systems often apply pressure sensors [10] or capacitive sensors [13] for localization and activity recognition. Braun et al. [1] uses a grid-layout with capacitive sensing to localize indoor and detect falls. The capacity will increase if the person is standing close to the sensing element. However, the measurable capacity is limited to the sensing element. If the load is already too heavy due to the existing furniture, the detectable measuring range is small, which can cause difficulties by detecting capacitive changes. Fu et al. [6] presented a solution in their work with a smart floor measuring the change of electric body charge due to movement in order to detect steps and perform localization and fall recognition. The grid layout can be placed under any non-conductive floor materials and is independent of the load. The ground-based approach is good that these systems are unobtrusive and respect the privacy of users, but they are difficult to install such a system. In most cases, the entire floor covering must be removed and re-installed.

Using acoustic signals is not new. Schroeder et al. [17] introduce in their work the detection of coughing, knocking, clapping and phone bell events by placing common microphones in the environment. Temko et al. [18] use microphones that are placed in a meeting room to classify 16 different events in an office context. However, using common microphones for event detection has similar privacy issues as in case of the camera setups, because it records audio signals as speech or sounds. Therefore using pickups has the advantage that only acoustic waves of the surface are recorded and any environmental sounds or speeches will not be directly recognizable.

Braun et al. [3] presented a smart furniture - CapTap - which combines capacitive proximity and acoustic sensing to create an interactive surface that provides the recognition of mid-air and touch gestures. They can localize the point of impact with an average localization error of 1.5 cm at touch distance and 5 cm with an elevation of 20 cm above the able. Harrison et al. [7] tracks the input using capacitive, optical or resistive surfaces and classify acoustic impacts using a medical stethoscope. They can distinguish tiny impacts of human finger like e.g. tip, pad, nail and knuckle on a surface like a smartphone device.

3   Acoustic Surface Wave

Applying force on a surface by, for example, walking or falling will create an acoustic signal. This can be described physically as a mechanical bump. It lets the surface vibrate and a mechanical wave propagates through the surface and transmitted to the surrounding air, resulting in secondary acoustic waves as explained in [12]. The particle movement is normal to the surface and parallel to the direction of propagation. The surface acoustic wave is called the Rayleigh wave. This mechanical wave transmitted through the surface can be sensed and sampled with acoustic sensors.

The sampling frequency in our application is 96 kHz, as this is the maximum supported sampling frequency of the M-Audio M-Track Quad audio device used in this project. The higher the sampling frequency, the more information can be reconstructed due to the Nyquist-Shannon sampling theorem as explained in [19]. It states that we can reconstruct a signal with the fastest frequency component up to 48 kHz without information loss for our chosen sampling frequency. This is especially important for sudden events like falls or steps which contain high-frequency components in the signal itself. According to the high sampling frequency, the time resolution will increase. With the sampling frequency of 96 kHz, we achieve a time resolution of 42.67 ms for a window length of 4096 samples and the time resolution decreases to 85.3 ms with an increased window length of 8096 samples. The given windows size is used to extract features for activity classification. We use the sliding window approach with an overlap of 50% between successive window frames.

4   Proposed Smart Floor System

In this section, we introduce our proposed system by first introducing the system hardware, then explaining how the indoor localization algorithm works, and finally extracting features for activity classification. The overall pipeline for the processing can be seen in Fig. 1. Each component will be briefly explained in the following sections.

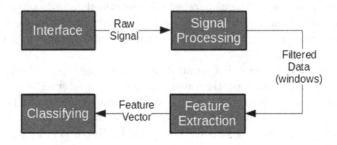

Fig. 1. Figure depicts the process pipeline.

4.1   Hardware Setup

The M-Audio M-Track Quad with four connected Schaller Oyster 723 Pickups is utilized for the pipeline interface and the dataset recording. Figure 2 shows this hardware.

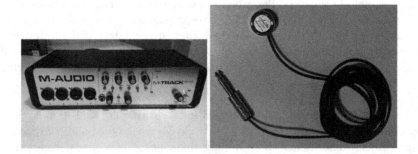

Fig. 2. Figure depicts the hardware used. The M-Audio M-Track Quad is depicted on the left and can connect up to four input channels. On the right is one of the four Schaller Oyster 723 pickup sensor used in our experiment.

The M-Audio M-Track Quad is an audio input and output device for recording and playing music. It is possible to add additional signal processing hardware. One advantage of this device is that it can handle four independent microphones. Onboard sound cards from laptops or computers support only one or maximal two channels. Every microphone input channel has its own amplifier control and can be set to the instrumental or microphone input handling. This device can be connected directly to the computer and handle four channels with the ASIO driver under Microsoft Windows.

4.2 Acoustic Localization

A general method used for localization in the time domain is the time difference of arrival (TDOA), as used in [14]. If we have one source of impact with unknown coordinate (x, y, z) and three receivers with known coordinates (x_i, y_i, z_i) with $i = 1 \ldots 3$, so the distance D_i between the source and the receiver i is given by Eq. (1).

$$D_i = \sqrt{(x - x_i)^2 + (y - y_i)^2 + (z - z_i)^2} \tag{1}$$

The difference of travel distance between source to receiver i and j is called D_{ij} and can be expressed by the Eq. (2).

$$D_{ij} = \sqrt{(x - x_i)^2 + (y - y_i)^2 + (z - z_i)^2} - \sqrt{(x - x_j)^2 + (y - y_j)^2 + (z - z_j)^2} \tag{2}$$

The difference of travel distance can be further expressed using the time difference of arrival τ_{ij} based on the following relationship

$$D_{ij} = \tau_{ij} \cdot v = (t_i - t_j) \cdot v \tag{3}$$

The time difference $\tau_{i,j}$ of the individual receiver pairs can be easily calculated from the received signals using signal correlation to find the optimum peak positions. Theoretically, an exact solution of the impact position can be calculated by using only three receivers as depicted in Fig. 3 left. But in the practice due to noise, it is not always possible to get the exact solution for the problem. Therefore we use an additional receiver to perform least square solutions, where we try to get a solution with minimum squared errors with respect to all receivers. This case is depicted in Fig. 3 right. Based on the TDOA approach, the exact position of the point of impact can be determined. Since the force of

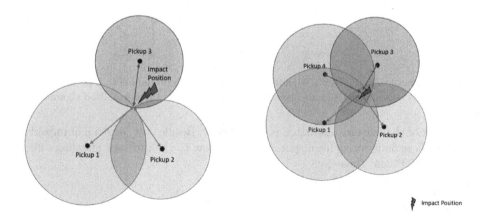

Fig. 3. Left: The concept of Tri-/Multilateration on the ground plane is depicted here. Right: Due to input noise, there is often no ideal solution for the TDOA. Therefore a least square approach is used to minimize the distance error towards the receiving sensors.

impact is directly on the ground, there is no z component and the equations above can be further simplified by inserting $z_i = 0$.

4.3   Activity Recognition

The next step is the feature extraction for the activity recognition. For time signals, there are basically three feature domains which are mostly used so far. They are either features from time domain, frequency domain or time-frequency domain. In the time domain, we investigate the pure signal form and extract features including zero-crossing or amplitude related features. In the frequency domain, Fast Fourier Transformation (FFT) [16] is often applied to get the spectral information of the signal. In time-frequency domain, we are interested in the spectral distribution of the signal over discrete time steps. This can be done using short time Fourier transformation (STFT) [8].

We perform normalization and synchronization as part of the data pre-processing, to achieve a better classification result. By observing different input signals from all input channels, we found out that there is a systematic offset in time for different input channels due to the device hardware. Since the error is systematic, we can easily remove this offset. Normalization helps to improve the received signal form. Since the amplitude is different for each input channel, it is of utmost importance to normalize the input signal before applying classification approaches. This can be seen in Fig. 4.

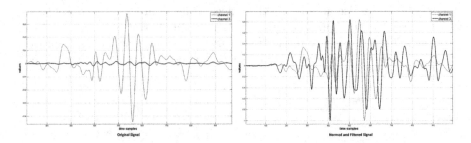

Fig. 4. Depicted are the input signals from channel 1 and channel 3. The left figure shows the un-normalized signals and the right figure shows the normalized signals.

A list of the features extracted is given below. Besides the location of impact, we use these features as input per sliding window to the different classifiers like SVM, CART, and BayesNet:

1. RMS value
2. Zero-Crossing value
3. The maximal FFT value index
4. The FFT value average
5. The FFT Standard Deviation
6. The FFT vector

The first two features are both extracted from the time-domain. The RMS value can be calculated by using the Eq. (4). x_i is the sampled time signal, and N is the number of samples within a chosen window size of 4096 or 8192 samples.

$$RMS = \sqrt{\frac{\sum_{i=1}^{N} x_i^2}{N}} \tag{4}$$

Zero crossing counts the number of zero crossings within a chosen window of N samples.

The FFT gives the spectral distribution of a time signal in the frequency domain. The Eq. (5) calculates the Fourier coefficients. $x(n)$ are the discrete sampled time signal and N is the number of FFT points used. $(k = 0, 1, ... N-1)$ represents the index of the Fourier coefficients.

$$X(k) = \sum_{n=0}^{N-1} x(n) \cdot \exp(-j\frac{2\pi}{N}nk) \tag{5}$$

The maximal FFT value index represents the strongest spectral power at a certain frequency and the average FFT value is calculated by $\bar{X} = \frac{\sum_{k=0}^{N-1} X(K)}{N}$ and its standard deviation is $s = \sqrt{\frac{\sum_{k=0}^{N-1}(X(K)-\bar{X})^2}{N-1}}$. The FFT vector consists of components $X(k), k = 0, 1, ... N - 1$ which are the Fourier coefficients.

5   Experiments and Evaluation

For the evaluation, four pickups are placed in a room with a parquet floor with the size of 3.9×3.42 m. In this room, there are various types of furniture (e.g., cupboards, tables and sideboard). The setup is illustrated in Fig. 5. Table 1 lists the positions of specific entities. For the evaluation setup, a wide range pickup sensor setup is used. The advantage of this setup type is the larger observation area. The amplifier of the M-Audio M-Track Quad is set to the maximal level to also detect small signal strength activities like *Walking barefoot* and to reduce missing signals. After setting up the environment, the activity signals from the pickups sensors are recorded. With the recorded data an offline analysis with the WEKA Explorer [9] is performed.

The evaluation starts with an analysis of the activity groups. We start with a basic activity group (AG-1), including only *walking, cupboard closing* and *falling*. We then try to expand this basic activity groups into various sub-activity groups with more precise activities. In AG-2, we divided the class of *walking* further into *walking barefoot, walking with shoes* and *walking with High-Heels*. In AG-3, we expanded the class of *cupboard closing* to 3 cupboards locating at different positions in the room. In the final activity group of AG-4 we combined all possible activities to verify the overall performance of the recognition. The different sets can be seen in Fig. 6. An example activity signals are depicted in Fig. 7 in time domain. Different activities have distinct signal patterns.

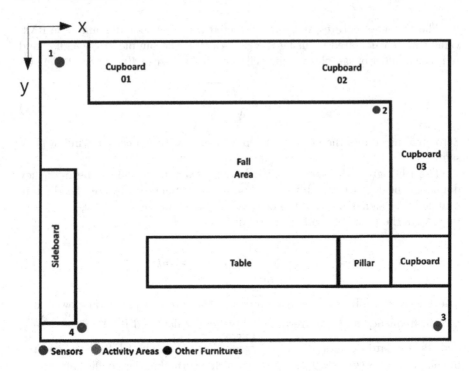

Fig. 5. Setup of the evaluation environment.

Table 1. The positions of specific entities in the evaluation environment.

Object	Position x	Position y
Pickup 1	0.32 m	0.37 m
Pickup 2	3.22 m	0.65 m
Pickup 3	3.81 m	3.26 m
Pickup 4	0.49 m	3.27 m
Cupboard 1	0.90 m	0.30 m
Cupboard 2	2.52 m	0.30 m
Cupboard 3	3.60 m	0.90 m
Fall area	2.20 m	1.30 m

For the evaluation, we invited 8 participants to perform the described activities in the physical setup as shown in Fig. 5. The test population consists of 3 females and 5 males, with an average age of 35 years old and body weight ranges from 65 kg–130 kg. There are no specific instructions given as how to perform this activities. The door of the cupboard can only be opened in one direction. Only the closing of the cupboard can be registered by our acoustic sensing system. It consists of in total 400 steps and 400 times of cupboard closings, in which these

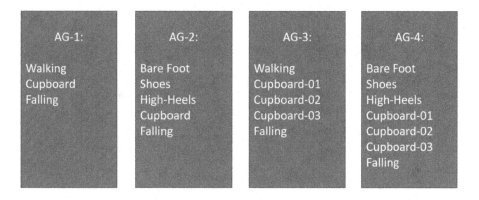

Fig. 6. Setup of the evaluation environment.

samples are further divided in sub-activities. *Falling* is a special case, because it is hard to simulate. A protection mat will distort the signal since it changes the consistency of the surface material. Therefore, the simulation can merely be performed carefully and not too often on the hard floor to prevent injuries. Therefore we only collected 50 times of falls. So the result feature vectors are upsampled multiple times to match the number of vectors of the other activities in the training dataset to avoid over-fitting. This way we can modify the dataset that we use to build our predictive model to have more balanced data classes. It is called over-sampling of our under-represented dataset [4]. The training dataset, based on the windowed-approach with an overlap of 50%, contains now 1000 feature sets each class. With this amount, the experiment results are considered to be significant. Each classification experiment with WEKA is performed with a window size of 4096 and 8192 samples and in each case with normalized windowed signals. To evaluate the performance of different classifier methods, some statistical measures like precision and area under curve (AUC) are given. The precision also known as positive predicted value gives a measure of the portion of correctly predicted class samples with respect to all predicted positive classes. The equation for precision is given by

$$Precision = \frac{TP}{TP + FP} \tag{6}$$

where TP stands for true positive and FP stands for false positive classes. The AUC is the integral of the receiver operation characteristic (ROC) curve and presents how well certain binary classifier works. The ROC curve is a plot of true positive rate (TPR) against false positive rate (FPR). It shows the performance of this binary classifier with respect to false rejection and false acceptance. An AUC value of 0.5 is close to a binary classifier with a random guess. The closer the AUC gets to 1, the better this binary classifier works.

Figure 8a shows the precision of different activity groups. The window size of 4096 samples was used and the time signal is normalized before feature extraction to make the channel difference smaller. SVM, CART, and BayesNET were

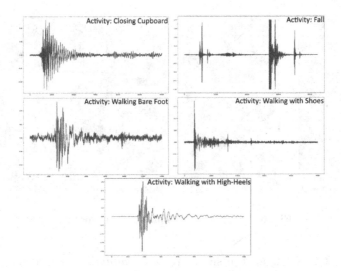

Fig. 7. Time-domain signals for the specified activities.

used as classifiers with 10-fold cross-validation to show the more generalized performance. We use the Bayes inference net as the baseline classifier, since it is a really simple model. CART with binary decision trees is used to better generalize the model. SVM is used in combination with grid search combining cross-validation approach to find the optimum hyper parameters. We used the radial basis function (rbf) kernel to separate the features. The regularization parameter C and γ is optimized by using grid search. Based on the training data, the final hyper parameter set is chosen such, that $C = 10$ and $\gamma = 10^{-3}$ are used as regularization parameter to avoid the classify from overfitting.

The classification of the three general classes in AG-1 can be achieved with a precision of more than 95%. The SVM shows superior performance in all classification results than CART and BayesNET. A regularization parameter C of 10 is chosen to avoid SVM from over-fitting. The SVM reaches the precision of 98.47% for AG-1, 94.26% for AG-2, 96.50% for AG-3 and 93.61% for AG-4. As expected, the precision decreases as the number of sub-classes increases, since the sub-activities are not fully independent from their main supper classes. The AUC for each classifier and each activity group can be extracted from Fig. 8b. The SVM shows more superior classification performance in all four set-ups regarding the higher AUC value.

The precision can be however increased by using a larger window size of 8192 samples as shown in Fig. 8c. The size of the samples within a window is of utmost importance to the performance of a good classification. It determines how well one activity is observed within the observation window. All features will be inferred from the chosen observation window. The final results of all activity groups are superior to the case of 4096 samples. The SVM reaches the precision of 98.90% for AG-1, 97.42% for AG-2, 98.42% for AG-3 and 97.23% for AG-4.

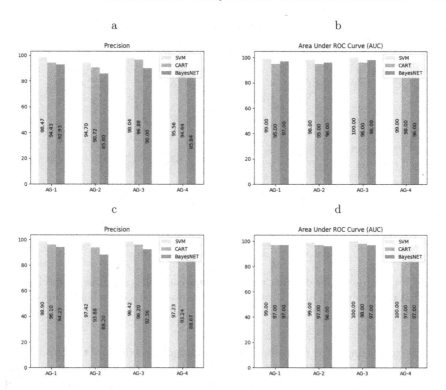

Fig. 8. Figure **a**: Precision score for different activity groups with a window size of 4096 samples. The SVM classifier uses a regularization parameter $C = 10$. Figure **b** shows the ROC Area combine for different activity groups. Figure **c**: Precision score for different activity groups with a window size of 8192 samples. The SVM classifier uses a regularization parameter $C = 10$. Figure **d** shows the ROC Area combine for different activity groups.

Table 2. Cross validation confusion matrix for SVM classification of AG-1. A window size of 8192 samples and normalized FFT coefficients are used for the input features.

	Cupboard	Falling	Walking
Cupboard	**977**	3	20
Falling	0	**1000**	0
Walking	5	5	**990**

The AUC for each classifier and each activity group for this window size can be extracted from Fig. 8d.

We further investigated the performance of using only one single input channel instead of using a combination of 4 pickups. We state the hypothesis that by using only one single pickup, the performance is inferior than the fusion. The result can be seen in Fig. 9. Since from previous results the SVM performs the

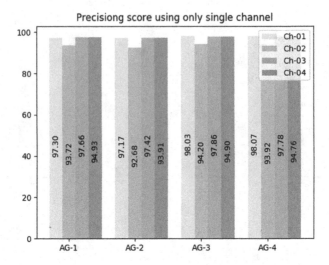

Fig. 9. Precision score for different activity groups each using only one single channel. The SVM classifier with a linear kernel is used. The precision score is built using 10-fold cross validation.

best, we keep using SVM as the best practice classifier to validate the hypothesis. Even the precision of using only one input channel is not worse in some cases; the fusion still outperforms the single input case. The overall performance of different channel inputs is not stable. Some of the input channels perform better than others. Besides, by using only one single input, we are missing the location information of the source of impact.

The confusion matrix for SVM classifier with 10-fold cross validation can be viewed in Table 2 for AG-1, Table 3 for AG-2, Table 4 for AG-3 and Table 5 for AG-4. In the extended activity use-cases, we can see the misclassification of different sub-activities. It is not surprising to see that certain sub-activities like *walking bare foot* or *walking with shoes* are getting confused sometimes, since they are not fully independent.

Table 3. Cross validation confusion matrix for SVM classification of AG-2. A window size of 8192 samples and normalized FFT coefficients are used for the input features.

	Cupboard	Falling	Bare foot	Shoes	High heels
Cupboard	**975**	2	14	9	0
Falling	0	**1000**	0	0	0
Bare foot	2	2	**926**	60	10
Shoes	0	2	14	**980**	4
High heels	1	1	1	7	**990**

Table 4. Cross validation confusion matrix for SVM classification of AG-3. A window size of 8192 samples and normalized FFT coefficients are used for the input features.

	Cupboard-01	Cupboard-02	Cupboard-03	Falling	Walking
Cupboard-01	**967**	2	31	0	0
Cupboard-02	0	**1000**	0	0	0
Cupboard-03	36	0	**964**	0	0
Falling	0	0	0	**1000**	0
Walking	2	3	0	5	**990**

Table 5. Cross validation confusion matrix for SVM classification of AG-4. A window size of 8192 samples and normalized FFT coefficients are used for the input features.

	Cupboard-01	Cupboard-02	Cupboard-03	Falling	Bare foot	Shoes	High heels
Cupboard-01	**965**	0	33	0	0	2	0
Cupboard-02	0	**992**	0	0	2	6	0
Cupboard-03	37	0	**959**	0	0	4	0
Falling	0	0	0	**1000**	0	0	0
Bare foot	0	0	0	2	**925**	62	11
Shoes	0	0	0	0	22	**976**	2
High heels	0	0	0	3	2	6	**989**

For the recording, it is necessary to start it and walk to the specific cupboard. Falling down can contain an initial step or steps after standing up to stop the recording. Therefore the falsely classified samples can be explained by not perfectly dividable class samples. Since the class of High Heels is also limited to only the female participants, it is unbalanced similar to the class of fall. Therefore, we have to use the Synthetic Minority Over-sampling Technique (SMOTE)[5] to oversample this class. However comparing the frequency components of the step class, high heels contains higher frequency components as expected. In this paper, we further discarded the non-activity class by using the impact detection step before classification. To avoid the continuous processing of each window, the heuristic that is outlined by Braun et al. [2] is used. To find the impact window, we computed the RMS value of each window and defined a MINRMS value to ignore any window with a RMS value that does not exceed this threshold. The window with the maximal RMS value between the first and last RMS value that crosses this threshold is chosen. To avoid choosing a local maximum, all peaks are ignored after selecting the first maximum until the RMS values fall below a CLOSINGRMS value. We further adapt this approach to our multi-channels application by using the following Eq. 7,

$$RMS_{window} = \sqrt{\frac{\sum_{i=0}^{N} RMS_c^2}{N}} \tag{7}$$

where N is the channel count and RMS_c is the RMS value of the channel c. Since the output of the SVM can be a measure of probability instead of one-hot decision, we can further combine SVM with threshold method to determine the correctness of the classified class.

6 Conclusion and Outlook

In this paper, we introduced a ubiquitous and unobtrusive smart floor system using four pickups. The system is easy to install, has low power consumption and is easy to maintain. The use of pickups has the further advantage that only acoustic waves of the surface are recorded and any environmental sounds or speech will not be directly recognizable. The computation effort is rather low compared to image processing and doesn't suffer from the problem of occlusion.

We use pickups to retrieve surface acoustic waves to track a basic set of user's daily activities, including *walking, cupboard closing* and *fall*. By exploring different algorithms, we achieved a desired precision of over 94%. Additionally, the activity classes *Walking* and *Cupboard closing* are further expanded into their sub-classes (shoe types and cupboard instances) and can be successfully distinguished with a relatively high precision rate. This goal can be achieved by using a fusion of multiple pickups instead of only a single input channel. We have shown that by using a combination of multiple pickups, the performance is more superior and stable than only using a single one of them. The best classifier turns out to be the SVM with an observation window size of 8192 samples compared to CART and BayesNET. The SVM reaches the precision of 98.90% for AG-1, 97.42% for AG-2, 98.42% for AG-3 and 97.23% for AG-4.

Limitation of the setup is the connection of the pickups to the ground surface. To perfectly pick up the surface acoustic wave created by the impact, a sound coupling of the sensing device and the ground surface is of utmost importance. To note, the ground surface used in the experiment is homogeneous. In case of an inhomogeneous ground surface, like, e.g., placing a carpet on the wooden floor, a calibration of the system is needed to keep a high recognition performance. It has been shown in our experiment, that carpet attenuates the acoustic surface wave and decreases the amplitude of the received signal. Since the received signal is relevant to the performance of our system, therefore it is recommended to use a homogeneous flooring material, which can perfectly conduct the surface acoustic wave.

For future research, the identification of more recognizable activities will be interesting by increasing the number of useful features. The current amount of monitored activities are less than the amount of what can be recognized by approaches with cameras or wearable. However as discussed, the advantages of the fewer privacy issues and the unobtrusiveness of the wearable sensors becomes apparent by using our system. It is to note, that the current system only works for single user. Multiple users would affect the time series which leads to modifying the extracted features and therefore decrease the classification performance. For multiple person, independent component analysis (ICA)[11] should be applied to isolate the individual contribution to the system. Based on the decomposed individual signal, further processing may be applied to determine the class of activities.

References

1. Braun, A., Heggen, H., Wichert, R.: CapFloor – a flexible capacitive indoor localization system. In: Chessa, S., Knauth, S. (eds.) EvAAL 2011. CCIS, vol. 309, pp. 26–35. Springer, Heidelberg (2011). https://doi.org/10.1007/978-3-642-33533-4_3
2. Braun, A., Krepp, S., Kuijper, A.: Acoustic tracking of hand activities on surfaces. In: Proceedings of the 2nd International Workshop on Sensor-Based Activity Recognition and Interaction, iWOAR 2015, pp. 9:1–9:5. ACM, New York (2015). http://doi.acm.org/10.1145/2790044.2790052
3. Braun, A., Zander-Walz, S., Krepp, S., Rus, S., Wichert, R., Kuijper, A.: CapTap: combining capacitive gesture recognition and acoustic touch detection. In: Proceedings of the 3rd International Workshop on Sensor-Based Activity Recognition and Interaction, iWOAR 2016, pp. 6:1–6:6. ACM, New York (2016). http://doi.acm.org/10.1145/2948963.2948969
4. Chawla, N.V.: Data mining for imbalanced datasets: an overview. In: Maimon, O., Rokach, L. (eds.) The Data Mining and Knowledge Discovery Handbook, pp. 853–867. Springer, Boston (2005). https://doi.org/10.1007/0-387-25465-X_40. http://dblp.uni-trier.de/db/books/collections/datamining2005.html#Chawla05
5. Chawla, N.V., Bowyer, K.W., Hall, L.O., Kegelmeyer, W.P.: SMOTE: synthetic minority over-sampling technique. J. Artif. Intell. Res. **16**, 321–357 (2002)
6. Fu, B., Kirchbuchner, F., von Wilmsdorff, J., Grosse-Puppendahl, T., Braun, A., Kuijper, A.: Indoor localization based on passive electric field sensing. In: Braun, A., Wichert, R., Maña, A. (eds.) AmI 2017. LNCS, vol. 10217, pp. 64–79. Springer, Cham (2017). https://doi.org/10.1007/978-3-319-56997-0_5
7. Ghosh, S., Ganguly, N., Mitra, B., De, P.: TapSense: combining self-report patterns and typing characteristics for smartphone based emotion detection. In: Proceedings of the 19th International Conference on Human-Computer Interaction with Mobile Devices and Services, MobileHCI 2017, pp. 2:1–2:12. ACM, New York (2017). http://doi.acm.org/10.1145/3098279.3098564
8. Gröchenig, K.: The short-time Fourier transform. In: Gröchenig, K. (ed.) Foundations of Time-Frequency Analysis, pp. 37–58. Birkhäuser, Boston (2001). https://doi.org/10.1007/978-1-4612-0003-1_4
9. Hall, M., Frank, E., Holmes, G., Pfahringer, B., Reutemann, P., Witten, I.H.: The WEKA data mining software: an update. SIGKDD Explor. Newsl. **11**(1), 10–18 (2009). http://doi.acm.org/10.1145/1656274.1656278
10. Holzinger, A., Röcker, C., Ziefle, M.: From smart health to smart hospitals. In: Holzinger, A., Röcker, C., Ziefle, M. (eds.) Smart Health. LNCS, vol. 8700, pp. 1–20. Springer, Cham (2015). https://doi.org/10.1007/978-3-319-16226-3_1
11. Hyvärinen, A., Oja, E.: Independent component analysis: algorithms and applications. Neural Netw. **13**(4–5), 411–430 (2000). https://doi.org/10.1016/S0893-6080(00)00026-5
12. Jack, M.A., Grant, P.M., Collins, J.H.: The theory, design, and applications of surface acoustic wave Fourier-transform processors. Proc. IEEE **68**(4), 450–468 (1980). https://doi.org/10.1109/PROC.1980.11674
13. Lauterbach, C., Steinhage, A., Techmer, A.: A large-area sensor system underneath the floor for ambient assisted living applications. In: Mukhopadhyay, S., Postolache, O. (eds.) Pervasive and Mobile Sensing and Computing for Healthcare, pp. 69–87. Springer, Heidelberg (2013). https://doi.org/10.1007/978-3-642-32538-0_3
14. Li, X., Shen, M., Wang, W., Liu, H.: Real-time sound source localization for a mobile robot based on the guided spectral-temporal position method. Int. J. Adv. Robot. Syst. **9**(3), 78 (2012). https://doi.org/10.5772/51307

15. Mettel, M.R., Alekseew, M., Stocklöw, C., Braun, A.: Safety services in smart environments using depth cameras. In: Braun, A., Wichert, R., Maña, A. (eds.) AmI 2017. LNCS, vol. 10217, pp. 80–93. Springer, Cham (2017). https://doi.org/10.1007/978-3-319-56997-0_6
16. Rao, K.R., Kim, D.N., Hwang, J.J.: Fast Fourier Transform - Algorithms and Applications, 1st edn. Springer, Dordrecht (2010). https://doi.org/10.1007/978-1-4020-6629-0
17. Schroeder, J., Wabnik, S., van Hengel, P.W.J., Goetze, S.: Detection and classification of acoustic events for in-home care. In: Wichert, R., Eberhardt, B. (eds.) Ambient Assisted Living, pp. 181–195. Springer, Heidelberg (2011). https://doi.org/10.1007/978-3-642-18167-2_13
18. Temko, A., Nadeu, C.: Classification of acoustic events using SVM-based clustering schemes. Pattern Recogn. **39**(4), 682–694 (2006). https://doi.org/10.1016/j.patcog.2005.11.005
19. Weik, M.H.: Nyquist theorem. In: Weik, M.H. (ed.) Computer Science and Communications Dictionary, pp. 1127–1127. Springer, Boston (2001). https://doi.org/10.1007/1-4020-0613-6_12654

Step by Step: Early Detection of Diseases Using an Intelligent Floor

Lisa Scherf[1], Florian Kirchbuchner[1,2]([⊠]) [iD], Julian von Wilmsdorff[1,2],
Biying Fu[1,2] [iD], Andreas Braun[1,2] [iD], and Arjan Kuijper[1,2] [iD]

[1] Technische Universität Darmstadt, Karolinenplatz 5, 64289 Darmstadt, Germany
[2] Fraunhofer IGD, Fraunhoferstr. 5, 64283 Darmstadt, Germany
{lisa.scherf,florian.kirchbuchner,julian.von.wilmsdorff,biying.fu,
andreas.braun,arjan.kuijper}@igd.fraunhofer.de
http://www.tu-darmstadt.de
http://www.igd.fraunhofer.de

Abstract. The development of sensor technologies in smart homes helps to increase user comfort or to create safety through the recognition of emergency situations. For example, lighting in the home can be controlled or an emergency call can be triggered if sensors hidden in the floor detect a fall of a person. It makes sense to also use these technologies regarding prevention and early detection of diseases. By detecting deviations and behavioral changes through long-term monitoring of daily life activities it is possible to identify physical or cognitive diseases. In this work, we first examine in detail the existing possibilities to recognize the activities of daily life and the capability of such a system to conclude from the given data on illnesses. Then we propose a model for the use of floor-based sensor technology to help diagnose diseases and behavioral changes by analyzing the time spent in bed as well as the walking speed of users. Finally, we show that the system can be used in a real environment.

Keywords: Disease detection · Behavior analysis
Activities of daily living · Smart home · Sensors

1 Motivation

Over the next 25 years, nearly every country will experience very rapid population aging [21]. This demographic change will be very challenging. Most people have the wish to live independently and to stay as long as possible in their familiar surrounding. At the same time, the number of seniors in need of care is rising. In most of the cases, family members are looking after them these days, but due to lower birth rates, this can not be considered as a long-term solution [12]. Together with the high costs of nursing home care, it is inevitable to develop alternatives which help older adults to age in their own homes.

In the era of Ubiquitous Computing, a technical solution seems to be the obvious answer. Smart Home systems can provide sufficient security standards

© Springer Nature Switzerland AG 2018
A. Kameas and K. Stathis (Eds.): AmI 2018, LNCS 11249, pp. 131–146, 2018.
https://doi.org/10.1007/978-3-030-03062-9_11

for emergencies. This can be achieved, for example, by using fall detection systems or help older adults with context-aware applications and services such as medication management tools. These technologies are using sensor events, which are generated while residents perform their daily routines in their homes. In this way, the activities of daily living can be monitored. Anomalies in those activities are associated with the cognitive health status.

There are many sensors that can be used for activity monitoring. These can be firmly integrated into the environment or have to be worn by the users on their bodies. Some are examined in more detail below and compared across a number of dimensions, such as privacy and accuracy. As an innovation and as an alternative to the well-known systems we propose the use of a floor-based localization system to record and monitor the sleep behavior and walking speed of persons in the long term for an early recognition of diseases. Floor-based systems offer the advantage that they can be installed inconspicuously, do not violate privacy and thus achieve a higher user acceptance [18].

2 Related Work

In this section, we show how Smart Home technologies can detect user activities and thus detect physical or mental illnesses.

2.1 Sensors for Health Monitoring and Activity Recognition

There is a variety of mobile and wearable sensors which can be used in Smart Homes. An overview of the most common ones is given in Table 1. An advantage of wearable health-monitoring systems is the possibility to measure a variety of physiological parameters like heart rate, blood pressure or body and skin temperature. This enables early detection and a better treatment of medical conditions as well as disease prevention [25]. Thanks to the proximity of these sensors to the human body, they are particularly suitable for the acquisition of physiological parameters. This makes it possible to record the state of health of a person, but also his or her activities.

Smartphones are also often used for activity recognition because most of them already include accelerometers, gyroscopes, the global positioning system (GPS), and other sensors. With the data of these sensors, it is possible to detect falls [7,13], monitor the health status or provide context-aware assistance [29].

Apart from wearable sensors, there are also many ambient sensors which can be used in intelligent assistance systems. In contrast to wearable sensors, they are integrated into our everyday environment, such as our home, in an unobtrusive way and sensitive and responsive to our needs, habits, gestures, and emotions [28].

One possible application is monitoring for emergency detection. There are many fall detection techniques which rely on cameras or other ambient sensors. Miaou et al. [22] used a MapCam (omni-camera) for fall detection which leads to a precision of 79,8% when personal information was used in addition. Since

Table 1. Body worn sensor types that can be used for health monitoring. Adjusted from [25]

Type of bio-signal	Type of sensor	Date rate
Temperature	Temperature probe or skin patch	Very low
Hart rate	Pulse oximeter/skin electrodes	High
Body movements	Accelerometer	High
Orientation	Gyroscope	High
Electrocardiogram (ECG)	Skin/Chest electrodes	High
Electromyogram (EMG)	Skin electrodes	Very high
Electroencephalogram (EEG)	Scalp-places electrodes	High
Blood glucose	Strip-base glucose meters	High
Oxygen saturation	Pulse oximeter	Low
Blood pressure	Arm cuff-based monitor	Low

only the ratio of peoples height and width was used as features, there are still problems with people standing side by side or shadows. These problems are common in vision-based systems. Apart from occlusion and light conditions, privacy concerns are important issues. In contrast to other sensors, cameras are often visible to the resident what can cause a feeling of being observed. On the other hand, camera-based systems provide rich information. The video material could, for example, be used by medical professionals for diagnostic purposes.

A less obtrusive way of monitoring daily activities is using microphones as sensors instead of cameras. Vacher et al. [33] proposed the system AUDITHIS for real-time activity and speech recognition based on eight microphone channels. It was tested in the Habitat Intelligent pour la Sant? of Grenoble [8]. The flats of these Smart Homes are equipped with microphones and presence-infra-red sensors (PIR) and door contacts. Together with the set of other sensors, the average percentage of correctly classified activities of daily life was 82.85% Falls could be detected in 76.19% of the cases. Gjorski et al. [10] also showed that a combination of sensors is well suited for the detection of falls. Theire fall-detection method detected all of the fast falls and minimized the false positives, achieving 85% accuracy. However, a combination of permanently installed sensors and portable sensors was chosen here.

Another possibility for fall detection are systems built into the floor. These systems are often based on pressure sensors [1] or capacitive sensors [5,19]. So far, the systems have been used as a localization solution and for fall detection. But a lot more information can be derived from this localization information. Therefore, a possible application scenario is to be proposed in this work.

2.2 Behavior Analysis and Prediction of Health Changes

The previously described Smart Home technologies can not only be used to detect urgent emergencies or provide context-aware services. The sensors in a

Smart Home can also be used for health monitoring. This means that the information of the sensors is used to extrapolate from gradual changes in the measurement to a health decline or a disease. In this way, an early medical treatment can be ensured. Monitoring the recovery from a disease or a surgery is another possible use case. When a worsening of the health status is detected, family, friends, or medical staff can be informed.

Skubic et al. [31] proposed a health change detection model, and they investigated features extracted from in-home sensor data to generate alerts. With these results, they identified different indicators for health-decline and used them to train and test a classifier. The health-alert system was tested on a small number of residents and helped to recognize early signs of urinary tract infections and other acute infections such as heart failure or hypoglycemia. After the year-long randomized control study, the intervention group showed significantly better health outcomes than the control group. Therefore some vital signs, such as pulse rate and breathing rate, were chosen.

Furthermore, a change in bed restlessness can also indicate a health decline. Closely linked to the total time in bed (TIB) is the activity in other rooms than the bedroom at night. If this activity level rises, the total TIB is shorter, so it can provide valuable information and is also included in the proposed model. There is evidence that both short and long sleepers are at increased risk of all-cause mortality. The risk of death is smallest for an average sleep of seven to eight hours. Short sleep is generally defined as a reported sleep less than seven hours on average per night and long sleep as more than nine hours. There is also evidence for an association between sleep and health outcomes [14]. They also rated some gait-related values as essential for health monitoring. In-home walking speed, stride length and stride time were included in the health change detection model. Sleep, gait and vital signs, therefore, seem to be important determinants of health. Other studies also confirm the importance of sleep behavior as an indicator of health. Stenholm et al. [32] analyzed the connection between sleep behavior and physical functioning decline.

The results showed an association between long sleep (nine hours) and poor functioning and health and some evidence that short sleep (six hours) is associated with a higher likelihood of mobility disability, hypertension, diabetes, and mortality. A strength of this study is the longitudinal design with the repeated measurements of physical function and sleep behavior. However, the oldest and most disabled persons were lost to follow-up and may have weakened the findings. Also, the total sleeping time was based on self-report and can differ from physiological sleep duration. It is possible that much of the time spent in bed might have been spent awake.

Furthermore, self-reported sleep duration or TIB might be imprecise because subjects with insomnia underestimate their sleeping times [12]. In the mentioned studies, sleep duration or TIB were accessed using self-report questionnaires. These measurements can be imprecise because the time can be under- or overestimated by the subjects. Another possibility to access sleep is given by different sensors. Skubic et al. [31] for example used a pneumatic bed sensor installed on the bed mattress which was used to capture sleep patterns. It can distinguish four levels of bed restlessness, as well as three levels of pulse and respiration rate. Some residents preferred to sleep in a recliner chair and therefore had the sensor installed in the chair. The features extracted from the collected data of this sensor included TIB, bed restlessness, pulse and respiration events.

Closely linked to the quality of sleep is the number of bathroom visits per night which gives information about the number of nocturia events. Nocturia is defined as waking up one or more times at night to void. The first void in the morning is not counted as a night-time void since that is a natural expulsion of the urine produced during the night [17]. It is a prevalent condition, especially in older age groups. Middelkoop et al. [23] reported a prevalence of 72% and 91% in woman and man over the age of 80, whereas woman and man of 50–59 years only showed a prevalence of 59% and 67%. An increasing number of voids per night compromises sleep and health-related quality of life [6]. There is evidence for an association between nocturnal micturition and mortality risk. An observation over 54 months showed that male pensioners with three or more nocturnal voiding episodes have a 1.9 times higher death rate compared to matched cohorts [3]. This is consistent with the results of the retrospective cohort study of Lightner et al. [20] which indicate that nocturia may be a marker for death in men over 60 years. A significant association with later development of diabetes mellitus or hypertension could not be found, so nocturia may not apply to predict these diseases before they occur. However, nocturia can be a symptom of different diseases. If an abnormally large volume of urine is produced at night, we speak of nocturnal polyuria. Causes can be various health conditions, such as autonomic dysfunction, congestive heart failure, or estrogen deficiency. Persons with nocturia, who do not have nocturnal polyuria, will most likely have a sleep disorder or problems related to the bladder storage. Sleep disorders which are potentially related to nocturia are, for example, insomnia, the restless legs syndrome, and parasomnias, as well as lung disease or cardiac diseases and sleep disorders related to neurological diseases, such as Alzheimers or Parkinsons. Sometimes it results from behavioral influences like excessive evening intake of fluid, caffeine, and alcohol. In this case, general lifestyle advice can be sufficient to solve the problem. Nevertheless, some persons experiencing nocturia are not bothered by their condition and do not desire treatment [17]. Moderate nocturia is therefore often defined as waking to urinate two or more times per night [20].

Most human movement is associated with goals, so walking also involves intention and therefore cognitive input. Hence, gait performance is related to cognitive impairment [30]. A decreased in-home walking speed and stride-length, for example, is here presented as a predictor of health decline, whereas the in-home stride time increases in case of a health decline. There is indeed evidence that gait velocity might allow the detection of elderly at risk for adverse events. A lower gait velocity (¡0.7 m/s) was correlated with hospitalization, the requirement of a caregiver and new falls [24]. The longitudinal study of Quach et al. [26] also showed a higher risk of indoor falls in slow walkers. A value under 0.6 m/s was considered as a slow gait speed. It was measured during a 4-m walk. These findings are already used for some in-home monitoring systems for elder-care which continuously monitor walking speed [2,11]. The so measured values turned out to be lower than the walking speed values measured by a therapist. This might be caused by the tendency of the subjects to improve their behavior when being assessed [2]. Sheridan and Hausdorff [30] also studied whether gait velocity could be sufficient to predict adverse events like for example hospitalization, the requirement for a caregiver or falls in healthy elderly persons. They agreed with the proposal that gait velocity could be used to detect adverse events. Apart from gait velocity, there are a lot more quantitative gait parameters which could be assessed.

Verghese et al. [34] analyzed different gait markers and their relationship to decline in cognitive domains and the risk of developing dementia. As a method, they carried out a prospective cohort study with 427 elderly over five years. Factor analysis reduced the quantitative gait parameters to three independent factors: pace, rhythm, and variability. The pace factor had strong loadings by velocity and length measures, such as stride length, whereas the rhythm factor reflected variables such as cadence, swing or stance time. The last factor variability loaded strongly on the stride length variability and the swing time variability. With these factors, 87% of the variance was explained. To access cognition and assign dementia diagnosis, the subjects performed tests to general cognition, memory, executive function and attention. The findings indicate that quantitative gait dysfunction predicts the risk of cognitive decline in initially non-demented elderly and risk of dementia. An increase in the pace factor predicted a decline in executive function. Rhythm and variability factors predicted the risk of developing dementia. The gait was measured with the GAITRite system which is widely used and has excellent reliability. With this system, many gait parameters could be considered. The described gait parameters are well suited for behavior analysis. An interesting value in connection with the prediction of falls is the path variability or tortuosity. It can, for example, be gauged using fractal dimension (Fractal D). It was shown that odds of falling increased with an increase in Fractal D. Tortuosity could, therefore, serve as an independent predictor of fall risk [15]. Kearns et al. [16] measured Fractal D of elderly residents in their daily-life with an ultra-wideband sensor network. The results revealed a significant and negatively related correlation with cognitive functioning. The cognitive status was captured with the Mini Mental State Examination (MMSE). Fractal D was able to account for 22% of the total variance in the MMSE score. There might be confounding variables such as age and disease status that werent evaluated in this study due to the small number of subjects. Moreover, a low MMSE score is an indicator of dementia.

There are already some systems using environmentally embedded ambient sensors to monitor gait to detect potential changes in health continuously. Rantz et al. [27] for example daily calculated gait speed, stride length, and stride time of older adults and sent automated health alerts to health-care staff if a change was detected. Besides, they also captured their respiration, pulse, and restlessness as they slept. To make such monitoring possible, motion and bed sensors, a Kinect depth camera, and a pulse-Doppler radar were installed in different apartments. Results showed that health changes could be detected ten days to two weeks before the person is aware of symptoms. This early detection allowed for a faster intervention of clinicians and led to a faster recovery with less functional decline. This was also confirmed by the results of a one-year pilot study where the intervention group showed significant improvement as compared to the control group. Diseases that could be found by early assessment were, for example, acute infections, heart failure, hypoglycemia or pneumonia.

3   Implementation of the Floor-Based System

As shown before, many features can be accessed in a Smart Home and used to monitor health and detect gradual changes. Various vital signs, the sleep behavior, as well as the nocturia and gait are frequently mentioned as indicators of health. However, to monitor all these features, different sensors are needed. To offer a method that can be used in everyday life and is accepted by a broad range of older adults, different factors have to be considered. The costs have to be kept as low as possible. This means that the number of different sensors has to be reduced. Also, a high number of installed sensors in an apartment can create the feeling of being observed. The technology should be as unobtrusive as possible. This concludes that the sensors should not disturb the everyday life of the resident which can be the case for some uncomfortable wearable sensors. Based on these considerations, our goal was to extend the use cases of a smart floor to be able to detect health changes without the need of additional sensors. This, of course, limits the range of possibilities, but there are still some features that might be accessible via the location of a person and are shown to be linked with health. Table 2 gives a rough overview. We chose three of these values which we thought would be accessible using our floor-based System. These values are the gait velocity, the number of bathroom visits in one night, and the sleep duration. As described above, there is evidence that these values are linked to health and can be used to detect diseases or a cognitive decline.

3.1   System Design

As described above, many parameters could be used as indicators to detect gradual changes in health. However, in the scope of this work, we will confine ourselves to values, which can be measured or calculated from the data collected with the floor-based system, proposed by Fu et al. [9]. The System only includes sensors to track the indoor location of a person. Physiological parameters, such as heart rate, breathing rate, or body temperature are therefore excluded from the outset. To measure these vital signs, additional wearable sensors would be needed.

The system we use is based on the principle of passive measurement of the electric field. Through a fine wire mesh under the floor covering, the sensors used to detect the smallest charge displacements that are generated by a person's

Table 2. Model for detection health decline with an floor-based Sensor System

Sensor-based parameter	Increase		Decrease		Measured by our floor-based system
	Day	Night	Day	Night	
Motion density	-	x	x	-	x
Bathroom density	x	x	-	-	x
Bedroom activity	-	-	-	-	x
Living room activity	-	x	-	-	x
Kitchen activity	-	x	-	-	x
Time away from home	-	x	x	-	x
Visitor activity	-	-	-	-	-
Total time in bed	x	-	-	x	x
Bed restlessness	x	x	x	x	x
Pulse rate	x	x	x	x	-
Breathing rate	x	x	x	-	-
In-home walking speed	-	-	x	x	x
In-home stride length	-	-	x	x	-
In-home stride time	x	x	-	-	-

movement. The system detects changes of the electric field with a frequency of 10 Hz corresponding to a measurement of every 100 ms. A small computer analyses the measured value and calculates the position of the person in the room. For this purpose, the system has a graphical user interface which makes it possible to load the building plan and to position the sensors and measuring electrodes. This makes it possible to determine the person's global position. It is also possible to subdivide the areas and mark regions of interest. Sophisticated algorithms recognize reliably whether a person is moving around the apartment where they are or whether a person has fallen. A detailed description of the system is referenced in [9] for further reading. For the communication with the building control system, the software generates an event upon entering the apartment which is updated with every movement registered. When a person leaves the apartment, the event is canceled. To protect the privacy of the users, the data is evaluated locally and is not outsourced to cloud-based services. All computing is done by a BeagleBone embedded computer with a Linux operating system. The BeagleBone Black is a power-saving, community supported platform, based on an AM335x 1 GHz ARM Cortex-A8 equipped with 512 MB DDR3 RAM and a 4 GB 8-bit eMMC onboard flash storage. All software is written in Java, using the Apache Karaf OSGi framework. That offers a modular software architecture which allows controlling the system remotely and update all components successively.

As previously described, sleep is an essential determinant of health. The possibilities to measure sleep quality or sleep duration are limited. To access sleep duration, we will use TIB as a measurement. As already mentioned, TIB can differ from the actual sleep duration. However, there is evidence for a significant correlation between TIB and health. To measure TIB with our floor-based system, the time between two events in the bedroom is measured and stored in a database, if it exceeds a given threshold. This threshold is used to sort out other activities in the bedroom, such as standing in front of the wardrobe or sitting down, which can also cause an extended period between two events. For the database db4o1 was chosen, which is object-orientated and easily embeddable to other programs with limited memory space. It is, therefore, possible to create classes for every health indicator and store objects of them in the database. The information is well organized so that it can easily be accessed, managed, and updated. Furthermore, to access the database the programming language Java can be used itself in the form of Native Queries and developers do not need to switch to string-based APIs. This allows, for example, to filter all stored TIB episodes easily. Since only this one bundle needs access to the database, the embedded mode was chosen (Fig. 1).

Another possible indicator of a gradual change in health is the gait of a person. To be able to compare the gait velocity of different days, it is necessary to measure it under similar conditions. Therefore, we decided to assess the gait velocity considering the same path at a similar time of day. We assumed that the way to the bathroom at night has a low variability between different nights and is hence suitable for measuring the gait velocity. The majority of older adults

Fig. 1. Test setup in the lab with electrode grid and sensors [9].

---

1 http://supportservices.actian.com/versant/default.html.

(72%) has to get up at least once at night to urinate [4]. If this is not the case, the walk to the bathroom in the morning can also be used. To ensure that the gait is only measured at night, a variable "sleptgait" is set to "true" if a TIB event is stored in the database. The measurement starts at the passage from the bedroom to the floor and ends at the passage from the floor to the bathroom. The parts of the path in the bedroom and the bathroom are not considered to avoid measuring the time to get up from the bed and other activities instead of only the continuous gait. If the person deviates from this path and is, for example, entering the kitchen, the measurement of the gait velocity is interrupted and not stored in the database. In this case, the variable "sleptgait" is again set to "false". Otherwise, the measured velocity is stored in the database together with the date of the current night. It has to be mentioned that for an exact measurement of the gait velocity, the length of the actual path would have to be divided by the time it takes the person for this path. The measured gait velocity may be imprecise with our approach because we define a regular route between bedroom and bathroom. However, since we assumed that the chosen path stays the same over different nights, the measured values are comparable, and gradual changes in the gait velocity are reflected in the measurements.

Besides gait velocity and sleep duration, the number of bathroom visits in one night is also stored in the database. With this intention, a variable "slept" is set when a TIB event is stored in the database. If the person then triggers an event in the bathroom, the bathroom visit is stored in the database together with the date. The variable "slept" is then again set to "false".

To identify short-term changes in health as well as gradual changes, a time window of two weeks is chosen. So all measured parameters are stored for the past two weeks, and an average value is computed. This value is then compared to the current measurement. If the current measurement has a higher deviation than the standard derivation times a multiplier compared to the mean of the past two weeks before, a significant change is identified. We used three as a multiplier inspired by the results of Skubic et al. [31]. They varied from 2.5 to 4 according to the relative importance of the parameter rated by a clinical research team. The exact values were not published. Further evaluation would be needed to determine the most suitable values. A compromise must be found between minimizing the false alarm rate and maximizing the likelihood of detecting critical health changes. The time in bed is only considered critical and stored in the database if it falls below six hours [32]. The same applies to the gait velocity for a value below 0.6 m/s. A gait velocity below this value is considered indicating a higher risk of indoor falls [26]. If one or more predictors show a significant change, a log message is generated. It informs about the predictor that showed a change and how the values changed.

3.2 Evaluation

As a first step, we carried out a short technical evaluation of the system set up in a laboratory environment. For this purpose, a smart floor measuring 2.40 by 3.70 m was used. The area equipped with sensors is smaller than an average apartment and is not covering different rooms, but at first, only the technical function should be shown. To be able to test the developed method, the area was separated into smaller regions of interest using the graphical interface of the floor-based system. The so generated sectors are representing different rooms. The "Bath-Room" was placed in the opposite corner as the "BedRoom" to ensure a long path to measure the gait velocity. Between these two areas, there is a hallway which is separated into two different parts: "Hallway1" and "Hallway2". Four different possible scenarios were tested. Every test case was performed five times.

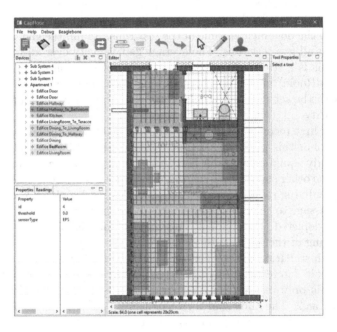

Fig. 2. The user interface of the smart floor with instant-scale plan of the tested Apartment. Predefined areas highlighted in different colours and named on the left. The red line marks the way to measure the speed.

The first scenario simulates a nocturnal visit to the bathroom. To do this, a stay in bed must first be recognized. Activity in the bedroom, followed by a pause (40 s), should first indicate the TIB. For test purposes, the threshold value was lowered to 30 s. After this, new events were generated following a given path to measure the gait velocity. In this case, the velocity was measured when crossing "Hallway1" and "Hallway2" in this order and then entering the "BathRoom". Besides the sleeping phase, the gait velocity and a bathroom visit should also be stored in the database when entering the "BathRoom" area.

The second test case was used to ensure that other activities in the bedroom, such as standing in front of the wardrobe for a few minutes, are not identified as TIB. The developed method is using a threshold to filter out these activities. The third scenario occurs when the resident is walking to the bathroom but is not using the direct way. The person could, for instance, walk into the hallway, return to the bedroom and then walk to the bathroom. If the way to the bathroom would then be divided by the time it took the person to reach the bathroom, a lower gait velocity would be mistakenly assumed. Therefore, the gait velocity should not be stored in the database. The last test case then simulates the case when a person wakes up in the night but does not walk into the bathroom.

As a result, in all test cases, the expected values were stored in the database. For all five test runs the time was stored together with the start and the end date of the TIB. The average duration of TIB overall test runs is approximately 38 s. This value is close to the measured 40 s. The stored start and end dates also correspond to the documented time of the test runs. Again, the gait velocity was determined in all five test runs. The average gait velocity over all test runs was 0.52 m/s. This is a reasonable value since the generating of events on the way from the "BedRoom" area to the "BathRoom" took approximately five seconds. Together with the set path length of 2.80 m, this would give a similar value for the gait velocity.

After this first technical test in the lab, we carried out tests in a real living environment. For this purpose, a senior citizens' residential complex was used, which is already equipped with our floor system. The apartment is also equipped with numerous other smart home sensors. The chosen apartment has a bedroom, a bathroom, a living room, and a combined kitchen and dining area, which also serves as a passage to the rooms mentioned above. In Fig. 2 the floor plan of the apartment is depicted. The resident is a female senior who has given her consent to the recording of the data.

After the installation of the developed software packages and an adjustment of the regions of interest, the nightly activities were recorded for 14 days. The gait velocity is only measured if the test person is passing the given path as depicted in Fig. 2. The threshold for recognizing inactivity in the bedroom as a TIB was set to five minutes because the resident said she would fall asleep relatively quickly. If two events are successively detected in the bedroom, the time in between is stored in the database if it exceeds this threshold.

However, the first series of tests led to technical problems since the sensor system interpreted occasional noise as a short-term movement. As a result, the recorded nocturnal movement patterns were not valid. Therefore, it was necessary to repeat the test series after recalibrating the floor system.

In Fig. 3 the overall TIB per night over the evaluation period is pictured. On average, the test person spent 6.4 h a day in bed. The duration varied between 5.5 and 7.3 h. The duration of the individual sleep phases is not shown. This means the time between individual activities, e.g., going to bed and the first visit to the toilet. The TIB varied between 1 and 3.5 h and lasted an average of 2.3 h.

The stored number of bathroom visits per night over the time of the evaluation period is pictured in Fig. 4. It shows a mean of 1.78 bathroom visits for one night with a standard deviation of 0.5. The highest number of bathroom visits is three.

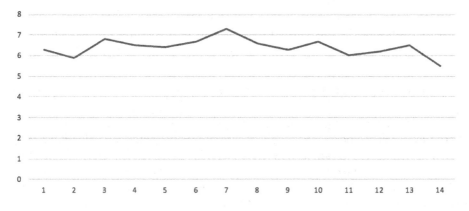

Fig. 3. Overall time in per night.

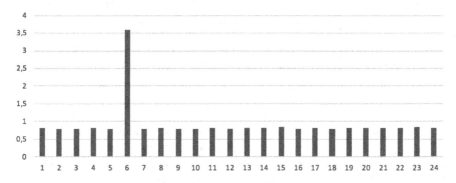

Fig. 4. Walking speed from 24 bath visits in 14 nights. Sample 6 is outlier, caused by some activity in the kitchen area.

An important result is that the speed for the nightly bathroom visit is almost constant. This is important because it proves that the chosen approach is suitable to use this fixed path as a reference value. The average walking speed is 0.81 m/s, with a variance of 0.1 m/s. One value deviates strongly with 3.6 m/s, which is to be evaluated as an outlier. This outlier is due to the fact that the path leads past the kitchenette. In this case, the participant stayed there longer to have a drink. However, the path sequence was followed correctly and therefore this time was included.

In order to prove the reliability of the values obtained, the test person was asked to document the times of getting up and going to bed, including the number of visits to the toilet. It was found that the database entries approximately corresponded to the self-documentation. All in all, the functionality of the recording could be shown. The smart floor has proven to be suitable for reliably recording the TIB, the number of bathing visits and the walking speed.

In the next step, the nocturnal data is recorded continuously and compared with the values of the previous 14 days as shown in the previous section. This investigation is still ongoing. So far, no anomalies have been registered.

4   Conclusion and Future Work

In this paper, we presented a model for health monitoring using only data collected by a smart floor. Considering the technical possibilities of this floor and based on existing work about health monitoring, three key factors were chosen: number of bath visits, duration of sleep, and gait velocity. All three values showed relations to the health status and were often used as indicators of health in different papers. The resulting developed method for behavior analysis consists of two parts. Each night these factors are derived from the sensor data and stored in a database. After this, the values for one night are compared with those of the previous two weeks to detect changes in behaviour. In such a case, a warning message with information about the suspicious value is generated. In the brief evaluation, it was shown that it is technically possible to collect relevant data. The next step is to record and evaluate this data over a long period. Moreover, a long-term study could verify the detection of significant changes in the stored values and if there is a correlation with a decline in health.

In conclusion, we proofed that many values related to health status could be accessed only using a smart floor. They cannot be measured directly, but are reflected in the sensor data. This is an important finding since smart floors are in many cases only used for fall detection or context-aware services. The usage for health monitoring demonstrates far more potential of smart floors for future applications. However, a significant limitation is that floor-based systems are expensive and laborious to install. Other solutions are cheaper - at least for short-term use. On the other hand, floor-based systems protect the privacy of the users. Additionally, they do not have to adjust their habits to new devices and they do not have to wear a portable token.

References

1. Addlesee, M.D., Jones, A., Livesey, F., Samaria, F.: The orl active floor [sensor system]. IEEE Pers. Commun. **4**(5), 35–41 (1997). https://doi.org/10.1109/98.626980
2. Aicha, A.N., Englebienne, G., Kröse, B.: Continuous measuring of the indoor walking speed of older adults living alone. J. Ambient. Intell. Humanized Comput. **9**(3), 589–599 (2018). https://doi.org/10.1007/s12652-017-0456-x
3. Asplund, R.: Mortality in the elderly in relation to nocturnal micturition. BJU International **84**(3), 297–301 (1999)
4. Barker, J.C., Mitteness, L.S.: Nocturia in the elderly. Gerontologist **28**(1), 99–104 (1988)
5. Braun, A., Heggen, H., Wichert, R.: CapFloor – a flexible capacitive indoor localization system. In: Chessa, S., Knauth, S. (eds.) EvAAL 2011. CCIS, vol. 309, pp. 26–35. Springer, Heidelberg (2012). https://doi.org/10.1007/978-3-642-33533-4_3

6. Coyne, K., Zhou, Z., Bhattacharyya, S., Thompson, C., Dhawan, R., Versi, E.: The prevalence of nocturia and its effect on health-related quality of life and sleep in a community sample in the usa. BJU International **92**(9), 948–954 (2003)

7. Dai, J., Bai, X., Yang, Z., Shen, Z., Xuan, D.: PerFallD: a pervasive fall detection system using mobile phones. In: 2010 8th IEEE International Conference on Pervasive Computing and Communications Workshops (PERCOM Workshops), pp. 292–297, March 2010. https://doi.org/10.1109/PERCOMW.2010.5470652

8. Fleury, A., Vacher, M., Noury, N.: SVM-based multimodal classification of activities of daily living in health smart homes: sensors, algorithms, and first experimental results. IEEE Trans. Inf. Technol. Biomed. **14**(2), 274–283 (2010). https://doi.org/10.1109/TITB.2009.2037317

9. Fu, B., Kirchbuchner, F., von Wilmsdorff, J., Grosse-Puppendahl, T., Braun, A., Kuijper, A.: Indoor localization based on passive electric field sensing. In: Braun, A., Wichert, R., Maña, A. (eds.) Ambient Intelligence, pp. 64–79. Springer, Cham (2017). https://doi.org/10.1007/978-3-319-56997-0_5

10. Gjoreski, M., Gjoreski, H., Lutrek, M., Gams, M.: How accurately can your wrist device recognize daily activities and detect falls? Sensors **16**(6) (2016). https://doi.org/10.3390/s16060800, http://www.mdpi.com/1424-8220/16/6/800

11. Hagler, S., Austin, D., Hayes, T.L., Kaye, J., Pavel, M.: Unobtrusive and ubiquitous in-home monitoring: A methodology for continuous assessment of gait velocity in elders. IEEE Trans. Biomed. Eng. **57**(4), 813–820 (2010). https://doi.org/10.1109/TBME.2009.2036732

12. Haustein, T., Mischke, J., Schönfeld, F., Willand, I.: Ältere Menschen in Deutschland und der EU. Statistisches Bundesamt (2016)

13. He, Y., Li, Y., Bao, S.D.: Fall detection by built-in tri-accelerometer of smartphone. In: Proceedings of 2012 IEEE-EMBS International Conference on Biomedical and Health Informatics. pp. 184–187, January 2012. https://doi.org/10.1109/BHI.2012.6211540

14. Hublin, C., Partinen, M., Koskenvuo, M., Kaprio, J.: Sleep and mortality: a population-based 22-year follow-up study. Sleep **30**(10), 1245–1253 (2007)

15. Kearns, W.D., et al.: Path tortuosity in everyday movements of elderly persons increases fall prediction beyond knowledge of fall history, medication use, and standardized gait and balance assessments. J. Am. Med. Dir. Assoc. **13**(7), 665–e7 (2012)

16. Kearns, W.D., Nams, V., Fozard, J.L.: Tortuosity in movement paths is related to cognitive impairment. Methods Inf. Med. **49**(06), 592–598 (2010)

17. van Kerrebroeck, P., Abrams, P., Chaikin, D., Donovan, J., Fonda, D., Jackson, S., Jennum, P., Johnson, T., Lose, G., Mattiasson, A.: The standardisation of terminology in Nocturia: report from the standardisation sub-committee of the international continence society. Neurourol. Urodyn. Off. J. Int. Cont. Soc. **21**(2), 179–183 (2002)

18. Kirchbuchner, F., Grosse-Puppendahl, T., Hastall, M.R., Distler, M., Kuijper, A.: Ambient intelligence from senior citizens' perspectives: understanding privacy concerns, technology acceptance, and expectations. In: De Ruyter, B., Kameas, A., Chatzimisios, P., Mavrommati, I. (eds.) AmI 2015. LNCS, vol. 9425, pp. 48–59. Springer, Cham (2015). https://doi.org/10.1007/978-3-319-26005-1_4

19. Lauterbach, C., Steinhage, A.: Sensfloor®-a large-area sensor system based on printed textiles printed electronics. In: Ambient Assisted Living Congress. VDE Verlag (2009)

20. Lightner, D.J., et al.: Nocturia is associated with an increased risk of coronary heart disease and death. BJU international **110**(6), 848–853 (2012)

21. McDaniel, S., Zimmer, Z.: Global ageing in the twenty-first century: challenges, opportunities and implications. Ashgate Publishing Ltd (2013)
22. Miaou, S.G., Sung, P.H., Huang, C.Y.: A customized human fall detection system using omni-camera images and personal information. In: 1st Transdisciplinary Conference on Distributed Diagnosis and Home Healthcare, D2H2, pp. 39–42, April 2006. https://doi.org/10.1109/DDHH.2006.1624792
23. Middelkoop, H.A., Smilde-van den Doel, D.A., Neven, A.K., Kamphuisen, H.A., Springer, C.P.: Subjective sleep characteristics of 1,485 males and females aged 50–93: effects of sex and age, and factors related to self-evaluated quality of sleep. J. Gerontol. Ser. A Biol. Sci. Med. Sci. **51**(3), M108–M115 (1996)
24. Montero-Odasso, M., et al.: Gait velocity as a single predictor of adverse events in healthy seniors aged 75 years and older. J. Gerontol. Ser. A Biol. Sci. Med. Sci. **60**(10), 1304–1309 (2005)
25. Pantelopoulos, A., Bourbakis, N.G.: A survey on wearable sensor-based systems for health monitoring and prognosis. IEEE Trans. Syst., Man, Cybern., Part C (Appl. Rev.) **40**(1), 1–12 (2010). https://doi.org/10.1109/TSMCC.2009.2032660
26. Quach, L., et al.: The nonlinear relationship between gait speed and falls: the maintenance of balance, independent living, intellect, and zest in the elderly of Boston study. J. Am. Geriatr. Soc. **59**(6), 1069–1073 (2011)
27. Rantz, M.J., et al.: A new paradigm of technology-enabled vital signs' for early detection of health change for older adults. Gerontology **61**(3), 281–290 (2015)
28. Rashidi, P., Mihailidis, A.: A survey on ambient-assisted living tools for older adults. IEEE J. Biomed. Health Inform. **17**(3), 579–590 (2013). https://doi.org/10.1109/JBHI.2012.2234129
29. Ribeiro Filho, J.D.P., e Silva, F.J.d.S., Coutinho, L.R., Gomes, B.d.T.P.: MHARS: a mobile system for human activity recognition and inference of health situations in ambient assisted living. J. Appl. Comput. Res. **5**(1), 44–58 (2016)
30. Sheridan, P.L., Hausdorff, J.M.: The role of higher-level cognitive function in gait: executive dysfunction contributes to fall risk in Alzheimers Disease. Dement. Geriatr. Cogn. Disord. **24**(2), 125–137 (2007)
31. Skubic, M., Guevara, R.D., Rantz, M.: Automated health alerts using in-home sensor data for embedded health assessment. IEEE J. Transl. Eng. Health Med. **3**, 1–11 (2015). https://doi.org/10.1109/JTEHM.2015.2421499
32. Stenholm, S., Kronholm, E., Bandinelli, S., Guralnik, J.M., Ferrucci, L.: Self-reported sleep duration and time in bed as predictors of physical function decline: results from the inchianti study. Sleep **34**(11), 1583–1593 (2011). https://doi.org/10.5665/sleep.1402
33. Vacher, M., Fleury, A., Portet, F., Serignat, J.F., Noury, N.: Complete sound and speech recognition system for health smart homes: application to the recognition of activities of daily living (2010)
34. Verghese, J., Wang, C., Holtzer, R., Lipton, R., Xue, X.: Quantitative gait dysfunction and risk of cognitive decline and dementia. J. Neurol., Neurosurg. Psychiatry (2007)

Prototyping Shape-Sensing Fabrics Through Physical Simulation

Silvia Rus[1,2](✉) [ID], Felix Hammacher[2], Julian von Wilmsdorff[1],
Andreas Braun[1] [ID], Tobias Grosse-Puppendahl[3], Florian Kirchbuchner[1] [ID],
and Arjan Kuijper[1,2] [ID]

[1] Fraunhofer IGD, Fraunhoferstr. 5, 64283 Darmstadt, Germany
{silvia.rus,julian.von.wilmsdorff,andreas.braun,
florian.kirchbuchner}@igd.fraunhofer.de
[2] Technische Universität Darmstadt, Karolinenplatz 5, 64289 Darmstadt, Germany
{silvia.rus,felix.hammacher}@stud.tu-darmstadt.de,
arjan.kuijper@mavc.tu-darmstadt.de
[3] Dr. Ing. h.c. F. Porsche AG, Porschestr. 911, 71287 Weissach, Germany
tobias@grosse-puppendahl.com

Abstract. Embedding sensors into fabrics can leverage substantial improvements in application areas like working safety, 3D modeling or health-care, for example to recognize the risk of developing skin ulcers. Finding a suitable setup and sensor combination for a shape-sensing fabric currently relies on the intuition of an application engineer. We introduce a novel approach: Simulating the shape-sensing fabric first and optimize the design to achieve better real-world implementations. In order to enable developers to easily prototype their shape-sensing scenario, we have implemented a framework that enables soft body simulation and virtual prototyping. To evaluate our approach, we investigate the design of a system detecting sleeping postures. We simulate potential designs first, and implement a bed cover consisting of 40 distributed acceleration sensors. The validity of our framework is confirmed by comparing the simulated and real evaluation results. We show that both approaches achieve similar performances, with an F-measure of 85% for the virtual prototype and 89% for the real-world implementation.

Keywords: Shape sensing fabrics · Sleeping posture
Simulation framework

1 Introduction

The rapid development towards miniaturized sensors and bendable electronics has led to new concepts for shape-changing and shape-sensing devices [3,9,12, 18,19]. Contrary to the traditional usage of cameras for shape-sensing, which suffer from occlusion, lack of mobility and lack of acceptance, sensors integrated into everyday materials can leverage fine-grained shape detection supported by developing bendable sensors [1,5,13,14,16].

© Springer Nature Switzerland AG 2018
A. Kameas and K. Stathis (Eds.): AmI 2018, LNCS 11249, pp. 147–161, 2018.
https://doi.org/10.1007/978-3-030-03062-9_12

Having a flexible shape-sensing fabric use-case, the engineer needs to decide on how to equip and distribute sensors across his shape-sensing surface. He has to try out different designs with solely his intuition to work with regarding type, number and placement of sensors. Even though supporting tools like simulators are well known in the robotics area they are only suited for rigid object simulation and not for flexible surface simulations [20]. We close this gap by providing a tool for designing virtual prototypes for shape-sensing fabrics.

The proposed simulation workflow, shown in Fig. 1, eliminates the need for designing and building the hardware equipment. First, the application developer scans a number of shape-sensing scenarios. With this representation, we provide the developer with a tool to estimate the desired level of accuracy, deciding on the trade-off between accuracy and amount of sensors suitable for this use case. Finally, when the application developer is satisfied, the system can be implemented.

As our central scientific contribution, we introduce and evaluate a simulation framework for shape-sensing fabrics, which enables developers to investigate designs of applications prototypes, before any hardware installation.

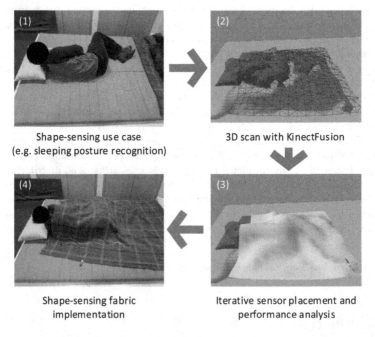

Fig. 1. To support better prototyping of shape-sensing fabrics, we introduce a simulation and refinement phase. First, we 3D-scan a number of scenarios e.g. sleeping posture recognition (1) to create a mesh representation (2). On this mesh, we place a virtual prototype of a shape-sensing fabric with simulated sensors (3). The classification performance is iteratively analyzed, allowing the application developer to implement the best-performing shape-sensing fabric (4).

Furthermore, we propose the work-flow for the prototype design process based on an exemplary use case: sleeping posture recognition. Based on our experiences with the simulated problem space, we implement a prototypical bed cover featuring 40 acceleration sensors arranged in a grid. By evaluating and simulating the problem with 10 different users, we show that the simulation data closely matches with the experiences made in an actual implementation.

2   Related Work

It is common to simulate prototypes in a virtual surrounding to see if the planned hard- and software is capable of fulfilling their desired purpose before they are built in real hardware [4,20], especially in robotics research. Several robotic simulators have been implemented that integrate virtual sensors and use them together with other virtual robots [17]. Since robots are mostly made of rigid materials, none of the robotic simulators were found to be able to attach virtual sensors to soft materials, like fabrics and thus simulate our shape-sensing fabric. However, there are multiple existing shape-sensing fabrics approaches which we address in the following.

2.1   Shape Sensing

Flexible, self-sensing objects, which know their current shape and report their deformation have recently been in the focus of different works using technologies like piezoelectric, resistive and capacitive sensors [5,10,11,13]. An example of a self-sensing flexible surface is FlexSense, a piezoelectric transparent foil which can sense if it is bent. It is used as input foil for tablet interaction [13]. PrintSense is a similar approach for manipulation detection of flexible surfaces using capacitive sensing [5]. Resistive sensors enable the users of the PaperPhone to interact with its bendable corners [10]. Lorussi et al. create a piezoelectric sleeve which detects the arm bending [11]. All of these examples have as a goal to determine their shape and use this information for the use case at hand.

Additionally, there are a few approaches using inertia and magnetic sensors added on flexible surfaces, in order to determine their shape [2,6–8,15,21,22]. The Three-Dimensional Capture Sheet measures its own shape only by using embedded inertia and magnetic sensors [8]. It produces a 3D-mesh without external devices, by attaching inertia sensors onto rigid links connected at their ends, forming a lattice structure. By determining the orientation of each attached sensor, the orientation of the corresponding link can be distinguished. The theory and a simulation of an exemplary 13×13 lattice structure shows the feasibility of using the orientation, measured via accelerometer and magnetic sensors, for shape reconstruction. However, only a small prototype with a 3×3 grid using 24 sensors, attached to the grid links, was realized. MorphoShape consists of a rectangular piece of fabric embedding a 3×3 grid of inertia sensors [15]. Although MorphoShape only uses 9 sensors (accelerometers and magnetometers), its reconstruction algorithm, based on curves, provides a realistic interpolation of the whole prototype. Hermanis et al. have developed two shape sensing prototypes [6,7]. The first was comprised of a 4×4 acceleration sensor grid used for body posture recognition. The sensors were attached to clothing on the back. The second prototype was based on inertia sensors sewed into two layers of freely bendable fabrics. The 63 embedded sensors are aligned in a 9×7 grid. In a similar manner Wang et al. have demonstrated Zishi, a wearable smart garment based on intertial measurement units monitoring the shape of the back of a person for rehabilitation purposes [21,22]. Demetyev et al. have developed a cuttable SensorTape, where each sensor node has inertial, infrared and light sensors gathered on a flexible substrate [2]. Demonstrating the capability of their rapid prototyping they attach the tape to the back of the person, recording and displaying its deformation.

We provide a tool for fast prototyping by simulating the use case for shape-sensing fabrics. Through this, we enable developers to analyze bigger prototypes, using heterogeneous sources of sensors. Developers can thus easily tailor the needed hardware to the use case.

3   Simulation Framework Use Case: Sleeping Posture Recognition

In order to show the workflow for simulation-aided prototyping of hardware and software, we choose sleeping posture recognition as application for shape-sensing fabrics. We cover a sleeping individual with a sensors embedded bed cover, which adapts to her body posture. The bed cover senses the shape of the person lying underneath and deduces her sleeping posture.

In this section we present the workflow, that supports planning the hardware for this specific use case like deciding on different dimensions of a prototype, the number of sensors and the sensor layout. This is achieved by creating a virtual prototype first. Subsequently, we describe the real prototype built according to its model, the virtual prototype. The description of the two prototypes, virtual and real-world prototype, is followed by a detailed comparison and evaluation in the validation section.

3.1   Virtual Prototype - Hardware Planning

Our proposed simulation framework offers tools to create and run a physical based simulation in real time. This simulation can not only contain physical objects interacting with each other, but also sensors attached to them. Instead of just being able to attach sensors to rigid bodies, like in most robotic simulators, sensors can also be attached to soft bodies. Thus it enables a user to simulate fabrics with embedded sensors. The sensors currently included in the simulation framework are acceleration sensors and combined acceleration and magnetic sensors.

Our shape-sensing fabric is comprised of a bed cover equipped with acceleration sensors. Before a hardware prototype is created, the simulation framework is used to test different sensor layouts which are suitable for the use case. The simulation framework provides a way to quickly generate sensor output for different virtual prototypes. Even huge amounts of sensors become manageable. Although a higher resolution of sensors leads to a more precise shape reconstruction, embedding more real sensors on a real prototype is very complex. To find the optimal solution for the trade-off between precision and complexity, the simulation framework is used. For this, we create the scene of the use case in the virtual environment of the simulation framework. The virtual bed cover consists of a soft body with 36×36 nodes and virtual sensors. Sensors can be attached to each of the nodes. This way, the behavior of the soft body only slightly changes because of the weight of the attached sensors. Different resolutions of nodes instead would cause a different behavior of the bed cover.

Virtualizing Real-World Sleeping Postures. For evaluating the analyzed use case in the virtual area of the simulation framework, the ground truth of the use case has to be gathered and virtualized. We have decided on detecting 6 common sleeping postures, depicted in Fig. 2: lying on the back, on the stomach, on the left and on the right side with stretched legs and lying on the left and right side in fetus position. This ground truth is gathered by using a depth camera, in this case we used the Microsoft Kinect v2 and the free software KinectFusion. The outcome of this process, a raw high-resolution mesh of a test person is shown in Fig. 3. After this initial 3D capture of a test person, all unnecessarily captured objects in the surrounding have to be eliminated. This is done be registering the persons 3D shapes against each other and cutting around the object of interest. The result from this process is a high-resolution mesh of the test person. In order to load this high resolution mesh into the simulation framework, a lightweight low resolution mesh of the test person has to be calculated. We chose to use Cloudcompare[1] for registration and Meshlab[2] for lowering the resolution of the 3D mesh. Finally, the lower resolution mesh is introduced in the simulation framework, shown in the upper right of Fig. 3. In the bottom right, the mesh of the sleeping posture is covered by a soft body, the bed cover, which is equipped with the virtually modeled sensors. The sensors provide virtual sensor data of

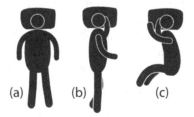

Fig. 2. Evaluated sleeping postures: (a) supine and prone; (b) straight left and right; (c) left and right fetal.

---

[1] http://www.danielgm.net/cc/.

[2] http://meshlab.sourceforge.net/.

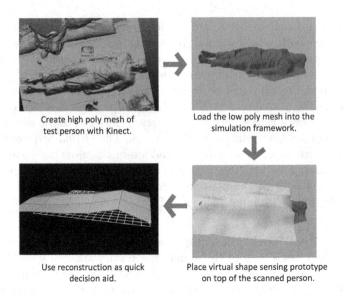

Create high poly mesh of
test person with Kinect.

Load the low poly mesh into the
simulation framework.

Use reconstruction as quick
decision aid.

Place virtual shape sensing prototype
on top of the scanned person.

Fig. 3. Virtual prototyping workflow: the high resolution mesh of a sleeping posture is created using a depth camera (upper left); this mesh is preprocessed creating a mesh of lower resolution, which is loaded into the simulation framework (upper right); the virtual bed cover equipped with sensors falls on the virtualization of the sleeping posture and delivers the according simulated sensor data (bottom right); the reconstruction of the surface calculated from the sensor data is displayed (bottom left).

the softbody covering the 3D mesh of a sleeping posture. This data is passed to the classification algorithm where the sensor data is classified using a Support Vector Machine (SVM). Using the reconstruction algorithm the reconstruction visualizes the sensed shape.

Preliminary Virtual Sensor Layout Evaluation. Initially, we have scanned two sets of sleeping postures from two test persons. We loaded the 3D shape data into the simulator using the process described in Fig. 3. The next step was to decide on the positions of the sensors on the virtual bed cover - the layout. Due to resource limitation, the maximum number of available sensors was 40. Hence this number was used as a starting point. However, in the validation section we describe evaluation results in more detail, where the number of sensors varies and further adapts to our use case. For now, this number of 40 sensors was used to compare three different virtual layouts: one where the sensors were equally dispersed on the bed cover, one where the sensors cover the person underneath and one where the upper part of the body and the sides of the bed cover are occupied by sensors (see Fig. 8). As a quick aid on deciding which layout was more suitable, we analyzed the reconstructed shape. The third layout showed the best recognizable shape for the human eye, hence we decided for the upper body covering layout. Even though, at this moment a human looking at the reconstructed image of the simulated sensor data was used to decide on the most suitable layout, further evaluations support this decision and are described in the validation section.

3.2   Real-World Prototype - Hardware and Software Implementation

As a result of the virtual prototype simulation, the layout with the best results in detecting the sleeping posture was identified. This input is used to build a real-world prototype consisting of 40 sensors, arranged in a 5×8 grid. As shown in Fig. 4, the extracted distances between the sensors from the simulated layout are 14 cm and 21 cm. These dimensions were chosen to cover a human torso using 40 sensors. The sensors are linked by three wires, two power-lines and a bus-line for communication. The wires are sewn to the bed cover. Since the bed cover is deformed by every underlying object, the power-lines as well as the bus-line have to withstand physical stress. In order to compensate for possible single point of failures in the links between the sensors, the links were built redundant on every side of the bed cover, as schematically depicted in Fig. 4. The reason to not link each sensor to its neighbors is to preserve the flexibility of the bed cover.

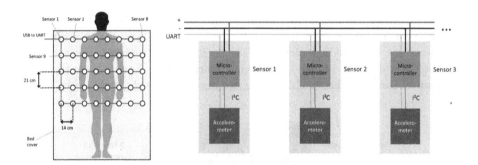

Fig. 4. Schematic of hardware implementation of posture recognizing bed cover. 40 sensors are aligned in a 5×8 grid, connected via bus and redundant power lines. Each accelerometer is connected to a microcontroller which communicates using the UART protocol. Dimensions and layout are outcome from the preliminary layout evaluation.

Each sensor uses an accelerometer to detect its current orientation. The accelerometer is connected to a 8 MHz microcontroller via I^2C. The microcontroller transfers the data using the UART protocol. This was chosen in order to minimize wire-usage, as only one is required for transferring data.

To transfer the data to a computer, we use a simple, yet fast protocol. Each sensor has a fixed, programmed address. The first sensor sends two start-bytes and the data of the accelerometer periodically in a fixed interval of time. The second sensor, as all other sensors, is counting the amount of data that was transferred over the bus. After the first sensor has sent all of its data, the byte-count of the sensor with address 2 will be $(sensoraddress - 1) *$ $NumberOfBytesPerSensorData$. Then the second sensor starts transmitting.

All other sensors follow the same procedure. The byte-count of all sensors is set to zero and the procedure is repeated if the start-byte, transmitted by sensor 1, is received. Using this method, all of the 40 sensors can be read at a rate of more than 20 Hz.

4   Validation of Simulation Framework

We used the simulation framework for designing a virtual prototype for the exemplary use case of sleeping posture detection. Following its virtual model, we have built a hardware prototype. In order to validate the correct results of the simulation framework, the results of the evaluation of the virtual prototype will be compared against the results of the hardware prototype. Hence, in the following sections we will describe the evaluation setup used to gather data which will be used for comparing the simulated and the real prototype. We will further analyze in more detail the influence of the number and placement of sensors for this use case.

4.1   Evaluation Setup

In order to compare the virtual and hardware prototype designed and built for sleeping posture detection, we asked 10 participants to carry out six different lying postures on a bed, depicted in Fig. 2. The set of participants was predominantly male, with 8 male and 2 female participants. Each person repeated a lying posture twice. For each posture, we executed the steps shown in Fig. 5.

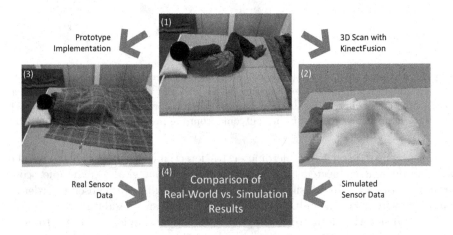

Fig. 5. Evaluation steps: (1) instruct test person to lie down; (2) the 3D shape of each posture is recorded and used in the simulation framework where the virtual prototype provides virtual sensor data; (3) the test person is covered with the real prototype gathering sensor data; (4) the real and the virtual sensor data are evaluated and compared.

First, we verbally instructed the participants to lie down in the different sleeping postures, not giving any further instructions. This assures highest resemblance to a natural setting. As a second step, we scanned the person in the sleeping posture using a depth camera. Next, we covered the person using the real-world prototype and gathered a sample of 500 sensor readings for each sensor. The whole process of scanning each of the six sleeping postures twice and gathering the sensor data using the real prototype lasted one hour per test person. The 3D shape of the test persons is used as input for the evaluation using the simulation framework. We have described the process of loading the 3D shape into the simulation framework, which is shown in Fig. 3. Once the shape is loaded, the virtual bed cover hung on top of the shape is released and falls on the test person. Using this setup, for each sleeping posture virtual sensor data is collected.

4.2 Matching the Two Worlds: Classification of Real and Simulated Data

As a result of the evaluation, we have collected sensor data corresponding to the sleeping postures from the real, as well as from the virtual prototype. To classify this data we used Weka's implementation of the Support Vector Machine (SVM) classificator LibSVM with adjusted parameters (SVMType: nu-SVC, normalize: true).

For each sleeping posture we have recorded a set of 500 data samples per sensor. We calculate the mean value per sensor per sleeping posture. Joining the data of all the sleeping postures, we recorded 12 sleeping postures, two times six postures, per test person. As a final result we have two data sets of the 10 test persons, one for the hardware prototype and one corresponding to the virtual prototype.

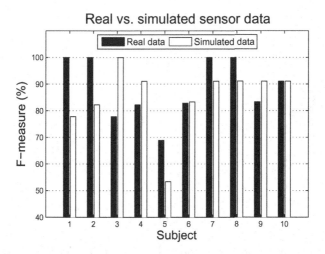

Fig. 6. Classification results of leave one subject out cross-validation of 10 test persons for real and simulated sensor data recorded by the hardware and virtual prototype for sleeping posture detection.

For each data set a leave one subject out cross-validation has been conducted, the results of which are shown in Fig. 6. The Figure shows the resulting F-measure for each test person by evaluating real and simulated data. We observe that the real and the simulated estimation are not far apart. The overall F-measure for the real data is 88.6% and 85.2% for the simulated data, resulting in a slightly more pessimistic F-measure of the simulated evaluation.

The small difference is caused by the slightly different execution of the simulated and the real evaluation. In the real evaluation we covered the test person with the bed cover. In the simulation the bed cover falls on the test person, causing the sensor node placement to be slightly different. Another influencing factor might be the parameters of the bed cover itself, which need to be set in the simulation framework. These slightly differ from the real bed cover.

4.3   Simulation: Determine the Optimal Number of Sensors

In order to find out which number of sensors would be optimal for our application, the simulation framework can be used to easily equip the virtual prototype with simulated sensors. Hence, the simulated bed cover has been equipped with different numbers of sensors, ranging from 4 to 676. We distributed the sensors homogeneously in order to cover the full surface of the bed cover. The simulated sensor data has been recorded by letting the bed cover with different numbers of sensors fall on the 3D shape of the 10 test persons. The same evaluation process, mean calculation of F-measure of the leave one subject out cross-validation using SVM, results in the mean F-measures depicted in Fig. 7.

We observe that in the interval of 4 to 40 sensors the highest F-measure gain is achieved, with its highest value at 40 sensors. Further increasing the sensor

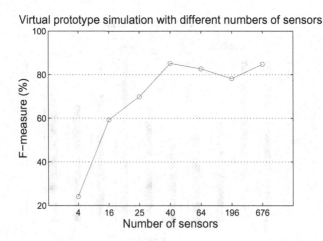

Fig. 7. Mean F-measure of total coverage layout with increasing number of sensors. Using the simulation framework up to 676 sensors are simulated on the prototype. The F-measure versus number of sensors trade-off is reached using 40 sensors.

count to 64, 196 and 676 does not significantly improve the results. Possible reasons might be that more sensors do not offer additional information that improves the feature selection. This is caused by the redundancy of information or because of over-fitting produced by sensors detecting small wrinkles in the bed cover. Hence, the simulation results confirm the trade-off between sensor count and improved F-measure as well as the decision of using the 5×8 grid of 40 sensors in the hardware implementation of the real prototype.

4.4   Simulation: Determine the Optimal Sensor Layout

By simulating different prototypes equipped with increasing number of sensors we have determined the optimal sensor count of 40 sensors. We used the general layout where all sensors are equally distributed on the bed cover prototype.

In this section we compare different possible layouts using the same sensor count of 40 sensors and evaluate these. Figure 8 shows the three evaluated sensor layouts. The left image of Fig. 8 shows the equally distributed sensors covering the entire prototype. In the middle we see the 5×8 sensor grid in a more constrained area, covering the entire body of the test person. The third image at the right shows a combination of the previous two layouts covering the upper body and the sides of the bed cover. Underneath the images, the mean F-measure per layout is shown, reaching the highest value of 85.2% with the upper body coverage layout.

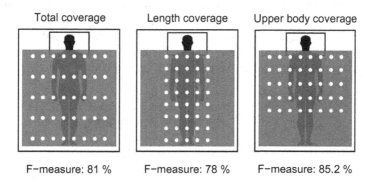

Fig. 8. Layout comparison of three different layout designs with 40 sensors evaluated using the simulation framework. The layout covering the upper body achieves the highest F-measure of 85.2%.

4.5   Optimized Amount of Sensors

In the previous sections we have derived the form of the implemented hardware prototype. We use a 5×8 grid of 40 sensors aligned on the bed cover in order to cover the upper body of the underlying person. In order to detect if some sensor data is still redundant we consider the upper body coverage layout with a growing subset of sensors. The different sensor subsets are depicted in Fig. 9.

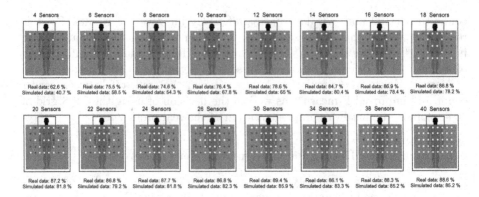

Fig. 9. F-measure of increasing sensor amount using upper body coverage layout with 40 sensors. For each sensor layout the mean F-measure is calculated by effectuating a leave one subject out cross-validation for simulated and real data.

Additionally to these sensor layout subsets, Fig. 10 shows the mean F-measure of the evaluation results. For each sensor layout subset a leave one subject out cross-validation has been effectuated for real and simulated data. Both are depicted on the same graph. We observe that in general better results are achieved evaluating the real prototype. The simulation data shows a clear gain in F-measure at the layout using a subset of 14 sensors. The real data similarly shows a high slope at the layout using 14 sensors. The mean F-measure values at this point are 84.7% for the real prototype and 80.4% for the virtual prototype. Looking up the corresponding 14 sensor layout subset from Fig. 9, we observe that it represents the minimum configuration covering the whole upper body of the test person as well as areas outside, where the bed cover lies on the bed.

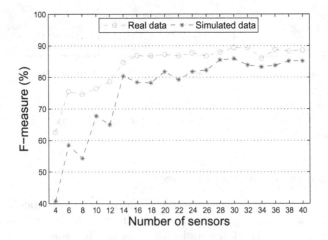

Fig. 10. F-measure of layout with increasing sensor number

We observe a second similar but smaller jump in F-measure by looking at the simulation data for the subset of 30 sensors. The real data mimics this small peak achieving the highest F-measure with 89.4%. Looking at the corresponding layout subset with 30 sensors, we observe that the improvement of results is generated by adding sensors to the first and last line, covering the shoulders and legs as well as the area lying flat on the bed.

5   Conclusion and Future Work

In this work we presented a simulation framework for shape-sensing fabrics. Even before the hardware is available developers can start designing and virtually evaluating their prototype for their individual shape-sensing application.

We proposed and demonstrated the workflow of a prototype designing process with shape-sensing fabrics by virtually planning a sleeping posture detecting bed cover. According to its virtual model we have equipped a bed cover with 40 acceleration sensors and evaluated it with 10 different users. Comparing the F-measures of 85% for the virtual and 89% for the real-world implementation we validate our proposed simulation framework for shape-sensing fabrics. We show further advantages of the simulation framework in terms of analyzing optimization potentials in order to find the suitable trade-off point for the required application. To our knowledge there is no simulation framework which includes soft-body simulation and attaches virtual sensors to them. Through our simulation framework we were able to provide a decision basis for developers when they need to decide on the trade-off between number of sensors, sensor placement and achieved accuracy.

In further development steps we would like to demonstrate the general approach of the simulation framework by extending the group of available sensors in the simulation framework and using this for planning further shape-sensing applications. Such shape-sensing applications in the field of ambient intelligence could be intelligent clothing which reports on its status (in drawer, washing bin, coat hanger, coat hook, if it is worn correctly, etc.) or an intelligent furniture cover which would detect on which furniture it is placed and provide the user with services such as posture detection, breathing frequency tracking, amount of movement.

References

1. Cheng, M.Y., Lin, C.L., Yang, Y.J.: Tactile and shear stress sensing array using capacitive mechanisms with floating electrodes. In: Proceedings of the IEEE International Conference on Micro Electro Mechanical Systems (MEMS), vol. 2, pp. 228–231 (2010). https://doi.org/10.1109/MEMSYS.2010.5442525
2. Dementyev, A., Kao, H.L.C., Paradiso, J.A.: SensorTape: modular and programmable 3D-aware dense sensor network on a tape. In: Proceedings of the 28th Annual ACM Symposium on User Interface Software & Technology, UIST 2015, pp. 649–658. ACM, New York (2015). https://doi.org/10.1145/2807442.2807507, http://doi.acm.org/10.1145/2807442.2807507

3. Du, J., Markopoulos, P., Wang, Q., Toeters, M., Gong, T.: ShapeTex: implementing shape-changing structures in fabric for wearable actuation. In: Proceedings of the Twelfth International Conference on Tangible, Embedded, and Embodied Interaction, TEI 2018, pp. 166–176. ACM, New York (2018). https://doi.org/10.1145/3173225.3173245, http://doi.acm.org/10.1145/3173225.3173245

4. Echeverria, G., Lassabe, N., Degroote, A., Lemaignan, S.: Modular open robots simulation engine: MORSE. In: 2011 IEEE International Conference on Robotics and Automation, pp. 46–51. IEEE, May 2011. https://doi.org/10.1109/ICRA.2011.5980252, http://ieeexplore.ieee.org/lpdocs/epic03/wrapper.htm?arnumber=5980252

5. Gong, N.W., et al.: PrintSense: a versatile sensing technique to support multimodal flexible surface interaction. In: Proceedings of the SIGCHI Conference on Human Factors in Computing Systems, CHI 2014, pp. 1407–1410. ACM, New York (2014). https://doi.org/10.1145/2556288.2557173, http://doi.acm.org/10.1145/2556288.2557173

6. Hermanis, A., Nesenbergs, K.: Grid shaped accelerometer network for surface shape recognition. In: Proceedings of the Biennial Baltic Electronics Conference, BEC, pp. 203–206 (2012). https://doi.org/10.1109/BEC.2012.6376852

7. Hermanis, A., Cacurs, R., Greitans, M.: Shape sensing based on acceleration and magnetic sensor system. In: 2015 IEEE International Symposium on Inertial Sensors and Systems (ISISS), pp. 2–3 (2015). http://ieeexplore.ieee.org/xpls/abs_all.jsp?arnumber=7102383

8. Hoshi, T., Shinoda, H.: 3D shape measuring sheet utilizing gravitational and geomagnetic fields. In: 2008 SICE Annual Conference, pp. 915–920. IEEE, August 2008. https://doi.org/10.1109/SICE.2008.4654785, http://ieeexplore.ieee.org/lpdocs/epic03/wrapper.htm?arnumber=4654785

9. Khalilbeigi, M., Lissermann, R., Mühlhäuser, M., Steimle, J.: Xpaaand. In: Proceedings of the 2011 Annual Conference on Human Factors in Computing Systems - CHI 2011, p. 2729. ACM Press, New York, May 2011. https://doi.org/10.1145/1978942.1979344, http://dl.acm.org/citation.cfm?id=1978942.1979344

10. Lahey, B., Girouard, A., Burleson, W., Vertegaal, R.: PaperPhone: understanding the use of bend gestures in mobile devices with flexible electronic paper displays. In: Proceedings of the SIGCHI Conference on Human Factors in Computing Systems, CHI 2011, pp. 1303–1312. ACM, New York (2011). https://doi.org/10.1145/1978942.1979136, http://doi.acm.org/10.1145/1978942.1979136

11. Lorussi, F., Rocchia, W., Scilingo, E.P., Tognetti, A., Rossi, D.D.: Wearable, redundant fabric-based sensor arrays for reconstruction of body segment posture. IEEE Sens. J. 4(6), 807–818 (2004). https://doi.org/10.1109/JSEN.2004.837498

12. Ramakers, R., Schöning, J., Luyten, K.: Paddle. In: Proceedings of the 32nd Annual ACM Conference on Human Factors in Computing Systems - CHI 2014, pp. 2569–2578. ACM Press, New York, April 2014. https://doi.org/10.1145/2556288.2557340, http://dl.acm.org/citation.cfm?id=2556288.2557340

13. Rendl, C., et al.: FlexSense: a transparent self-sensing deformable surface. In: Proceedings of the 27th Annual ACM Symposium on User Interface Software and Technology, UIST 2014, pp. 129–138. ACM, New York (2014). https://doi.org/10.1145/2642918.2647405, http://doi.acm.org/10.1145/2642918.2647405

14. Rus, S., Grosse-Puppendahl, T., Kuijper, A.: Recognition of bed postures using mutual capacitance sensing. In: Aarts, E. (ed.) AmI 2014. LNCS, vol. 8850, pp. 51–66. Springer, Cham (2014). https://doi.org/10.1007/978-3-319-14112-1_5

15. Saguin-Sprynski, N., Jouanet, L., Lacolle, B., Biard, L.: Surfaces reconstruction via inertial sensors for monitoring, July 2014. https://hal.inria.fr/hal-01020418/

16. Schwesig, C., Poupyrev, I., Mori, E.: Gummi. In: Proceedings of the 2004 Conference on Human Factors in Computing Systems - CHI 2004, pp. 263–270. ACM Press, New York, April 2004. https://doi.org/10.1145/985692.985726, http://dl. acm.org/citation.cfm?id=985692.985726
17. Staranowicz, A., Mariottini, G.L.: A survey and comparison of commercial and open-source robotic simulator software. In: Proceedings of the 4th International Conference on PErvasive Technologies Related to Assistive Environments - PETRA 2011, p. 1. ACM Press, New York, May 2011. https://doi.org/10.1145/ 2141622.2141689, http://dl.acm.org/citation.cfm?id=2141622.2141689
18. Steimle, J., Jordt, A., Maes, P.: Flexpad: highly flexible bending interactions for projected handheld displays. In: Proceedings of the SIGCHI Conference on Human Factors in Computing Systems - CHI 2013, pp. 237–246 (2013). https://doi.org/ 10.1145/2470654.2470688, http://dl.acm.org/citation.cfm?doid=2470654.2470688
19. Tan, D., Kumorek, M., Garcia, A.A., Mooney, A., Bekoe, D.: Projectagami. In: Proceedings of the 33rd Annual ACM Conference Extended Abstracts on Human Factors in Computing Systems - CHI EA 2015, pp. 1555–1560. ACM Press, New York, April 2015. https://doi.org/10.1145/2702613.2732801, http://dl.acm. org/citation.cfm?id=2702613.2732801
20. Žlajpah, L.: Simulation in robotics. Math. Comput. Simul. **79**(4), 879–897 (2008). https://doi.org/10.1016/j.matcom.2008.02.017, http://www.sciencedirect. com/science/article/pii/S0378475408001183
21. Wang, Q.: Designing posture monitoring garments to support rehabilitation. In: Proceedings of the TEI 2016: Tenth International Conference on Tangible, Embedded, and Embodied Interaction, TEI 2016, pp. 709–712. ACM, New York (2016). https://doi.org/10.1145/2839462.2854106, http://doi.acm.org/10.1145/ 2839462.2854106
22. Wang, Q., Toeters, M., Chen, W., Timmermans, A., Markopoulos, P.: Zishi: a smart garment for posture monitoring. In: Proceedings of the 2016 CHI Conference Extended Abstracts on Human Factors in Computing Systems, CHI EA 2016, pp. 3792–3795. ACM, New York (2016). https://doi.org/10.1145/2851581.2890262, http://doi.acm.org/10.1145/2851581.2890262

Analysing Physiology of Interpersonal Conflicts Using a Wrist Device

Junoš Lukan[1]([✉])(iD), Martin Gjoreski[1], Heidi Mauersberger[2],
Annekatrin Hoppe[2], Ursula Hess[2], and Mitja Luštrek[1]

[1] Jožef Stefan Institute, Jamova cesta 39, Ljubljana, Slovenia
{junos.lukan,martin.gjoreski,mitja.lustrek}@ijs.si
[2] Department of Psychology, Humbold-Universität zu Berlin,
Unter den Linden 6, Berlin, Germany
{heidi.mauersberger,annekatrin.hoppe,ursula.hess}@hu-berlin.de

Abstract. We present a study in which 59 participants logged their interpersonal conflicts while wearing an Empatica E4 wristband. They marked the beginnings and endings of the conflicts, as well as their intensity. In this paper, the dataset is described and a preliminary analysis is performed. We describe data segmentation and feature calculation process. Next, the interrelationships between the features and labels are explored. A logistic regression model for conflict recognition was built and significant features were selected. Finally, we constructed a machine learning model and proposed how to improve it.

Keywords: Interpersonal conflicts · Context · Real life
Wrist device · Machine learning

1 Introduction

It is well known that understanding the user's context is essential for ambient intelligence. Most research is dealing with physical context, while psychological context remains a challenge. In this work we tackle perceived interpersonal conflicts in the workplace, an important source of stress [13] whose management could contribute to workers' satisfaction and productivity.

The psychophysiology of interpersonal conflicts has already been studied [e.g. 5,9,14]. The physiological data in these studies, however, is limited to short recordings and gathered in a laboratory setting. There have also not been, to our knowledge, any attempts to develop machine learning models of physiological responses during interpersonal conflicts.

In this study, participants tracked their interpersonal interactions with a focus on conflicts. They were asked to log their conflicts in the workplace for several

Data collection for this study was supported by a grant to Heidi Mauersberger from the structured graduate program "Self-Regulation Dynamics Across Adulthood and Old Age: Potentials and Limits". Junoš Lukan's expenses were covered by Slovenian Research Agency (ARRS, project ref. N2-0081).

A. Kameas and K. Stathis (Eds.): AmI 2018, LNCS 11249, pp. 162–167, 2018.
https://doi.org/10.1007/978-3-030-03062-9_13

days and fill out a questionnaire after each such interaction. At the same time, they were wearing Empatica E4 wristbands to track their physiological data.

For the first time, to our knowledge, a large dataset of physiological data was thus collected in a field study and labelled with times and durations of interpersonal interactions. The dataset could turn out to be a valuable resource for building physiology-based models of interpersonal conflicts.

2   Data Collection and Analysis

Physiological Data. A total of 59 participants, 35 women and 24 men, with a mean age of 32.5 years ($SD = 11$ years) participated in this study. The participants, full-time employees, wore an Empatica E4 wristband throughout their work day for several days, resulting in 43.7 h of data per participant on average.

The following physiological signals were collected: (a) three-axis acceleration, (b) blood volume pulse (BVP) from a photoplethysmograph, (c) electrodermal activity (EDA), (d) heart rate and interbeat intervals as calculated from BVP on device, and (e) skin temperature.

Description of Conflicts. The participants were asked to keep track of their interpersonal interactions in the workplace, paying particular attention to disagreements. They were instructed to note the time and duration as soon as possible and no more than 15 min after the conflict took place.

The participants reported 379 conflicts. They were further classified into task (304) or relationship conflicts (58) or both (17 conflicts). This referred to answers to two questions:

- Did you experience disagreements with your interaction partner regarding content or the implementation of the work being done?
- Did you experience personal attacks during the interaction?

The participants also answered other questions pertaining to the interaction, such as assessing its intensity and positive and negative affect during the interaction.

In a couple of days of data collection, each participant logged 6.7 conflicts on average (see Fig. 1). The mean duration of all conflicts was 10.9 min, however, almost half of them were shorter than 5 min. The distribution of the conflicts' durations is shown in Fig. 2.

Data Segmentation. To analyse the physiological data, we divided it in shorter segments on which features were calculated. We defined three periods related to each conflict: pre-conflict period, which acts as a baseline, a gap, which accounts for transitory changes before the interaction, and the conflict itself. The length of the pre-conflict period was chosen as 25 min and the length of the gap was 5 min.

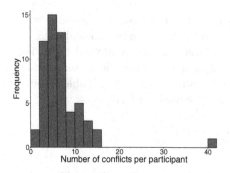

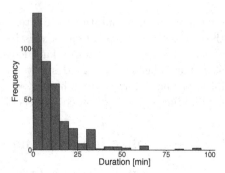

Fig. 1. The distribution of participants by the number of conflicts each of them logged. A couple of participants logged a high number of (short) conflicts.

Fig. 2. The distribution of conflicts by their reported durations. Almost half of the conflicts fall within the first bin of width 5 min.

The pre-conflict and conflict periods were split into two-minute segments, so that they could be compared without the effect of period duration. This length was chosen, because that is the lower bound for the frequency-domain methods used to calculate heart rate variability (HRV, see [7]).

Feature Calculation. Features that can be calculated from Empatica signals are multiple and varied (for a good overview of commonly used ones see Alberdi et al. [1], and for heart rate variability, specifically, see Malik et al. [7]). Table 1 lists the features used in this work.

Table 1. Features calculated from each signal.

Signal	Features
Skin temperature	mean, median, standard deviation
Heart rate	mean, median, standard deviation
Interbeat intervals	mean, median, SDNN, SDSD, RMSSD, pNN20, pNN50, $\sqrt{SDNN}$, $\sqrt{\lvert 2SDSD^2 - 0.5SDNN^2 \rvert}$, VLF, LF, HF, LF normalised, HR normalised, LF/HF
Electrodermal activity	mean, median, standard deviation, first and third quartile, interquartile range, mean derivative, number of SCRs, rate of SCRs, sum of amplitudes of SCRs, mean amplitude of SCRs, mean phasic component, mean tonic comp., mean derivative of tonic comp., integral of tonic comp. in different regions
Physical activity	mean, standard deviation, mode

For definitions of commonly used abbreviations in heart rate variability, see Malik et al. [7].

The electrodermal activity signal was first filtered using a fourth-order low-pass filter with a cut-off frequency of 1 Hz. Next, using `peakutils` Python library [8], the signal was separated into a tonic and phasic component, where the former is a slowly changing baseline and the latter characterises fast changing skin conductance responses (SCRs).

A custom algorithm was used to identify peaks in blood volume pulse and calculate interbeat intervals [12]. These were transformed using a Lomb-Scargle periodogram [6,11] from `SciPy` [4] and typical heart rate variability features [7] were calculated.

To determine the physical activity from the acceleration data, another custom algorithm was used [3], which classifies activities into either lying, sitting, walking or standing, and running or cycling. Besides using the mode of these categories as a feature (see Table 1), they were also assigned activity intensity 1, 2, 4, and 5, respectively, so that the mean and standard deviation could be calculated.

Finally, the features were normalized. This was done within person, i.e. for each person, their mean was subtracted and the result divided by the standard deviation.

3 Results

After segmentation of the data and calculation of features, performed as described in Sect. 2, relationships between features and labels were explored. In Fig. 3, a correlation matrix of representative features is shown. Some correlations follow from the interrelatedness of definitions of features, such as the one between the rate of skin conductance responses (SCRratePeaks) and the sum of their amplitudes (SCRpeaksAmpSum) and some of these were intentionally excluded from the matrix in Fig. 3. Others illustrate that different features contain different information: for example, there is no correlation between the standard deviation of heart rate (HRsd) and another measure of heart rate variability, normalized power in the lower part of the spectrum (LFnorm). There are also some weak correlations between unrelated physiological parameters, such as skin temperature and galvanic skin response, specifically their standard deviations.

There are weak correlations between standardized features and conflict intensity and duration. For example, heart rate variability is somewhat lower in longer and more intensive (relationship) conflicts, which is in line with results from some existing literature (see, for example, Alberdi et al. [1]). To capture these relationships, a logistic regression model was fitted to classify conflicts and pre-conflict periods. Only conflicts longer than 2 min were analysed.

A hierarchical logistic regression model was built step-wise. Predictors from each physiological domain were included using the "forward" method, i.e., only the predictors which significantly decreased the Akaike information criterion (AIC) were retained in the model. This procedure yielded the following features: median skin temperature; normalized power in high-frequency spectrum of heart rate variability; interquartile range of electrodermal activity, and mean of skin conductance responses. No feature describing physical activity decreased AIC significantly.

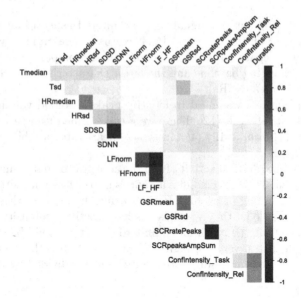

Fig. 3. Correlation matrix between selected standardized features and intensity of two types of conflicts and their durations.

Finally, a model containing the selected features was built, in which all predictors were statistically significant at $p < 0.1$ level. The interquartile range of electrodermal activity had the highest standardized coefficient $\beta = 0.096$ with $z = 2.94$ and $p = 0.003$.

An attempt to construct a machine learning predictive model was also made. Implementation of logistic regression in `scikit-learn` [10] was used. Specifically, a leave-one-subject-out (LOSO) cross-validation procedure was used [see e.g. 2], where one subject was taken as a test set, while all the others were put in the training set. The average accuracy obtained in this way was 65.8% when distinguishing the pre-conflict period from the labelled conflicts themselves. Because the pre-conflict periods were longer than the average conflict, they made up the majority of instances, which was 63.0%.

4   Conclusion and Outlook

In this paper, we presented a large real-life physiological dataset labelled with interpersonal conflicts. To our knowledge, this is the first example of such data being tackled by ambient-intelligence methods. Detecting conflicts in physiological data appears to be challenging and requires further work.

Several improvements to the machine learning model have already been tested. The dataset was limited to task conflicts only or conflicts with higher intensity were considered. Another way of reducing the dataset is to select only some participants. A model with subjects with more than 60 min of conflicts was tested. Different lengths of pre-conflict periods were tried out. Various types of machine learning models were also tested for predictive power, such as random forest, support vector machines etc.

None of these modifications improved the results significantly. A likely reason are the labels of the conflicts themselves. A possible workaround might be to search for the beginning of conflicts by considering significant changes of features.

In conclusion, an interesting dataset was collected with more possible pathways of analysis. The dataset is available on request.

References

1. Alberdi, A., Aztiria, A., Basarab, A.: Towards an automatic early stress recognition system for office environments based on multimodal measurements: a review. J. Biomed. Inform. **59**, 49–75 (2016). https://doi.org/10.1016/j.jbi.2015.11.007
2. Arlot, S., Celisse, A.: A survey of cross-validation procedures for model selection. Stat. Surv. **4**, 40–79 (2010). https://doi.org/10.1214/09-SS054
3. Gjoreski, M., Gjoreski, H., Luštrek, M., Gams, M.: How accurately can your wrist device recognize daily activities and detect falls? Sensors **16**(6) (2016). https://doi.org/10.3390/s16060800
4. Jones, E., Oliphant, T., Peterson, P., et al.: SciPy: open source scientific tools for Python (2001–2018). http://www.scipy.org/
5. Lavoie, K.L., Miller, S.B., Conway, M., Fleet, R.P.: Anger, negative emotions, and cardiovascular reactivity during interpersonal conflict in women. J. Psychosom. Res. **51**(3), 503–512 (2001). https://doi.org/10.1016/S0022-3999(01)00217-3
6. Lomb, N.R.: Least-squares frequency analysis of unequally spaced data. Astrophys. Space Sci. **39**, 447–462 (1976). https://doi.org/10.1007/BF00648343
7. Malik, M., et al.: Heart rate variability. Eur. Hear. J. **17**(3), 354–381 (1996)
8. Negri, L.H., Vestri, C.: lucashn/peakutils: v1.1.0, September 2017. https://doi.org/10.5281/zenodo.887917
9. Neumann, S.A., et al.: Cardiovascular and psychological reactivity and recovery from harassment in a biracial sample of high and low hostile men and women. Int. J. Behav. Med. **18**(1), 52–64 (2011). https://doi.org/10.1007/s12529-010-9110-0
10. Pedregosa, F., et al.: Scikit-learn: machine learning in Python. J. Mach. Learn. Res. **12**, 2825–2830 (2011)
11. Scargle, J.D.: Studies in astronomical time series analysis. II - Statistical aspects of spectral analysis of unevenly spaced data. Astrophys. J. **263**, 835–853 (1982). https://doi.org/10.1086/160554
12. Slapničar, G., Luštrek, M., Marinko, M.: Continuous blood pressure estimation from PPG signal. Informatica **42**(1), 33–42 (2018). http://www.informatica.si/index.php/informatica/article/view/2229
13. Stephenson, E., King, D., DeLongis, A.: Coping process. In: Fink, G. (ed.) Stress: Concepts, Cognition, Emotion, and Behavior, Chap. 44, pp. 359–364. Academic Press, San Diego (2016). https://doi.org/10.1016/B978-0-12-800951-2.00045-5
14. Tada, M., et al.: Fear conditioning induced by interpersonal conflicts in healthy individuals. PLoS One **10**(5), 1–14 (2015). https://doi.org/10.1371/journal.pone.0125729

Ambient Intelligence in Education

Raising Awareness for Water Polution Based on Game Activities Using Internet of Things

Chrysanthi Tziortzioti[1,2], Giuseppe Andreetti[3], Lucia Rodinò[3], Irene Mavrommati[1,2], Andrea Vitaletti[3], and Ioannis Chatzigiannakis[2,3(✉)]

[1] Hellenic Open University, Patras, Greece
tziortzio@gmail.com, mavrommati@eap.gr
[2] Computer Technology Institute and Press, Patras, Greece
[3] Sapienza University of Rome, Rome, Italy
andreetti.1339193@studenti.uniroma1.it, luciatomb@gmail.com,
{vitaletti,ichatz}@diag.uniroma1.it

Abstract. Awareness among young people regarding the environment and its resources and comprehension of the various factors that interplay, is key to changing human behaviour towards achieving a sustainable planet. In this paper IoT equipment, utilizing sensors for measuring various parameters of water quality, is used in an educational context targeting at a deeper understanding of the use of natural resources towards the adoption of environmentally friendly behaviours. We here note that the use of water sensors in STEM gameful learning is an area which has not received a lot of attention in the previous years. The IoT water sensing and related scenaria and practices, addressing children via discovery, gamification, and educational activities, are discussed in detail.

1 Introduction

Raising awareness among young people regarding the environmental resources and supporting a better understanding of the factors at play, is key to changing their behaviour towards achieving a sustainable planet. Moreover, reinforcing the educational community on educating new generations has a multiplier effect for understanding the resources and for reducing our environmental footprint; it is the sustainable behaviour at school or social gaming activities that can impact the home behaviour, as children communicate their newly acquired knowledge to parents.

The work presented here focuses on raising awareness for water pollution since most of the planet is covered in water: about 79% of the surface of the Earth is covered by water. Water has multiple importance as being a source of life as it provides the ability to produce food, minerals and energy, is a key factor for the renewal of the oxygen we breathe, and the means of transporting goods (trade, energy transfer/information). However, in order to achieve a better understanding of the potential of water, its uses, and at the same time to effectively protect it, a detailed study is required [1].

© Springer Nature Switzerland AG 2018
A. Kameas and K. Stathis (Eds.): AmI 2018, LNCS 11249, pp. 171–187, 2018.
https://doi.org/10.1007/978-3-030-03062-9_14

The approach proposed is to develop a set of educational scenario that use a series of sensors to measure physical and chemical water parameters. As already observed in Sect. 2, bringing the IoT into large aquatic environments is still very difficult, for this reason, the focus assumed here is on surface sampling activities that are more affordable in the context of STEM educational activities. This can serve as the first step towards better understanding aquatic resources.

Via the pedagogical steps of awareness, observation, experimentation and action, children using portable and inexpensive equipment will be able to carry out relevant measurements and submit them to a database. The mathematical and scientific thinking developed in the above process can be exploited in various ways by the online application, or the tutor, in the context of teaching mathematical and scientific skills, not only in the science courses but also in cross-thematic approaches that combining such observations and analyzes the economic, social and other aspects of our effort for clean water, and, in subsequent steps, clean seas.

With a systematic, stepwise research approach as a goal, this paper describes the first steps towards this broader direction. With the initial aim to enable children to get involved in the scientific process, of measuring and understanding aquatic parameters, a set of educational scenaria is described; based on these a game has been devised and implemented, deploying a basic IoT sensor-set for measuring water parameters, with the initial goal to measure sweet water resources in one's hometown.

2   Related Work

Overall, the play was the most typical feature of childhood and was characterized by great autonomy [2]. Several serious games seeking to cultivate environmental awareness, e.g., "Greenpeace" from [28] or the "2020 Energy Game" [3] from the EnergyBits project. However, these are generic Web-based "games", designed and implemented on top of mostly statically defined scenarios, i.e., they do not take into account real data originating from energy meters; also, they do not utilise unique aspects of modern smartphones like location awareness - information presented is the same no matter where the users are located or do not take into account proximity settings. [25] is an example of a browser-based serious game by Siemens, allowing players to test different energy-efficient scenarios in a city-wide planning game. While such designs provide useful insight, they are not paired with real-world data; we will additionally utilise the real-world data produced by the buildings participating in the project. Another example of an energy-focused game is [15], which is being deployed in cooperation with PG&E, a major US utility company, also discussed in [26].

Regarding the work presented here, [12] discusses pedagogical aspects of integrating real-life data into playful scenarios and serious games; [14,21] are additional examples of such dimensions, that we intend to use while designing and implementing games. [11] discusses the implementation and evaluation of a platform for a multiplayer pervasive game in public open spaces, that we intend to utilise to support our envisioned activities. An example of such activities is discussed in [10], where a university corridor was metamorphosed into an interactive public space. Together with omnipresent devices such as smartphones, an engaging and meaningful experience is brought to life.

Regarding measuring environmental conditions via an IoT network, most of the works focus on terrestrial applications. Even when offshore infrastructures or vessels are considered, IoT devices are mostly deployed in "dry" surfaces and only some specific transducers are actually deployed into the water. The underwater environment is hostile, and consequently, underwater IoT devices are very expensive. If you only consider a reliable water-proof housing for shallow water, it costs at least 2 or 3 order of magnitude more than terrestrial solutions and much more if you consider deep water scenarios. Underwater operations are complex and challenging. As an example, the fast growth of algae or microorganisms can suddenly affect the quality of sensors readings that have to be often cleaned. Underwater communications are still extremely difficult and energy-hungry; RF propagates only a few centimetres and only acoustic or optical communications can be used for longer distances. Due to these reasons, the availability of underwater IoT data is still very limited. One of the few attempts to provide a federation of underwater testbeds for the Internet of Underwater Things is the EU project SUNRISE [22]. While SUNRISE clearly showed us the potential of exploring underwater data, it was not originally conceived for STEM educational activities, and both the complexity of the tools and the costs of the equipment are not yet suitable to be operated by students. Despite these difficulties, there are already some efforts for more affordable tools for underwater investigations [6,20] and is, however, possible to design significant STEM activities (see Sect. 4) that focus on shallow water and/or surface sampling that significantly lower the above-discussed difficulties. Indeed, the focus on the shallow water and/or the sea surface allow us to (a) engage students in participatory sampling (i.e. they are directly involved in the sampling procedure at sea), (b) deploy relatively simple networking infrastructures capable to deliver the data acquired by possible underwater traducers employing standard wireless technologies (e.g. Lora, GPRS or even WiFi).

In the case reported in this paper, a stepwise approach is assumed, by first attempting to measure qualities of sweet water reserves and water resources that are used every day, such as drinking water.

3   IoT and Real-World Data in STEM

The aim of this research is to put users in the loop of monitoring as a first step towards raising awareness, but also for gaining knowledge and skills on how to conduct an experiment, and gather information and data with appropriate methods. The concept of users in the loop of monitoring is central in the area of participatory sensing [8] in which personal mobile phones of users are used to collect relevant data for a number of applications such as urban planning, public health, cultural identity and creative expression, and natural resource management. This approach has been employed by the Cornell Laboratory of Ornithology [7] in a science education project on bird biology, while in [19] the authors describe trials for air quality, water quality and plant disease monitoring. Similarly to the context, of this paper [30] presents a solution combining a deployed and participatory sensing system for environmental monitoring.

In [18] the authors discuss the value of participating to project like these for students, concluding that "Students are gaining deep domain-specific knowledge through their citizen science campaign, as well as broad general STEM knowledge through data-collection best practices, data analysis, scientific methods, and other areas specific to their project".

The GAIA platform [4,5,9] is among few IoT systems that focus on the educational community. The goal of GAIA is to include the users in the loop of monitoring the energy consumption in the buildings they use daily, thus making the first steps towards raising awareness, connecting the educational activities carried out at schools with their activities at home. A real-world IoT deployment is spread in 3 countries, monitoring in real-time 18 school buildings in terms of electricity consumption and indoor and outdoor environmental conditions. GAIA's IoT devices are either open-design IoT nodes (based on the Arduino popular electronics prototyping platform, see [24]) or off-the-shelf products acquired from IoT device manufacturers. The data collected is used as part of a series of education scenarios whose goal is to educate, influence and attempt to transform the energy consumption behaviour of elementary school students. Feedback mechanisms notify the students on current energy consumption at school and in this way assist towards raising awareness regarding the environmental effects of energy spending and promote energy literacy by educating the users. Since the GAIA IoT deployment is multi-site it can motivate identification of energy consumption patterns in different geographic locations, and can also serve as the basis for competitions, promoting energy efficiency awareness and sustainability.

The integrated sources of input are utilized to continuously provide direct feedback, custom-tailored to each particular learner/audience. Direct feedback is provided via real-time displays (RTDs) installed at central locations in the buildings, published on school websites, posted on social media, and also displayed on the users' smartphones and tablets. Direct feedback mechanisms are developed to address the immateriality of energy [23] and make it a visible entity by connecting it to the daily activities of students. Visual analytics are combined with recent advances in IoT sensing and pervasive computing technologies to provide an interactive environment that *stimulates behavioural change on a frequent basis.*

The energy consumption topic is included in the pedagogical activities of the schools incorporating educational aspects to promote energy literacy, convey information regarding historical data and comparative information with other buildings of similar characteristics. A series of social-networking applications are provided to set community-based incentives for pro-environmental behavioural change and promote collective consuming of resources. These applications utilize the already established relationship between users of the same school/department to provide *community-based initiatives* to reduce their overall environmental footprint and increase environment-friendly activities. A series of *game-based competitions* further engage the students in learning how to improve the energy efficiency, and to encourage them to actually follow the learned practices. Research suggests that competitions can be effective in promoting environmentally responsible behaviour [17]. Historical data collected from the IoT infrastructure allows students to compete with each other on periodic intervals (e.g., per week/month/season) to further motivate eco-friendly behaviours. A combination of *direct competition* among other groups of similar size, climate zone, socio-economic characteristics and past years against each group's own performance is followed. These competitions *encourage spreading the word to larger groups*, allowing related persons, such as parents, friends, or neighbours, to participate and also *appeal to positive emotions*, such as hope and enjoyment, as ways to changing individuals' behaviours.

4   A Game for Raising Awareness for Water Pollution

A set of new educational activities are proposed targeting preliminary/secondary/high schools and addressing the pedagogical needs of existing curricula in aspects related to the environmental impact of water usage and environment-friendly behaviours. The educational scenarios are based on the principle that authentic problems cannot be faced using discrete disciplines that are taught in schools [13]. Quite often students cannot be involved in the learning process because they cannot be engaged in the context in which the problems are embedded [16, 29].

The goal of working on water pollution activities using the Internet of Things is to lead to a STEM approach, so the learning becomes connected, focused, meaningful, and relevant to students. As Sanders argues "the focuses of STEM education should apply knowledge of mathematics, science and engineering, design and conduct experiments, analyze and interpret data, and communicate and corporate with multidisciplinary teams" [27].

The educational activities are complemented by game-based methods that offer rich opportunities for a student to learn through engagement with the water quality measurement activities. A meaningful experience is a key to the success of the educational game. Players should voluntarily and actively engage with the game. This is a problem with a lot of serious games that are too much focused on teaching specific content. Especially with students from 13–18 years old, who often dismiss anything that feels like educational content. Games are great at providing systems to experiment with, spaces to explore and meanings to be deducted by the players themselves. Meaning that is inherent in the world, the game mechanics, the systems and the narrative of the game. If the educational content is too much focused on forcing specific text-book style knowledge on the players, they will be put off. The work presented here tries to carefully balance the educational content and the freedom of the player to ensure students will become aware of their energy consumption in an unobtrusive manner.

In the educational scenarios proposed, a series of sensors are used to measure physical and chemical water parameters. Using sensors within a water environment for various aspects of water quality is complex and quite challenging. If one only considers a reliable water-proof housing for shallow water, it costs at least 2 or 3 order of magnitude more than terrestrial solutions and much more if the device needs to be submerged into water, and in particular sea water. Underwater communications are still extremely difficult and energy-hungry; RF propagates only a few centimetres and only acoustic or optical communications can be used for longer distances. The energy cost of underwater communications strongly limits the device lifetime, that is usually in the order of few months at best and requires frequent replacements of the batteries, an annoying, time-consuming and difficult task. These are just a couple of examples that explain the very limited availability of underwater IoT. For this reason, the approach presented here focuses on surface sampling activities that are more affordable in the context of STEM educational activities.

The steps of the pedagogical activities followed are awareness, observation, experimentation and action. School students use portable equipment to carry out relevant measurements that are submitted automatically to a central database. Depending on the teaching needs and priorities, students can collect and analyze the following:

- current values and any fluctuations of them during the observation period of the activity,
- changing values for longer periods of time, e.g. making comparisons between different times of the day, between months, seasons, or years,
- the variance of the phenomena between different areas.

Scientific skills can be developed out of the combination of such observations and utilisation of the system from tutors of various subjects.

4.1   Educational Scenarios and Goals

Students use sensors to monitor physicochemical parameters in their hydrographic network area such as temperature, turbidity, pH, dissolved oxygen (DO) and conductivity. With the accurate and continuous recording of the parameters, they can describe the current physical, chemical and biological state of the water body. The systematic concentration of values creates a database for water quality conditions which can be used to compare data in the future.

The aim is to design and implement systematic research to identify any water quality problems in the water body. Initially, the students use a map of the area to select the position for sampling measurements. Using appropriate sensors, they record the parameter values, plot graphs with spatial and chronological variations, analyze the data, and end up with conclusions on the quality of water. It is important to compare and contrast the effects of water quality parameters, especially the relationship between temperature–DO, turbidity–DO, and pH–turbidity.

Scenario 1: Observation of Water Temperature as one of the most easily measured parameters of water quality and one of the most important factors in the workings of an aquatic ecosystem. Students are asked to make assumptions about the factors on which water temperature depends, such as depth, the hour of day that the measure has been taken, the season of year, mixing of water due to wind and rain, degree of stratification of the water system, the temperature of water flowing from tributaries, and human actions such as drainage of warm water used for cooling water in industrial plants (thermal pollution).

Students with the help of the instructor, conclude that water temperature affects other water quality parameters such as DO and pH. For example, students count a difference at DO levels as they take measurements early in the morning when the water is cool and then late in the afternoon when the water temperature has increased. Also, there may be a difference in DO levels at different depths of the water if there is a significant change in temperature with depth. The same conclusion will be reached if they measure DO levels at different times of the year. In spring and summer, the upper layer of water gets a higher temperature and mixing between this surface water and the cooler water below. In autumn the air temperature decreases, the surface water becomes more and colder and its density increases. As the surface water is sinking, mixing of the water column is caused. During winter, temperatures remain fairly constant from upper to lower levels (in shallow systems). Considering the above, we expect the students to conclude that water at higher temperatures dissolve lower DO levels than water at a lower temperature.

Scenario 2: Observation of Water Acidity-Alkalinity by measuring PH as a measure of the balance of acid and alkaline compounds dissolved in water. Generally, natural water has pH between 5 and 9 and most aquatic organisms survive in this range, so pH is a key indicator of water quality. Water with low pH increases the solubility of nutrients such as phosphates and nitrates.

Scenario 3: Observation of Water Turbidity as another physical parameter that measures the number of suspended particles in the water at a specific time and is an indicator of water quality. It depends on suspended solids, such as phytoplankton, mud, sewage, organic matter and industrial waste. High levels of turbidity occur due to natural causes (soil erosion, sediment transfer by rainwater, seasonal conditions like spring melt) and can be caused by human activities (sewage, land use, pollution).

Students are expected to combine high turbidity values with low DO levels in water and raised temperature. Students are also expected to observe that pH values are affected by turbidity (e.g., disorganized vegetation produces organic acids that lower the pH), bacterial activity, photosynthesis rate, and chemical components that end up in the aquatic system.

Students are expected to conclude that the turbidity value is not generally constant along the water column but depends on the depth, seasonality, water mix caused by the wind, storms and tides, the flow of rivers and pollution from human activities.

Scenario 4: Observation of Dissolved Oxygen as an indication of the presence of organisms, particularly microbes, within the water. These organisms with oxidative reactions metabolize organic substances by consuming for this process the oxygen dissolved in the water. Because oxygen has relatively little water solubility, it is quickly consumed when there is a high organic load resulting in anaerobic conditions. Concentration less than 7 mg/lt means oxygen deficiency resulting in the non-survival of fish and other aerobic organisms. Physiological values of DO range above 7 mg/lt.

The systemic nature of the measurements, as seen above, can be difficult to handle directly. In order to start addressing the problem of understanding water resources aided by IoT sensors, the proposal described in this paper is to start with a small subset of water sensing, and take this into the context of a gaming activity to familiarise oneself with sensors, taking measurements, and the quality of more accessible water, such as springs and drinking water sources.

4.2   Game Design

Sensor data are used in the game, as well as location and time data, for following the condition of water sources. The players have to adopt, follow, record and document the data from different water sources. They have to compare between different water sources, but also between the same water source at different times of the day or of the year. They have to make a hypothesis to explain what they observe and document it, and then support their hypothesis by providing facts and related measurements.

For example, if the PH is high, will the organisms live? Which will live and which will die? Until what value will the system maintain its sustainability? One should also try to give a possible explanation why the change occurs, should be able to discuss with others the various possible reasons, and if possible cross checks other parameters to support the given explanation. For example, PH increase may mean someone has thrown something in the water and has contaminated it. Players need to take decisions on what to do in order to remedy the problem, if they can, and restore the system to the previous state of balance. Differences in turbidity, in PH value, or in temperature may be observed, while the different values may happen due to location, time of the day, time of the year, and human-related activities.

Players take their IoT-water explorer sensor kit that contains: a Turbidity sensor, a PH sensor, a Water Temperature Sensor. What the little explorers then do is the following:

1. They are given a kit for water sensing and an accompanying application.
2. They find a water source in their neighbourhood.
3. They use their mobile phones to pin the source location on google map.
4. They take photos of the area and the water source and add it as extra information about the water source they have adopted.
5. They plunge the sensors (Turbidity, PH, and Temperature) in the source, and record the values.

6. They compare the data they have gathered, with a table of related data that shows ranges of normal values.
7. They do it all over again to collect as much water data as possible and expand their area with more sources (a crowd sensing process for water data).

By doing this exploration they develop certain skills: understanding and describing the problem space, documenting aspects of the problem space, taking measurements, following the steps of a so-called scientific process, etc.

The players can play individually, or as part of teams, which compete in an exploration quest. The more records they take, the more they expand their influence area in the city map. The more data and the more sources they document, the more points they gather, in their quest. Later, in different time of the day, and at different seasons during the year, they may return to the water source and take new measurements with their sensor kit, in the water sources that have been previously measured. A diary can be used to view the sensor data added, but also for taking notes on other related activities.

A game scenario can be the following: A set of friends set out to play a scouts game. The goal is to cover an area, by taking measurements in water sources in as many spots in the map as possible. The journey can, in more complete versions, be specific or thematic: one can select seawater, lakes and rivers, drinking water (taps and springs), or thematic (Archeological journey, park journey, temples route, etc).

From the initial deployment, an issue observed relates of grading in the sensors used in IoT games, and the accuracy of sensor data. This "slack" in measurements also affects the results of appropriateness, in a given acceptable range. For example, PH water measurements in drinking water should be between 6,8 and 8. If the measurement is outside this scale in a city tap, there may be an issue regarding the validity of the sensor reading. This may owe to the way the measurement is taken, therefore repeating the measurement is encouraged, or to the sensor itself (the grading of sensors has a slack when compared to a more accurate organ). To remedy this, once a measurement is taken and is seen to be outside of the expected range, the player is given an instant warning message to have the sensor graduation checked and repeat the sampling, in order to opt out a measuring error, by taking a second measurement from the same water source. Thus the player learns gradually to make sure that (s)he takes thorough and valid measurements. The players are encouraged (by messages and highlighted map locations) to return to take sensor readings at different time intervals (during the day, week, month, or in different seasons. If other players take measurements they co-own the area, and the rights of the previous players are weakened. Furthermore, they can compare explanations and exchange opinions with tutors and with their groups.

5   Deployment and Testing in Real-World Environments

The design of the IoT system, the educational scenarios and corresponding gamification activities are evaluated to measure the relevance of a realized system with the goals initially identified. The evaluation follows an experimental app-roach examining the performance of certain technical components through an operation in real-world environments. Moreover, the complete system is to be evaluated from the end-users perspective as an integrated interaction experience.

5.1 Hardware Prototype

A hardware prototype device was developed for the realization of the measur-ing kit provided to the end-users. The measuring kit is developed to offer a simplified interaction with the students that do not require the combination of multiple devices for the storage and transfer of data or for the power. It is expected that through a simplified experience the students will focus on car-rying out the gaming elements. For this reason, the device was developed to operate independently from any other device, such as a smartphone or tablet. The board B-L072Z-LRWAN1[1] was used as the basis, with the following key technical characteristics:

CPU – an STM32L072CZ offering an Arm® Cortex®-M0+ core, with 192 Kbytes of Flash memory, 20 Kbytes of RAM and 20 Kbytes of EEPROM.
POWER – an on-board compartment on the bottom side that holds 3xAAA-sized battery.
NET – an SX1276 transceiver that features the LoRa® long-range modem including a 50 ohm SMA RF antenna, providing ultra-long-range spread spec-trum communication and high interference immunity, minimizing current con-sumption.
UX – four LEDs and two push-button offer simple interaction mechanisms.
IO – Arduino™ Uno V3 connectors that allow extending the boards with sensors.
COST – The cost of the board is €52.70.

The prototype device is equipped with two sensors for measuring pH and turbidity. Low-cost sensors were selected to reflect the budget usually available for school projects. In a usual scenario, multiple such devices will be needed for a single class to carry out the educational activities. Moreover, being handled by students and operated in environments with running water might lead to situations where certain hardware elements are damaged. Note that at the time of the development of the board it was not possible to identify and acquire a low-cost temperature and dissolved oxygen sensor kit. In more details:

Water Acidity-Alkalinity – analog PH meter (SKU: SEN0161)[2] operating an gain adjustment potentiometer and a pH electrode. The sensor achieves ±0.1 pH accuracy when measuring water at 25 °C. A standard solution whose pH value is 7.00 is provided to calibrate the sensor. The response time of the sensor is about 1 s. The cost of the sensor kit is €25.40.

---

[1] https://www.st.com/resource/en/user_manual/dm00329995.pdf.
[2] https://www.dfrobot.com/wiki/index.php/PH_meter(SKU:_SEN0161).

Water Turbidity – analog Turbidity sensor (SKU: SEN0189)[3]. It uses light to detect suspended particles in water by measuring the light transmittance and scattering rate, which changes with the amount of total suspended solids (TSS) in water. As the TTS increases, the liquid turbidity level increases. The response time of the sensor is about 500 ms. The cost of the sensor kit is €8.50.

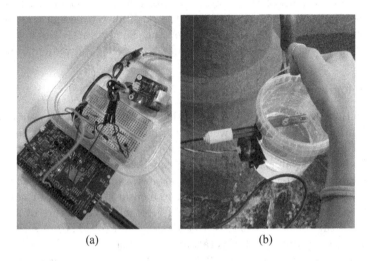

(a)   (b)

Fig. 1. Compartment for IoT device (left) and Box with sensors for sampling water (right)

Finally, we also attach a simple GPS receiver on the board so that we can automatically identify the location of the measurement. The board, the sensors, and all other components are positioned within a simple enclosure while the two sensors are attached on the side of a small bucket to hold the water that will be sampled. Figure 1 depicts a simple implementation of the prototype using DIY components.

5.2   Cloud Services

The values measured by the prototype device are transmitted via the LoRa LPWAN connection to the nearest gateway provided by The Things Network[4]. A cloud service is registered to collect the data retrieved by the LoRa network and store them within a simple key-value NoSQL database. The cloud service also provides the front-end through a Node.js implementation.

---

[3] https://www.dfrobot.com/wiki/index.php/Turbidity_sensor_SKU:_SEN0189.
[4] https://www.thethingsnetwork.org/.

5.3 Mobile App Prototype

A mobile application is provided as an accompanying component for the students that are on the move, engaged in the educational activities and making measurements. The mobile application acts as a diary for the students to record any remarks they might have related to the specific measurement. The main activity of the application is the display of the positions where a measurement took place on the map of the city. A secondary activity provides an overview of the values collected for a single point, the possibility to assign a label to the measurement, reposition it and add a comment. The two activities are depicted in Fig. 2. The mobile application was developed for the Android environment.

5.4 Deployment Evaluation

The evaluation started with the examination of the sensor components and the values acquired while measuring water of various qualities. Initially, the pH sensor was calibrated by positioning the pH electrode within the standard solution provided whose pH value is 7.00. In the sequel, the acidity of different liquids which contain acid or base at room temperature was used to test the accuracy of the sensor. When the finalised device used to measure the quality or normal tap water, the device provided the pH value of 7.14 and temperature of 23 °C and providing the turbidity value of close to the pure water (492 mV). A series of tests were carried out at different temperatures to further test the prototype device. A lemon juice was measured at pH 2.3, a tomato juice at 4.7, tap water at 6.98, distilled water at 7.02, and soap water at 12.09. For the case of turbidity, the highest value was recorded for distilled water 492 mV, a water mixed with a little dirt gives 374 mV while a water mixed with a lot of dirt gave a value of 62 mV.

The next step of the evaluation focused on testing the device while carrying out measurements at outdoor. The goal was to examine the connectivity of the LoRa® long-range modem included in the main board. The device was tested in the city centre of Rome, in areas close to the Department of Computer, Control and Management Engineering (DIAG) where a LoRa® gateway device was located. In total 12 fountains were identified within a range of 700 m and the water coming out from these fountains were sampled 10 times. All 1200 measurements were properly received by the cloud service.

The third experiment involved a class of students aged 9 years old that were asked to use the prototype device in order to measure the water coming out from a fountain. The process of measuring water quality was explained to the students, the technical details of the particular prototype device and the individual components that constitute it was presented, and the process of taking a water sample and measuring the water as well. Moreover, it was explained to the students that the device is developed only for educational purposes and as such, it should be treated with care making sure that water does not enter the delicate hardware parts. After the presentation that lasted about 1 h within the classroom, the students were organized in groups of 3 and each group was asked to measure the water coming out of 4 fountains positioned within 200 m

(a)   (b)

Fig. 2. Mobile application presenting the points of measurements and corresponding values

Fig. 3. Explaining the game assignment to the class

from their school. For ensuring a reasonable quality on the measurements, the students were asked to take 3 measurements on each fountain. On average each group took about 40 min to carry out all the measurements. A single measurement required about 3.4 min, where the time was measured from the timestamps received from consecutive measurements. At the end of the experiment, all students managed to use the device properly without reporting any difficulty or damaging the device. The battery used was sufficient to sustain the operation of the device for the full day.

6 Discussion and Conclusions

The main objective of sustainability education and raising awareness for environmental issues is making students aware that their actions may have a direct impact on the environment. Simple behaviour changes and interventions may have a tangible impact towards reversing water pollution. To this end, IoT technologies can support such initiatives with immediate feedback regarding the impact of their actions. This allows, on the one hand, better-informing people and enabling them to make informed decisions, and on the other to enable a different set of applications, like gamification bridging the virtual world with the real one.

The availability of actual measurements of parameters for water quality enables a number of diverse education-related applications and scenarios. For example, teachers can use collected data and analytics during class to explain phenomena related to the parameters monitored. Another example involves teachers organizing projects where students/groups monitor environmental parameters in class/home. In this direction, one major issue noted in this experiment is that IoT sensing (based on cheaper sensors and more sensitive to wear and tear) can provide values that are lacking in accuracy. The initial deployment has shown that there is often a slack between the measurements produced from the IoT sensors, that are inexpensive and are not meant as scientific measurement tools to start with. Similar differences in values of sensor readings have also been noted in the GAIA project [5], also reporting a similar approach of IoT environmental sensing used for education.

Nevertheless this slack in measuring parameters can result in important differences to the conclusions drawn; for example, during the game, water can be measured and found outside the limits of drinking values. It is therefore very important, to ensure, from the start of such games but also at regular intervals during the whole process, the appropriateness of degradation of the measurements tools used. It is important for children learning the scientific method, to learn to take correct measurements and therefore to question and grade the tools they use. Correction in degradation can be done by the school tutors themselves before they hand in the IoT sensors to their pupils, but the children need also to be notified. If one parameter is outside the acceptable margin, a warning message in the application can provide appropriate feedback and encourage to check the grading of the measurement tool, cross-check perhaps with another tool, (before drawing the wrong conclusions) and repeating the sampling actions in the same location.

Providing appropriate feedback via the application used is essential in IoT sensing systems used in citizen science and education. When the measurements taken are not in the acceptable range or after several uses (when the worn IoT sensors may need fixing or replacement), feedback for action is néeded in order to check and re-grade the IoT sensor, (and possibly provide step by step suggestions on related possible actions), so as to then repeat the measurement.

Recent technological developments allow us to extend the IoT infrastructure in order to monitor several, unforeseen before, environmental parameters, such as for example aquatic measurements. Towards this, the deployment of sensors in water is gradually introduced and promoted, with the potential aim to address more complex aquatic measurements and form appropriate underwater sensor networks for monitoring the aquatic sectors of our planet. A series of educational scenaria is proposed to this end, that utilize the collected data to further promote sustainability awareness and behavioural change. These are coupled by a gamification application, enabling the data collection as well as visualisation, and a packaged set of IoT sensors aiming specifically for water parameters. Future steps of the deployment described here is to further evaluate it, for assessing the motivation and engagement of the students for practising science and for sustaining the environment, and develop it further in the different aspects it pertains.

This research further supports that education-focused real-world IoT deployment can help to form a better understanding of our environment and promote sustainable activities, starting at a school level. By using inexpensive and easily available IoT infrastructure to measure, and then visualise and reflect on the data combinations, a more meaningful understanding of our very environment is informed, while at the same time citizen science is supported by adding to data sets.

Given the combination of technical difficulties with pedagogical goals presented in this work, it is critical to continue by a stepwise approach where advancements in the technical prototype are matched by enhancements in the gamification techniques. Detailing on the educational scenarios and how they are paired with gamification approaches are to be further researched. Likewise, it is important to carry out a high-level evaluation of the effectiveness of the proposed approach and the adoption of environmental healthy behaviour, as the ultimate goal.

Acknowledgements. We would like to thank Adriano Pimpini and Gabrio Tognozzi, students of the Sapienza University of Rome that helped in the development of the prototype system. This work has been partially supported by the EU research project "Green Awareness In Action" (GAIA), funded under contract number 696029 and the research project Designing Human-Agent Collectives for Sustainable Future Societies (C26A15TXCF) of Sapienza University of Rome. This document reflects only the authors' view and the EC and EASME are not responsible for any use that may be made of the information it contains.

References

1. Green paper marine knowledge 2020, mapping to ocean forecasting. Technical report, Luxembourg: Publications Office of the European Union, COM (2012) 473 final (2012). ISBN: 9789279-25350-8
2. Whitebread, D., et al.: A report on the value of childrens play with a series of policy recommendations. Technical report, Written for Toy Industries of Europe (TIE) (2012)
3. Energy Serious Game. http://www.2020energy.eu/game
4. Akribopoulos, O., Chatzigiannakis, I., Koninis, C., Theodoridis E.: A web services-oriented architecture for integrating small programmable objects in the web of things. In: Developments in E-systems Engineering (DESE), 2010, pp. 70–75. IEEE (2010)
5. Amaxilatis, D., Akrivopoulos, O., Mylonas, G., Chatzigiannakis, I.: An IoT-based solution for monitoring a fleet of educational buildings focusing on energy efficiency. Sensors **17**(10), 2296 (2017)
6. Baichtal, J.: Building Your Own Drones: A Beginners' Guide to Drones, UAVs, and ROVs, 1st edn. Que Publishing Company, US (2015)
7. Brossard, D., Lewenstein, B., Bonney, R.: Scientific knowledge and attitude change: the impact of a citizen science project. Int. J. Sci. Educ. **27**(9), 1099–1121 (2005)
8. Burke, J., et al.: Participatory sensing. In: Workshop on World-Sensor-Web (WSW06): Mobile Device Centric Sensor Networks and Applications, pp. 117–134 (2006)
9. Chatzigiannakis, I., et al.: True self-configuration for the IoT. In: 3rd International Conference on the Internet of Things (IOT) 2012, pp. 9–15. IEEE (2012)
10. Chatzigiannakis, I., Kröller, A., Mavrommati, I.: Indoors multi-visitors pervasive installations using mobile sensor networks. In: Proceedings of the 2011 International Conference on Indoor Positioning and Navigation (IPIN 2011), September 2011
11. Chatzigiannakis, I., Mylonas, G., Kokkinos, P., Akribopoulos, O., Logaras, M., Mavrommati, I.: Implementing multiplayer pervasive installations based on mobile sensing devices: field experience and user evaluation from a public showcase. J. Syst. Softw. **84**, 1989–2004 (2011)
12. Chryssafidou, E., et al.: Developing tools that support effective mobile and game based learning: the collage platform. In: Architectures for Distributed and Complex M-Learning Systems: Applying Intelligent Technologies (2010)
13. Czerniak, C.M., Weber Jr., W.B., Sandmann, A., Ahern, J.: A literature review of science and mathematics integration. Sch. Sci. Math. **99**(8), 421–430 (1999)
14. Dimaraki, E.V., Schmoelz, A., Koulouris, P.: Scenarios as pedagogical devices: designing activities for game-based learning. In: Proceedings of the International Conference of Education, Research and Innovation (in print)
15. Free Energy Game, PG&E. http://www.freeenergygame.com/
16. Frykholm, J., Glasson, G.: Connecting science and mathematics instruction: pedagogical context knowledge for teachers. Sch. Sci. Math. **105**(3), 127–141 (2005)
17. Göbel, S., Hardy, S., Wendel, V., Mehm, F., Steinmetz, R.: Serious games for health: personalized exergames. In: Proceedings of the International Conference on Multimedia, pp. 1663–1666. ACM (2010)
18. Heggen, S.: Participatory sensing: repurposing a scientific tool for stem education. Interactions **20**(1), 18–21 (2013)

19. Kotovirta, V., Toivanen, T., Tergujeff, R., Huttunen, M.: Participatory sensing in environmental monitoring - experiences. In: 2012 Sixth International Conference on Innovative Mobile and Internet Services in Ubiquitous Computing, pp. 155–162, July 2012

20. Mallon, E., Beddows, P.: The Cave Pearl Project: Developing a Summersible Data Logger System for Long Term Environmental Monitoring. https://thecavepearlproject.org

21. Koulouris, P., Dimaraki, E.: Engaging school communities in the design of game-based learning to foster creativity. In: Proceedings of the LD-Skills: The Future of Learning Design Conference (2012)

22. Petrioli, C., Potter, J., Petroccia, R.: Sunrise sensing, monitoring and actuating on the underwater world through a federated research infrastructure extending the future internet. In: Proceedings of EMSO 2013, Rome, Italy, 17 November 2013 (2013). Demo also presented

23. Pierce, J., Paulos, E.: Materializing energy. In: Proceedings of the 8th ACM Conference on Designing Interactive Systems, pp. 113–122. ACM (2010)

24. Pocero, L., Amaxilatis, D., Mylonas, G., Chatzigiannakis, I.: Open source IoT meter devices for smart and energy-efficient school buildings. HardwareX (2017)

25. Siements, Power your World serious game. http://www.powermatrixgame.com

26. Reeves, B., Cummings, J.J., Scarborough, J.K., Flora, J., Anderson, D.: Leveraging the engagement of games to change energy behavior. In: Smari, W.W., Fox, G.C. (eds.) CTS, pp. 354–358. IEEE (2012)

27. Sanders, M.E.: Stem, stem education, stemmania (2008)

28. SAVE ENERGY FP7 project. http://www.ict4saveenergy.eu/

29. Shahali, E.H.M., Halim, L., Rasul, M.S., Osman, K., Zulkifeli, M.A.: Stem learning through engineering design: Impact on middle secondary students interest towards stem. EURASIA J. Math. Sci. Technology. Educ. **13**(5), 1189–1211 (2017)

30. Sun, W., Li, Q., Tham, C.K.: Wireless deployed and participatory sensing system for environmental monitoring. In: 2014 Eleventh Annual IEEE International Conference on Sensing, Communication, and Networking (SECON), pp. 158–160, June 2014

Investigating Secondary Students' Stance on IoT Driven Educational Activities

Dimitrios Glaroudis[1], Athanasios Iossifides[1,2(✉)],
Natalia Spyropoulou[1], and Ioannis D. Zaharakis[1,3(✉)]

[1] Computer Technology Institute and Press (CTI) – Diophantus, Patras, Greece
{dglaroudis,aiosifidis,nataliaspy,jzaharak}@cti.gr
[2] Department of Electronics Engineering,
Alexander Technological Educational Institute of Thessaloniki,
Thessaloniki, Greece
[3] Computer and Informatics Engineering Department,
Technological Educational Institute of Western Greece, Patras, Greece

Abstract. This paper presents and analyses a set of data that reveal secondary education students' stance on the educational activities that were realised during a UMI (ubiquitous, mobile computing and the Internet of Things) Summer School. This Summer School deals with an IoT based recycling management application development and is part of UMI-Sci-Ed project that provides a training framework on UMI learning, for students aged between 14–16, with the use of properly designed educational scenarios and communities of practice (CoP) by setting UMI technologies as learning means and learning outcomes, simultaneously. The analysis focuses on the students' satisfaction and engagement (observed through a set of questionnaires) in relation with students' potential to follow the activities, the perceived, by the students, easiness, enjoyment and usefulness while setting as parameters the student gender and age. The results clearly show high student acceptability and engagement with the designed IoT-driven activities and reveal certain differentiations with respect to gender and age in these aspects. These findings, together with the observations that high student satisfaction does not translate to equally high engagement and that enjoyment is a critical factor, provide a basis for future adjustment of the educational scenarios and activities scope and design in order to enhance the UMI-Sci-Ed impact on student preference for a future career in the UMI technologies domain.

Keywords: Ambient intelligence education · Ubiquitous Computing
Mobile computing · Internet of Things · STEM education

1 Introduction

While the computer science research is focused on a practical and user-centred implementation of technology, there is a growing body of research about emerging technologies, such as Ubiquitous Computing (UbiComp), Mobile Computing (Mobi-Comp) and the Internet of Things (IoT), collectively mentioned in the literature as UMI technologies [12]. Nowadays these technologies attempt to move computer technology

© Springer Nature Switzerland AG 2018
A. Kameas and K. Stathis (Eds.): AmI 2018, LNCS 11249, pp. 188–203, 2018.
https://doi.org/10.1007/978-3-030-03062-9_15

beyond the confines of tool usage towards a pervasive penetration of everyday life; however in a decade or less they will prevail in our everyday life and greatly enhance human activities supporting them with "everyware" personalized action, suggestion and/or decision. This means that today's youngsters are the natives of this technology and must be able to think creatively, apply new knowledge in an effective way, become continuously competitive in a highly demanding working environment and thus be able to stand up for all the challenges that this new era brings.

Based on the abovementioned requirements, UMI-Sci-Ed,[1] (Exploiting Ubiquitous Computing, Mobile Computing and the Internet of Things to promote Science Education) is a Horizon 2020 project related to the innovative ways to make science education and scientific careers attractive to young people and aims to provide efficient practices into this technology training issue. The UMI-Sci-Ed approach introduces several model educational scenarios that incorporate UMI technologies, in order to cultivate relevant competences to high school students. Along these lines, UMI technologies emerge both as educational means but most importantly as support mechanism for developing powerful careers through ambient intelligence education.

In the context of UMI-Sci-Ed project and in an effort to raise young boys' and girls' motivation in science education and to increase their prospects in choosing a career in UMI technologies, we carried out a UMI Summer School event. The event was held in four cities in parallel and involved 63 secondary students. The students were introduced to the basics of UMI technologies and then they interacted with a novel educational scenario, so as to design and implement an IoT application for recycling. During the event, the students filled a set of questionnaires evaluating several aspects of the event, the technology used and the knowledge/experiences they gained.

The main research objective of this work is to examine in what extent the use of UMI (and especially IoT) technologies can be well accepted (satisfaction) by secondary education students both as educational means (e.g., to teach math and science) and learning outcomes (e.g., contemporary, advanced engineering and technology) and to investigate the students' stance on further attending IoT-related activities, properly organised in STEM educational scenarios (engagement-intention). These aspects are examined in relation to the students' view of self-competence to follow the event (control), their perception of easiness of the educational activities (easiness), the joy and excitement they felt during the training process (enjoyment) and, the perceived value of the educational activities (usefulness). In this context, student gender and age are set as independent variables and their impact on the above mentioned aspects is analysed.

This work attempts to fill a gap in the literature, since the relevant research efforts focus more on just presenting UMI to students or on the programming or technical aspects of IoT and less in using UMI technologies as main learning tools to reinforce STEM education and to investigate the students' engagement in IoT learning activities. Notable exceptions include the work of Mavroudi et al. [8], in which an analysis is conducted on a case study where four groups of lower secondary school students participated in a workshop and undertook the demanding role of designers of IoT

---

[1] http://umi-sci-ed.eu/.

applications and the case study presented in [6], that incorporates an IoT-based learning framework into a Software Engineering (SWE) embedded system analysis & design course. Both works focus on the learning gains of using IoT as a tool to design learning activities, evaluate the derived activities through survey questions and discuss the motivation aspect for teachers and students. Our work further evaluates the secondary education students' stance (satisfaction, intention/engagement) on IoT driven educational activities and correlates it with gender and age aspects, on the basis of the perceived, by the students, easiness, enjoyment and usefulness. The major findings of the data analysis can be summarised as follows:

- Overall, the UMI educational activities were found to reach high levels of satisfaction and engagement. However these levels were significantly lower for female students.
- The ability to follow and easiness of the activities do not seem to have significant role in the overall evaluation, mainly due to girls and older students. However, the activities should probably be easier for smaller ages.
- Enjoyment and usefulness enhance, almost linearly, student satisfaction and engagement. However, high satisfaction does not translate to equally high engagement and intention to follow similar activities in the future.

The rest of the paper is structured as follows: the next section describes the UMI-Sci-Ed educational methods and tools, while the third section presents the UMI Summer School event and the educational scenario for teaching IoT technologies in classroom settings. Subsequently, the fourth section, describes the evaluation methodology and the fifth section provides the results and data analysis on how the students interacted with UMI technologies and in what extent they believe that such training framework helps them during the learning process or initiates and inspires them to attend similar educational activities. The last section summarizes the outcomes and describes future steps of analysis on other aspects of the adopted approach.

2 UMI-Sci-Ed Educational Methods and Tools

The UMI-Sci-Ed project focuses on the investigation of the introduction of UMI technologies in education, putting these state-of-the-art technologies in practice, so as to make attractive the prospect of pursuing a career in domains pervaded by UMI. The main objectives of the project are stated in terms of delivering (a) novel educational services, which enable learners to understand, use and develop UMI applications, (b) career consultancy services, encouraging students to visualise a career in UMI technologies, (c) supporting software tools, through the development of an online platform and (d) supporting hardware tools, through the use of a dedicated hardware kit.

2.1 Educational Methods

In order to achieve such targets, the UMI-Sci-Ed educational framework provides an open, integrated and collaborative digital environment, where technology support the stakeholders of education, such as the educational community, the industry, career consultants and educational authorities and policy makers, with the formulation of dynamic online Communities of Practice (CoPs).

A CoP is a network of people distinguished by a common interest or a passion and learn how to do it better as they interact regularly [11]. In UMI-Sci-Ed project, the role of UMI-Sci-Ed CoPs is to create, develop and disseminate new tools, systems, and resources based on applications developed via UMI technologies. The creation and support of the UMI-Sci-Ed CoPs is based on the model of Snyder and Briggs [10], which consists of five stages, i.e., discovering the potential, coalescing, maturity/growth, advocacy and transformation. For the CoPs formulation, these stages are crucial in order to identify the key contents, the target population, the definition of the roles, the processes of involving key stakeholders and the recruit of participants.

In this context, UMI technologies are emerging both as learning tools and as learning objectives. With their exploitation by UMI-Sci-Ed CoPs, new educational services are designed and developed by applying innovative pedagogical methods to enhance creativity, socialization and scientific participation for both students and teachers. The core educational elements towards this direction are the educational scenarios.

An educational scenario is a structured plan of an educational program that aims to guide the teacher during the educational process. According to the learning objectives of each educational scenario, specific educational methods are used, which define the flow of the educational activities, the appropriate tools and the role of the teacher [3]. At UMI-Sci-Ed project several UMI educational scenarios have been developed by different research teams based on student-centred approaches and techniques, promoting creative thinking and problem-solving skills. These educational scenarios may be used as templates, however, they are flexible and teachers may adapt them according to their students' needs and create their own UMI projects; a specific application of an educational scenario based on the whole or some aspects of it. A more detailed description of UMI educational scenarios can be found in the UMI-Sci-Ed platform (which is presented in the next section), while each UMI project may be linked to the platform's available tools, and facilitate creators and participants (teachers, students, field specialists, field professionals, etc.) share their experiences, utilize different ways of using the provided educational material, or/and create and share new material [4]. All these supported services of the digital environment are aligned with the EU policy open access to scientific publications and to research data and conformed to ethical principles and data protection legislation based on EU guidance on responsible research innovation.

2.2 Educational Tools

Apart from the educational and the career consultancy services, the UMI-Sci-Ed training framework provides open-source software based learning environment as a facilitating mechanism for UMI learning in the context of science education, aiming to support all stakeholders to form CoPs through the UMI-Sci-Ed platform. In addition, the UMI-Sci-Ed framework provides a range of hardware supporting tools that includes low cost modular kit and several peripherals, packaged in handy suitcases, which were delivered to selected schools to teach and promote UMI technologies.

The software tools are packaged in the UMI-Sci-Ed platform[2], a web-based and open-source platform, which supports all stakeholders to form CoPs as a facilitating mechanism for UMI learning. In this context, the platform includes a portal on top of the architecture that is the showcase and interaction areas of the UMI-Sci-Ed consortium as well as future participants and actors with the society. The platform, among other characteristics, provides CoPs for UMI youths that aim to promote STEM, synchronous/asynchronous communication tools (chat, forum, wikis, blogs), educational material about STEM disciplines, entrepreneurship trainings delivered through and supported by UMI and peer learning opportunities and mentoring services. The platform is also a very useful tool for all interested parties as they can find projects and results developed by the students, teachers, experts as well as research results on educational approaches and methodologies, tools for information extraction, management and diffusion of the produced knowledge [4].

The hardware tools are packaged in a handy suitcase, called Udoo-Edu kit, which is meant to support young students to realise their UMI ideas. The main device is the Udoo Neo board[3], an all-in-one solution for UMI applications. It can be used both as a headless device and as a computer, by exploiting the USB, Ethernet and wireless connectivity (Wi-Fi and Bluetooth) ports as well as its 1 GB of RAM. The board is compatible with most Arduino shields, sensors and actuators and can be powered via a standard 12 V power supply or a micro USB cable. Although it has the same capabilities with a desktop computer, it has small size, realising a perfect solution for mobile and IoT applications. Udoo Neo is powered by GNU/Linux, a free operating system running on millions of devices worldwide, and is compatible with Arduino programming through Arduino IDE. The accompanying peripherals are specifically designed for helping students to learn science and to interact with the physical world. They include many sensors, such as temperature, humidity, light, gas, presence, distance, and actuators, e.g., a LED matrix display, a motor, various LEDs, buttons etc., and thus the students can tinker with the accessories by connecting them to the Udoo Neo board and program their own applications.

3 UMI Summer School Design and Realisation

3.1 Scope and Setup

The purpose of the Summer School was in line with the goals of the UMI-Sci-Ed project and it was twofold: (i) to familiarize secondary students with cutting-edge IoT technologies and provide them with a first level of understanding of the role of IoT in future life and (ii) to inspire them to envision and follow a career path in this particular domain. The summer school was based on a properly designed educational scenario entitled "Hands on... the Internet of Things" in which the students learned how to tackle the real-life problem of optimizing recyclable waste collection through the design and experimental realization of a simplified – yet full – IoT application.

---

[2] https://umi-sci-ed.cti.gr/.

[3] https://www.udoo.org/udoo-neo/.

The main axes of the application included: (i) recycle bin waste level and volume measurement/calculation with the use of Udoo devices and ultrasound sensors, and (ii) generation of notifications of specific events either locally or via an IoT platform so that to facilitate garbage truck fleet management. Physics, math, basic electronics and programming were the main STEM disciplines involved. The major learning outcomes can be summarized as follows:

- Connect UMI technologies with the physical world and the personal experience of the students.
- Understand the role of IoT in future life.
- Investigate the possibilities arising for developing new applications for life improvement with IoT.
- Apply, use and exploit technologies related with IoT.
- Envision a future career in IoT and UMI technologies in general.

The event was held during June 25–28, 2018, in four different Greek cities (Athens, Thessaloniki, Patras and Larissa) in parallel, in order to be addressed by students of different major geographical areas of the country, comprising a four days – four hours per day educational program that was realised in standard Greek secondary school labs, properly checked and setup beforehand. The only prerequisite that participating students had to meet was being between 14 and 16 years old. The event was disseminated through social media and Greek secondary schools authorities in the four geographic regions under consideration and attracted an unexpectedly high number of applications. The student selection process was set in a "first to apply – first to be chosen" basis. More than one hundred and ninety students applied to participate in the Summer School (the application deadline was moved earlier than it was originally scheduled), out of which eighty (80) students were accepted due to space and equipment limitations and finally sixty-three (63) of them fully attended the event.

Six secondary school teachers, three electronic/IT engineers and three members of the UMI-Sci-Ed CTI research team were involved in the in-class activities. The teachers were the main actors with the rest of the people (academics, researchers and technicians) supporting the educational activities and equipment. Overall, including the design phase, fifteen people contributed in the organisation and realisation of the Summer School over a period of two months.

3.2   Educational Scenario Description

Based on the scenario-based approach (SBL), the educational activities were designed with the aim to promote collaborative problem-solving and critical thinking skills, through a practice-oriented educational scenario [1, 2]. The scenario was designed by the CTI research team involved in UMI-Sci-Ed project and was divided in sixteen, in total, activities, with four activities per day, comprising twelve core activities, two auxiliary, an introductory and a concluding activity, as shown in Table 1. The UMI-Sci-Ed educational scenario template was used for the guidance of the teachers; the worksheets and educational material (documents, codes, presentations, etc.) were mainly developed from scratch by the research team and were accompanied by proper and carefully selected relative material freely available in the Internet.

Table 1. Summarization of summer school educational activities

Day	Activity	Type of activity	Title of activity
1	1.0	Introductory	Welcome activity
1	1.1	Core	Internet of Things in our service
1	1.2	Core	The UMI-Sci-Ed educational platform
1	1.3	Core	IoT tools: Introduction to the Udoo-Edu kit
2	2.1	Auxiliary	Let's play with the words
2	2.2	Core	Voltage, current and resistance
2	2.3	Core	Hands on…Udoo
2	2.4	Core	Ultrasound physics and distance measurement
3	3.1	Auxiliary	Let's play with the words
3	3.2	Core	The problem of recyclable waste collection
3	3.3	Core	From sensors to the Cloud
3	3.4	Core	From the Cloud to our cell phones
4	4.1	Core	Who are involved with the Internet of Things?
4	4.2	Core	Analysis and action
4	4.3	Core	UMI community discussion
4	4.4	Concluding	Reflections and completion of questionnaires

Welcome Activity. The summer school started with an introductory activity where a video conference among the four schools took place (Fig. 1). After a general welcome to all participants, a simple UMI application was demonstrated, in which the students were able to turn on and off with their mobile phones a light bulb that was placed in a different region of Greece. Next, a warm up activity was performed so as the students to introduce themselves, getting to know with each other and the trainers and to set the ground rules (timeline, in-class behaviour etc.) for the duration of the event.

Core Activities. The *Internet of Things in our service* activity was the first core activity of the *first day*. The tutors, starting from the issue of effective recyclable waste collection, facilitated a discussion/brainstorming towards "smart" solutions and triggered the discovery of the key concepts of IoT (e.g., sensors, data analytics, actuating) through a proper video. Next, students were divided in groups, searched through the Internet for relevant material as well as IoT applications over other fields and presented their findings. Finally, a video related to IoT followed by a presentation concluded the activity, aiming to define what IoT is, its characteristics and architecture.

The first day continued with two activities providing a description of the available UMI tools, i.e., the UMI-Sci-Ed educational platform and the Udoo-Edu kit. The teachers described the platform's environment, main features and capabilities (e.g., UMI projects, blog, forum, chat, etc.) and the students were logged in the platform to create new content and upload the material that was gathered during the previous activity. Next, the teachers briefly described the technical characteristics of Udoo-Edu kit, i.e., the Udoo Neo board, the available sensors and electronic components and enabled students to come in a first acquaintance and interaction with the devices.

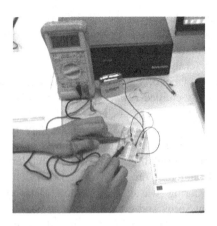

Fig. 1. UMI Summer School activities: welcome video conference left); performing voltage measurements during *Voltage, Current and resistance* activity (right)

Day two included three hands on activities. Initially, in the context of the *Voltage, current and resistance* activity (Fig. 1), the students created (in groups) a simple electrical circuit using a battery, ohm resistors and a LED so as to turn on the LED and to get familiar with the concepts of voltage and current. Next, the students were introduced to the different methods of interacting with Udoo board and the use of its input/output pins (*Hands on…Udoo* activity); they wrote and executed their first Arduino code on Udoo Neo board using the Arduino IDE environment (Fig. 2). During the next activity, i.e., *Ultrasound physics and distance measurements*, the students were first introduced to the physics of ultrasound technology, the natural quantities and their practical values and units involved in a distance measurement procedure with ultrasonic sensors. Then, they developed the necessary circuitry for connecting an ultrasonic sensor with the Udoo board and experimented with an Arduino code for reading the sensor values and monitoring the distance of different objects.

Fig. 2. UMI Summer School artefacts: The first Udoo board application during the *Hands on… Udoo* activity (left); the final construction measuring waste level with the ultrasonic sensor mounted on top of the recycle bin model (right). (Color figure online)

On *day three*, the UMI Summer School reached its peak. As a first step (*The problem of recyclable waste collection* activity), the teacher presented the problem of automating the measurement of waste level in a recycle bin that students had to solve and set the targets of the application that the they had to design and implement with their own efforts, using the obtained knowledge from the previous activities. During the activity entitled *From sensors to the Cloud*, the students constructed a circuit with the Udoo board, resistors, LEDs and an ultrasonic sensor properly mounted on the lid of an experimental recycle bin. Next, they programmed the Udoo device, following the appropriate mathematical formulas in order to read the waste level and calculate the volume, providing, in addition, conditions to check if and when the bin was empty or full and turn on green or red, respectively, LEDs (Fig. 2). Finally, they practiced transfering waste level/volume data to the open-source IoT Cloud Mathworks ThingSpeak and created time-data graphs. In the final activity of the third day, *From the Cloud to our mobile phones*, the students learned how to access the Cloud data and graphs with their mobile phones via web browsers, widgets or mobile applications.

Day four began with the activity *Who are involved with the Internet of Things*, through which the students, triggered by proper photos, searched (in groups) contemporary and future professions that are related with IoT in various domains and presented the corresponding skills and competences involved. The second activity, *Analysis and Action*, started with a discussion on data analytics, data exploitation and decisions that could be made in order to facilitate and optimize recyclable waste collection over a broader geographical (neighbourhood, town, city) and temporal (daily, monthly) basis. Concepts like truck fleet management, authorities and citizens' notifications, etc., were mentioned by the students. Then, students learned how to use control values and simplified programming of the ThingSpeak IoT platform to include control conditions and triggering for alerts' production via Tweeter.

During the *UMI Community Discussion* activity, an overall discussion via the UMI-Sci-Ed platform forum took place among all students and teachers who participated in the Summer School. CoP experts also participated in the discussion either by answering questions or by posing issues for further reflection. The aim of the activity was to strengthen the bonds of the community members and to allow the students to feel that they could use valuable advice or guidance by external experts, as well as for teachers and experts to recognize new, and maybe unpredictable issues or queries that can arise when students interact with innovative technologies for the first time. In this discussion, many topics were set, like the extensions of smart IoT recycling application, the limitations of the application, security and privacy issues in the IoT field, etc. The students' participation in this activity was surprisingly wide.

Auxiliary (Warm up) Activities. In the beginning of the second and third days warm up activities took place in order to review key concepts and strengthen the willingness of the students to participate. Both days started with an enjoyable word puzzle under the name *Let's play with the words* in which the students were separated in groups and one student from each group was trying to guess a word related to the material taught in the previous day, based on the descriptions that the other students of the group gave her/him. The group finding most of the words was the winning one.

Concluding Activity. The final activity of the event began with a concluding in-class free discussion and ended up with the completion of a set of questionnaires aiming at the overall analysis and evaluation of the Summer School. These questionnaires, properly designed in the context of the evaluation methodology of UMI-Sci-Ed (briefly discussed in next section) were provided by the UMI-Sci-Ed platform.

4   Evaluation Methodology

UMI-Sci-Ed has developed a holistic evaluation methodology aligned with current state-of-the-art instructional design methodologies, based on ADDIE model [9]. In this context, all the different aspects of the project, e.g., learning gains, learning tools usefulness and usability, stakeholders' engagement, CoPs development, user activity and experience as well as career consultancy services are evaluated via a plethora of tools comprising the UMI-Sci-Ed evaluation and research toolbox [7]: online surveys, artefact analysis, interviews, checklists, log files and web metrics (learning analytics), think aloud and observation protocols as well as cognitive tests and activity tracking. Data collection is both quantitative and qualitative to enable triangulation and provide a rich and robust data set. In all cases, data management and analysis follow strict rules on privacy and security aspects [5]. The present paper is focused on data evaluation collected by online surveys, mainly because the surveys produced straightforward and reliable quantitative results about students' perceptions.

The main purpose of this study is to obtain a first but clear evidence of the students' stance on the UMI and STEM oriented educational activities that were realized in the framework of the Summer School. In specific, students' perceived *satisfaction*, meaning fulfilment of their expectations when executing the educational UMI activities or more emphatically their expressed pleasure during these activities, as well as students' engagement and *intention* to follow similar activities in the future are set in the core of the analysis. These aspects are examined and discussed both directly and comparatively in relation to students' perceived potential (in terms of self-knowledge and self-ability) to attend the activities (*control*), how easy they believe they were (*easiness*), if they enjoyed them (*enjoyment*) and how useful they believe they were (*usefulness*). The correlation of satisfaction and intention aspects with the above mentioned parameters is examined in order to discover which factors affect mostly or "trigger" the students' stance on the activities or reveal the connections among them.

The above mentioned aspects/categories (satisfaction, intention, control, easiness, enjoyment and usefulness) are evaluated by close ended self-assessment question-naires, with responses in a 1 to 7 Likert-type scale, where, 1 means strongly disagree (negative) and 7 strongly agree (positive), following the UMI-Sci-Ed project evaluation methodology [7]. Table 2 summarizes the questions related to the aspects under consideration. These questionnaires were filled in once at the end of the Summer School referring to all the activities that were realised.

As a second step, the data are analysed with respect to students' gender and age in order to reveal important differences that should be taken into account in improving the educational activities.

Table 2. Evaluated categories with the corresponding questions for UMI learning activities

Satisfaction	Easiness
• I am satisfied with the activity • I am pleased with the activity • My decision to attend the activity was a wise one	• The activity was easy • I found the activity flexible • The process of the activity was clear and understandable • It was easy for me to attain skills with the activity
Intention	**Enjoyment**
• I intend to attend the activity in the future • My general intention to attend the activity in the future is very high • I will regularly attend similar activities in the future	• Attending the activity was enjoyable • Attending the activity was exciting • I was feeling good in the activity
	Control
	• I was able to follow the tasks of the activity • I have the knowledge and the ability to follow the tasks of the activity
	Usefulness
	• I found the activity useful • The activity improves my performance in science and technologies • The activity enhances the effectiveness in science and technologies • The activity increases my capabilities in science and technologies

Table 3. UMI summer school participant statistics

	Participants	Questionnaires	Male	Female	Age 14	Age 15	Age 16
Students	63	58	41	17	22	17	18

5   Results and Discussion

Table 3 summarizes the statistics of the participants' questionnaires that were taken into account in the analysis. The ones excluded provided too few answers over the full set of questions of Table 2.

5.1   Basic Data Analysis

Table 4 presents the mean values of the student responses per category (aspect). The ensemble mean values (excluding easiness), being well beyond 4 (median value of Likert scale), show a very positive view of the students in all aspects. Especially, the satisfaction and intention computed mean values of 5.66 and 4.96, respectively, indicate that the summer school was overall considered by the students to be successful. The perceived, by the students, easiness, on the other hand, was expected to be lower, since the scenario was considered as "intermediate" by the designers. However, it is

Table 4. Mean category values with respect to gender and age

Category	Ensemble mean	Gender		Age		
		Boy	Girl	14	15	16
Control	5.20	5.39	4.74	5.50	4.94	5.39
Easiness	4.88	5.10	4.35	5.13	4.73	5.33
Enjoyment	5.37	5.52	5.00	5.71	5.52	5.27
Usefulness	5.62	5.83	5.12	5.57	5.81	5.60
Satisfaction	5.66	5.78	5.35	5.89	5.85	5.56
Intention	4.96	5.19	4.41	5.07	4.94	5.24

important to note, that while the scenario was not easy, most of the students thought that they had the potential (control aspect) to follow the activities.

A differentiation with respect to gender is evident from the mean category values. It is clearly noticed that all the mean category values of male students are higher compared to those of female ones, in all categories. Taking into account the fact that the number of boys was double than the population of girls (41/17), it is clear that the high ensemble means are mainly due to the boys. This may be explained by the general fact of a positive predisposition of male students to STEM activities and new technologies. On the other hand, it shows a necessity to adjust the activities towards girl interests as much as possible and, especially, find methods to increase their engagement and intention to follow similar activities.

The mean values with respect to the age criterion do not reveal a specific trend. Overall, the younger (age 14) students seem surprisingly positive in all aspects while the older ones' (age 16) responses present the least differences among the categories, revealing more maturity and a change in attitude that takes place when the students enter the Greek Lyceum (the upper three years of secondary school).

Figure 3 illustrates intention with respect to satisfaction over the whole sample. The circles' radii indicate multiple identical samples, ranging from 1 to 6. A least squares fitted line over the scattered data is given together with a reference line joining the points (1,1) and (7,7). Clearly, satisfaction and intention are highly correlated while sharing high mean values (most samples are concentrated in the top-right part of the diagram). The fitted line presents a slope of one and a clear displacement with respect to the reference line. This, together with the mean category values presented in Table 4, i.e., 5.7 for satisfaction and 5 for intention, indicates that high student satisfaction does not necessarily translate to equally high intention and engagement. This may be due to the short and compact duration of the Summer School. However it necessitates further consideration for the next broad pilot phase of the project.

5.2   Data Correlation Analysis with Respect to Gender and Age

In order to get further insight into the way that student attending ability (control), the perceived, by the students, easiness, enjoyment and usefulness affect satisfaction and intention/engagement, we present in Figs. 4 and 5 the corresponding data after averaging the categories' responses over their constituent questions per student. In both

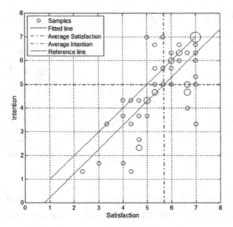

Fig. 3. Student satisfaction vs. intention (engagement). Circles' radii are proportional to the number of identical multiple samples.

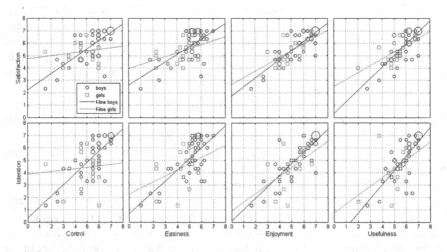

Fig. 4. Results of satisfaction and intention (engagement) vs. perceived control, easiness, enjoyment and usefulness aspects, categorized with respect to gender.

figures the vertical (y) axes describe the satisfaction (upper part of the figures) and the intention (lower part of the figures) values, while the horizontal (x) axes describe the perceived control, easiness, enjoyment and usefulness values. Both axes are calibrated to the 1–7 Likert scale. The marks represent the distribution of data with their size being proportional to the number of identical multiple values. Figure 4 distinguishes between boys and girls while Fig. 5 includes different marks with respect to age. Again, least squares regression lines are used to illustrate the observed values' trend.

Figure 4 shows that, overall, the perceived by the students control and easiness (for which the numerical analysis showed a high correlation factor of 0.82) do not significantly affect intention and satisfaction; especially when girl responses are

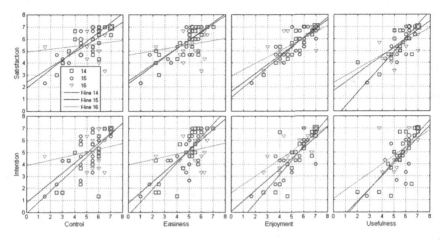

Fig. 5. Results of satisfaction and intention (engagement) vs. perceived control, easiness, enjoyment and usefulness, categorized with respect to age.

considered. Low easiness and (mainly) control values may well lead to high satisfaction and intention values. This leads to small slopes of the fitted lines that further indicate small correlation between perceived control/easiness and satisfaction/intention. Therefore, the original ability of the students (especially girls) to follow the activities and the difficulty of the scenario do not seem to be critical for student satisfaction and engagement. This has to do with proper design of the educational scenario, reasonable succession of the activities and quality of the accompanying material; preparation and performance of the tutors has to be pointed out as a major factor as well. Either way, the results attest that the activities were well accepted despite their difficulty.

In Fig. 5, the age analysis referring to the perceived control/easiness and satisfaction/intention aspects, clearly shows that the sixteen years old students did not correlate their positive perspective for satisfaction and intention to the easiness of the activities or their potential to attend. The opinions of lower aged students (14 and 15 years old) are more diverted and seem to relate strongly the easiness and ability aspects with their satisfaction and intention/engagement, although they still share positive feelings as the older ones. This outcome reveals a more "mature" behaviour of the 16ths towards UMI technologies, indicating, on the other hand, that the educational scenarios should probably be easier to satisfy and engage lower ages.

The students' gender and age analysis with respect to enjoyment-satisfaction and enjoyment-intention categories, as described in the corresponding diagrams of Figs. 4 and 5, reveals an almost linear dependence between the enjoyment-intention and especially enjoyment-satisfaction values. The individual samples present small dispersion and their distances from the corresponding fitted lines are low. To further enhance this relation, numerical analysis showed a correlation factor of 0.8 between enjoyment and satisfaction and 0.74 between enjoyment and intention. These are important features indicating that if or when the students' enjoyment increases, it is most likely that both satisfaction and intention scores will rise up. From this point of view, the design of future UMI, educational scenarios should be orientated to reinforce the interest, joy and excitement of the participants.

The ensemble mean usefulness value of 5.62 (Table 4), as well as the related to usefulness diagrams, for all student ages (Fig. 5) and both genders (Fig. 4), in which data is concentrated mainly in the top-right part of the graphs, provide clear evidence that the students considered the UMI learning activities to be very useful, and set usefulness (probably unexpectedly for these ages) as an important parameter towards high satisfaction and engagement. This outcome is significant and strongly indicates that the UMI event was successful and fulfilled its main scope.

Finally, it should be noted that in all types of questions, girls provided responses with scores of low average fluctuation. On the other hand, boys answered with significantly higher fluctuation in their opinions, while in all categories, especially in the intention one, their scores were higher. This might suggest that boys are more enthusiastic with UMI technologies or they better interact with their educational use, but still they can be more easily frustrated.

6 Conclusions

The UMI-Sci-Ed approach introduces model educational scenarios that incorporate UMI technologies both as educational means and learning outcomes, in order to promote novel and effective educational services while helping students to envision a future professional career in this scientific field. The objective of this work was to present the UMI-Sci-Ed training framework and especially one of its practical implementations, that is, the UMI Summer School 2018 event, the corresponding students' opinions gathered through properly designed surveys and their first analysis.

Setting student satisfaction and intention to follow similar activities at the core of the analysis in relation to student perceived ability, activity easiness, enjoyment and usefulness, certain useful inferences were drawn. Overall, the ensemble mean scores were found to be high in all evaluation aspects. However, deeper analysis revealed that female students provided more conservative results in comparison with male ones. Activities' perceived easiness and student ability to follow the activities was found to be less critical for girls and higher aged (16 years old) students. Usefulness and especially enjoyment, on the other hand, showed a clearer significance for satisfaction and intention (engagement) in all student categories. Finally, the analysis indicated that high student satisfaction rates do not necessarily combine with high engagement rates, an issue that needs reconsideration for the next steps of the project.

The above mentioned observations will be taken into account to improve the educational scenarios and activities in view of the broader phase pilots of the UMI-Sci-Ed project. As a next step, the presented results will be triangulated with semi-structured interviews, web metrics and in-class observations collected during the Summer School, so that to be cross-justified and enriched with further conclusions that will enhance the project educational methods' effectiveness and its potential impact on the design of novel future educational services via UMI technologies.

Acknowledgments. The UMI-Sci-Ed project has received funding from the European Union's Horizon 2020 research and innovation programme under grant agreement No 710583.

References

1. Bartel, A., Figas, P., Hagel, G.: Using a scenario-based approach for learning software engineering. In: Hagel, G., Mottok, J. (eds.) ECSEE – European Conference Software Engineering Education. Shaker, Aachen, pp. 167–179 (2014)
2. Elmore, B., Mariappan, J., Hays, G.: Improving performance through simulation - a scenario based learning approach. White Paper, Experia Solutions (2003)
3. Findeli, A.: Rethinking design education for the 21st century: theoretical, methodological, and ethical discussion. Des. Issues **17**(1), 5–17 (2001)
4. Goumopoulos, C., et al.: The UMI-Sci-Ed platform: integrating UMI technologies to promote science education. In: 10th International Conference on Computer Supported Education, vol. 2, pp. 78–90. SciTePress, Funchal (2018)
5. Iossifides, A., Zaharakis, I.D., Stefanis, V.: D1.1 – data management plan (v2.0), Public Deliverable, Horizon 2020 Project UMI-Sci-Ed, No. 710583 (2017)
6. Jing, H., Lo, D.C.-T., Ying, X., Lartigue, J.: Integrating internet of things (IoT) into STEM undergraduate education: case study of a modern technology infused courseware for embedded system course. In: 2016 IEEE Frontiers in Education Conference (FIE), pp. 1–9. Erie, PA, USA (2016)
7. Mavroudi, A., Divitini, M., Fragou, O., Giannakos, M.: D7.1 – evaluation concept-framework and piloting, public deliverable, Horizon 2020 Project UMI-Sci-Ed, No 710583 (2017)
8. Mavroudi, A., Divitini, M., Gianni, F., Mora, S., Kvittem, D.R.: Designing IoT applications in lower secondary schools, In: 2018 IEEE Global Engineering Education Conference (EDUCON), pp. 1120–1126. IEEE, Tenerife (2018)
9. Reiser, R.A., Dempsey, J.V.: Trends and issues in instructional design and technology. Pearson Merrill Prentice Hall, Upper Saddle River (2011)
10. Snyder, W., Briggs, X.N.D.S.: Communities of practice: a new tool for government managers. November 2003 Series Collaboration. IBM Center for the Business of Government (2003)
11. Wenger, E.: Communities of practice: a brief introduction. University of Oregon (2011)
12. Zaharakis, I.D., Sklavos, N., Kameas, A.D.: Exploiting ubiquitous computing, mobile computing and the internet of things to promote science education. In: 8th IFIP International Conference on New Technologies, Mobility & Security (NTMS 2016), pp. 1–2. IEEE, Cyprus (2016)

Rapid Prototyping Internet of Things Applications for Augmented Objects: The Tiles Toolkit Approach

Francesco Gianni[✉], Simone Mora, and Monica Divitini

Department of Computer Science, Norwegian University
of Science and Technology, Trondheim, Norway
{francesco.gianni,simone.mora,monica.divitini}@ntnu.no

Abstract. Designing and prototyping for IoT have historically required a diverse range of skills and a set of tools that individually supported only a fraction of the whole process, not being designed to work together. These tools usually require a certain level of proficiency in design methods, programming or electronics, depending on the phase addressed. Previous works on the Tiles Ideation toolkit and the RapIoT software framework demonstrated how the design phase can be democratized and how a simple programming paradigm can make coding for IoT a task accessible to non-experts. With this work we present and evaluate the process and the technologies involved in the programming and prototyping phase of an IoT application. The Tiles Square and the Tiles Temp are introduced, these two electronic devices complement and support IoT prototyping. They are designed to work in conjunction with the Tiles Ideation toolkit and are supported by the RapIoT software framework, allowing non-experts to augment and program everyday objects. We illustrate the potential of this approach by presenting the results obtained after workshops with 44 students. We conclude by discussing strengths and limitations of our approach, highlighting the lessons learned and possible improvements.

Keywords: Augmented objects · IoT · Rapid prototyping

1 Introduction

The Internet of Things (IoT) was originally introduced by Kevin Ashton in 1999 [2]. It encompass computers that embed everywhere in the physical environments that surround us, collecting data and independently sensing. Many technologies and architecture paradigms have historically found a place under the umbrella of Internet of Things, two prominent areas are wireless sensor networks (WSN) and solutions for machine-to-machine (M2M) networks. Less attention has been reserved to human-centered IoT, for example in the field of human computer interaction (HCI) [12]. Few works researched how IoT enables novel interaction modalities based on physical manipulation [1,6,13]. With our research we focus

© Springer Nature Switzerland AG 2018
A. Kameas and K. Stathis (Eds.): AmI 2018, LNCS 11249, pp. 204–220, 2018.
https://doi.org/10.1007/978-3-030-03062-9_16

on IoT as an enabling technology for object augmentation [14, p. 254], allowing the users to create tangible interfaces for direct physical interaction [7]. Smart objects and "things" become enabling artifacts for shared, collective, and collaborative activities [3]. Object augmentation is employed as a design strategy, as an expression of a creative process [15]. We also envision IoT as an ecology of devices which are small, untethered and energy efficient, wireless connected and operating on batteries. This approach aims to overcome the lack of mobility, which is a typical limitation of common IoT devices [4]. Being IoT a multifaceted concept, it is often difficult to grasp by people not directly involved in the field. Building an IoT system has always been a task reserved to engineers with a strong background in electronics, embedded systems and low level programming. These factors pose high entry barriers for IoT adoption and knowledge building. This situation has improved in the latest years, thanks to tools like Arduino [17], which facilitate microcontroller programming and standardize electronic assembly techniques. We aim at further extending the Arduino approach in lowering the entry barriers, allowing non-expert users to quickly prototype IoT applications for object augmentation and tangible interfaces. We define non-experts as users that do not have any skill in electronics, networking, or configuration of IoT devices. They do have instead some proficiency in the basic paradigms used by high-level programming languages such as JavaScript, Python, etc. Upper secondary school students often belong to this category. Despite the potential implications in terms of learning outcome and creative expression, few toolkits are able to support non-experts in rapid prototyping IoT applications involving ecologies of augmented objects [9]. We define an ecology as a group of networked devices and people that seamlessly exchange information. Our hands-on, workshop based approach envisions a learning journey about the concepts of IoT which starts from idea generation and brainstorming. The Tiles Ideation toolkit [19] has been successfully employed in support of this first step. Tiles is a card based toolkit to generate IoT ideas which tackle modern smart cities challenges through the ideation of novel applications for augmented objects. After completing this initial brainstorming phase, the students are able to switch to the actual implementation of the IoT application logic, prototyping the augmented objects just envisioned. The RapIoT framework [9] promises to simplify the wiring, reduce costs and time needed to create an IoT application, allowing students to focus only on the implementation, refinement and test of the application logic. This set of technologies supports the transition from the design brainstormed with the cards, to the prototyping of the augmented objects, including the programming phase of the application logic pictured. We use the term *prototyping* to describe the quick and tangible exploration in the physical world of the ideas generated by the users. The building blocks introduced with the Tiles Ideation toolkit are recalled and enriched during the programming and prototyping phase, progressively building knowledge without introducing new and overly complicated abstractions during each phase. In this paper, we present a study where 44 students created a working prototype of an IoT application based on ideas generated with the Tiles Ideation toolkit [19]. Everyday objects have been augmented through sensors and actuators. We designed and tested two electronic devices which are able to provide sense and feedback capabilities: the Tiles Square and the Tiles Temp. These devices are compatible with the RapIoT software framework and can (i) sense user interaction with the objects to which they are attached, (ii) provide sensor data about the objects itself, (iii) add sensory feedback capabilities to the objects, animating them with sound, vibration or light. We report how the students translated the ideas into code for the augmented objects, how they interacted with the development environment and how they used the electronic devices to create smart objects. More precisely, our research objectives concentrate on the evaluation of (i) how the participants grasped and acquired prototyping proficiency in the coding paradigm used, (ii) if they managed to prototype any augmented objects application designed with the Tiles Ideation toolkit and (iii) the outcomes in terms of knowledge, supporting a meaningful learning experience.

2 Related Work

Hardware Prototyping – Most hardware toolkits presented in literature are providing hardware modules small enough to be embedded into everyday objects and generic enough to be programmed for different scenarios. Their focus is on untethered operation, modularity and reusability. Untethered operation, meaning wireless connectivity and embedded power supply (batteries), is an enabling factor for the development of technologies that can disappear into everyday objects. In this perspective DUL Radio [5] provides tiny generic modules with an accelerometer embedded, to experiment prototyping sensor-based interactions. Modules stream their raw data to a PC over a serial link, making it available to other applications, and can run up to five days on a standard coin battery. Aiming at lowering the threshold of technical skills required for hardware development, BRIX [23] provides modular electronics embedded into Lego bricks while "Blades and Tiles" [21] presents a library of reusable hardware components. These works provide hardware modularity as a means to simplify prototyping. They hide into physical blocks the complexity of dealing with designing, soldering and wiring electronics. In this way, adding functionality (e.g. a temperature sensor or a vibration motor) to a device becomes as simple as snapping two Lego bricks together, requiring only writing the software. Modularity opens for reusability and scalability of components: functionalities can easily be added, removed or swapped across different prototypes, speeding up the design iterations and reducing costs, as demonstrated by [21]. The focus of these toolkits is however on hardware development, no support for writing the software to model the system behavior is provided.

Software Support for Prototyping – Hardware toolkits often require to be programmed with low level procedural languages which are usually oriented towards production rather than prototyping. On the other side, designers and non expert developers are more likely familiar with higher level and less complex programming languages, like web scripting ones. Abstractions can be provided in the form of proprietary textual or visual languages, APIs or wrappers for already existing languages. Arduino is a very popular prototyping platform which includes both a microcontroller-based board to which sensors and actuators can be wired to, and a software library and development environment [17]. The Arduino library spares developers from learning microcontroller-specific instructions or acquiring other electronic knowledge. Due to the simplicity and expressive power of the platform, a large community sharing open source code and schematics quickly grew after the public release. Modkit [18] extends the Arduino platform providing a block-based visual programming language based on the Scratch project [16], further expanding Arduino user base to non-professional developers such as kids and artists. Focusing on developing interfaces based on simple input/output feedback, Bloctopus [20] provides a platform based on self-contained, PC-tethered, modules with coupled sensors/actuators, and a hybrid visual/textual programming language. A different approach consists in providing developers with APIs that allow to control the hardware from third-party languages, therefore making the software development process language agnostic. This approach dramatically extends the user base, devices can be controlled by applications written in languages designed for simplicity or optimized towards performances. Several toolkits have taken this approach, Phidgets [10] provides APIs to control hardware modules via a programming paradigm similar to the ones used by graphical interfaces, while VoodooIO [22] provides APIs for a number of devices that can be freely arranged on a malleable control structure, to create fluid user interfaces.

The Tiles Position – Compared to the existing toolkits, the novelties of the tools presented in this article reside in (i) the complete and organic support from brainstorming to prototyping, (ii) the flexibility to operate with ecologies of interconnected, untethered devices, (iii) the focus on speed of development and simplicity, allowing to ideate and prototype an IoT application in less than a day, which is particularly beneficial when supporting learning in the educational domain.

3 Toolkits Employed and Prototyping Devices

We designed and manufactured the Tiles Square and Tiles Temp electronic devices to enable the creation of user-programmable augmented objects. Both the devices embed a bluetooth low energy (BLE) microcontroller and a rechargeable lithium battery. They use ultra low power components and have a battery life of several hours, while maintaining a compact form factor. The creative and educative process to generate an IoT application starts with the design and brainstorming phase, for which the Tiles Ideation toolkit is used. Students can then program the application logic using the RapIoT software framework. Finally they can build a prototype using augmented objects, thanks to the Tiles Square and Tiles Temp electronic devices. The logic of the IoT application can be programmed using a simplified DSL[1] based on JavaScript. The Cloud9[2] online IDE[3], which is integrated in the RapIoT software framework [9], is used to write the code.

Design and Brainstorming: Tiles Ideation Toolkit – The Tiles Ideation toolkit [19] is composed of several decks of cards and a workshop protocol to engage non-experts in idea generation. The toolkit also includes: (i) a cardboard, that scaffolds the use and placement of the cards, facilitates group collaboration, and contains a storyboarding and reflection phase, (ii) a playbook to guide the users step-by-step in the ideation process, (iii) user-centered design artifacts such as *personas* and *scenarios*, to address specific problem domains [8]. The ideation workshop starts with the selection of an arbitrary number of every-day objects, represented in the *things* cards. These objects are then *augmented* through the addition of sensing and actuation capabilities: *sensors*, *services* and *human actions* cards allow to trigger a specific reaction in the object when data coming from the ambient or from online services is received, or when the object is physically manipulated by a human being [8]. *Feedback* cards are used to specify how the object reacts when triggered. In addition, *connectors* cards can be used to indicate a condition that joins the behaviour of two or more smart objects. Finally, *missions* and *criteria* cards are used to stimulate divergent-convergent thinking and promote reflective learning [8]. All the card decks adopt the same graphic style and are color coded to be easily recognizable. Each deck has a *custom card*: a blank card that can be personalized directly by the users during the ideation workshop. This ideation phase usually lasts less than two hours, and produces a concrete application idea, together with one or more use cases visualized in the storyboard. The Tiles Ideation toolkit has been previously evaluated [19] and it's not the object of the user test reported in this article.

Programming: RapIoT – The RapIoT software framework is a collection of software tools targeting non-expert developers. RapIoT aims at facilitating rapid prototyping and coding of IoT applications for augmented objects. It is centered around a simple, event-based API, which also defines the messaging protocol. Data is exchanged in a human readable format, the messages are composed of comma separated text fields, and called input or output primitives (ex. *"temp, 23"*, or *"led, on, red"*). Augmented objects can generate one or more input primitives which are usually triggered by user interaction or represent sensor data. Output primitives are instead sent to the objects to provide feedback to the user, like sound, vibration or light. The objects are connected to the cloud through a mobile application for smartphones, which acts as a gateway. Using RapIoT, the functionalities exposed by different sensors and actuators are immediately available to the programmers through the integrated IDE. The electronic devices can be employed immediately, without flashing the firmware of the microcontroller or connecting them to a pc. RapIoT allows coding

---

[1] Domain Specific Language.

[2] https://c9.io.

[3] Integrated Development Environment.

applications that make use of ecologies of IoT devices. A single application logic can orchestrate input/output primitives received from and transmitted to different augmented objects.

Prototyping: Tiles Square and Tiles Temp – The Tiles Square (Fig. 1) is designed to sense user interaction with objects and provide sensory feedback. It measures 45×45 mm and has onboard an accelerometer, a touch controller, an RGB led, a buzzer to provide audible feedback, and a vibration motor for haptic feedback. The firmware of the device is programmed to expose a set of input and output primitives, which abstract the complexity of dealing directly with the electronic sensors and actuators. The Tiles Temp device (Fig. 1) is able to provide measurements of temperature and relative humidity of the objects which is attached to. It measures 60×25 mm, mounts two separate high-accuracy, ultra low power sensors for temperature and relative humidity. It also mounts an RGB led that can be used to provide a simple visual feedback.

Fig. 1. The Tiles Squares, Tiles Temp and Tiles cards representing the input primitives.

An Holistic Approach to IoT – Looking at Fig. 1 (right), the connection between all the tools presented is made apparent: the *temperature* and *humidity* cards of the Tiles Ideation toolkit are also implemented as RapIoT primitives, these primitives are generated by the Tiles Temp electronic devices and forwarded to the cloud through the smartphone app, which acts as a BLE-WiFi gateway. This approach simplifies the transition between the three phases since the workshop participants can reuse and enrich the concepts learned in the previous steps. Another advantage is the possibility to easily extend or adapt the experience to specific domains. If a new electronic device for prototyping is introduced, the user only need to have a description of its primitives to use it, and eventually create the corresponding cards.

4   Field Deployment

We tested the prototyping process and tools with 3 classes of students aged 14 to 17, for a total of 44 users. More than 80% of them declared to have a rather limited experience in coding, while only 3 declared to have advanced or expert coding skills. Almost 70% of the students had very limited or no experience at all in JavaScript, the language adopted by RapIoT to program the application logic. None of them declared to be an expert in JavaScript, in fact more than 65% knew Python best. The students were divided in groups of 4–5, each group had at its disposal (i) a 10 pages booklet with step by step instructions about how to set up the development environment and the electronic devices, a list of coding tasks and some sample code, (ii) a list of all the input/output primitives available, (iii) a laptop used to access the online IDE and program the IoT applications using the RapIoT framework, (iv) 3–4 Tiles Square and Tiles Temp electronic devices, (v) a smartphone used as gateway to connect the electronic devices to internet, (vi) some paper tape and rapid prototyping material to attach the electronic devices to real object, (vii) a set of Tiles cards representing objects, input and output primitives, together with the Tiles cardboard used as a tabletop game board to organize the cards. A picture of the workshop setup is reported in Fig. 2. The groups were given 2–3 h to follow the instructions in the booklet, coding as many tasks as possible. The instructions on the booklet were intended to be followed in autonomy by the students, but at least one researcher was always available to support the groups if required. The participants were also asked to arrange the Tiles cards on the cardboard to reflect the code written in the application, as well as to change the code based on a provided card configuration.

Fig. 2. A group of students programming the Tiles Squares. In the picture are also visible the booklet, the list of primitives, the Tiles cards and the cardboard.

The very first task the students were called to complete was the test of some sample code provided, in order to familiarize with the development environment, the deployment and testing process, and the Tiles electronic devices. As a second task, the students were asked to develop an application from scratch, following the requirements provided in the task description. To present to the students the desired behavior of the final application, a picture of six Tiles cards placed on the cardboard was also used. The next tasks challenged the students into modifying the application just created, for example using different objects or input/output primitives, while at the same time connecting to the card-based representation. Finally, in the last task the students were asked to develop a new application which made use of both the Tiles Temp and Tiles Square devices.

Data Collection and Analysis – We collected data through questionnaires, observations during the workshops, direct feedback provided by the students during the activities and analyzing the code of the IoT applications produced. The data from the questionnaires came from 39 students, since 5 of them didn't complete it. In the questionnaire, the students were also asked to answer five test questions related to a specific snippet of code reported, which contained new primitives and objects, not previously used during the workshop coding session. This small test was intended to further assess their understanding of the programming paradigm, based on input/output primitives. We analyzed the data from the questionnaires using a spreadsheet software, extracting relevant statistics connected to the research objectives reported in Sect. 1. Transcriptions of the observations were reviewed to extract insights, spot weaknesses and identify recurring patterns. The code of the IoT applications developed was reviewed, checked for errors and consistency with the coding tasks provided. To frame our analysis we used deductive analytic approaches, in connection with our research objectives described in Sect. 1. The deductive analysis examined the ways in which observed behaviors and reported perceptions contributed to the narrative framed by the research objectives, in either a positive or negative way. In addition, we employed inductive approaches to allow new themes to emerge from the data. Finally we reflected on the complete result set, discussing the experience from a bird's-eye view of the deductive/inductive analysis and the results emerged from quantitative data.

5 Findings

In Table 1 the statements contained in the questionnaire are reported. Their ID is used as a reference when presenting the statistics regarding the answers.

Open Ended vs Goal Oriented Activities – The students started the workshop reading the instructions and following the first coding task contained in the booklet, which provided a high level description of the behaviour of the applications to be developed. Several participants followed the instructions only until they managed to get the first lines of code working, basically making the Tiles devices react to some kind of physical input. At that point they decided to deviate from the original task to experiment with different input/output primitives, sometimes also revising the application logic. We noticed their excitement and enthusiasm every time they experienced the outcomes of their own code on the physical world, through the Tiles devices. This state of euphoria steered away their attention from the playbook and the intended workshop program, shifting their interest towards more open ended activities.

Connecting Design and Prototyping – All the groups had at their disposal a set of Tiles cards and a cardboard, to complement and connect the coding tasks with a representation of the IoT application normally used during the design

Table 1. Questionnaire statements.

ID	Statement
St1	I liked the prototyping workshop
St2	The workshop was something fun to do
St3	I feel that i learned something new
St4	The scenarios given for prototyping were easy to understand
St5	The scenarios given for prototyping were easy to implement with code
St6	The provided technical documentation was all i need to do the activity
St7	The provided technical documentation was easy to understand
St8	It was easy to setup the prototyping environment
St9	The steps of the prototyping process were easy to follow
St10	I managed to run and use the application i prototyped
St11	I have some ideas about how to extend my application
St12	Now i feel i can build more prototypes without help

and brainstorming phase. Only a couple of groups however used the cards and the board as indicated in the booklet. While these groups performed the tasks involving the cards without difficulties, the rest of the groups simply skipped such tasks. On one side this suggests a path of continuity between the Tiles model used for ideation and the prototyping phase, but it should also be noted that the participants demonstrated scarce interest in connecting back to the Tiles cards during the prototyping phase. The limited time at disposal didn't help either, students preferred to concentrate their efforts in the coding and prototyping activities, avoiding to switch back to the design phase.

The Coding Experience – Although the RapIoT integrated IDE was designed for a single user, as soon as the participants realized it was browser based, they asked to use it in a collaborative way: *"can we code together?"*. Unfortunately that was not possible. However, in one of its latest versions the online IDE introduced the option to code the same application simultaneously from different workstations, enabling the possibility to add the collaborative programming feature in a future release of RapIoT. Despite the lack of support for simultaneous coding, pupils often paired when programming the application. They usually teamed in number of 2–3 to write, test and debug the code. They confirmed their preference about the size of the group in the comments section of the questionnaire: *"Make smaller groups so that we can do more work individually. You don't really need more than two people in one group to work on the tiles"*. Others code-related comments expressed the need to simplify the JavaScript DSL used to encapsulate the primitives. Several participants commented that it may be useful to *"explain some of the code"*, and that *"[was difficult to] understand why the code was put where it was"*. On the other hand, several other students commented that the easiest task during the workshop was *"[to] code"*, *"programming"*, *"follow the steps, and write in the code"*, *"solve the code"* and *"writing the actual code"*. This led us to believe that the paradigm of the primitives is simple enough to be mastered, but the DSL is too verbose and not self-explicative, confusing the participants especially when reading the very first examples, before writing any code. A more intuitive DSL or programming paradigm might improve code readability and be less intimidating for non-expert developers approaching the platform for the first time. The questionnaire data reported in Fig. 3, recorded a positive sentiment regarding the support provided by the toolkit, the workshop format and the documentation provided to the students. The data confirmed our observations during the workshops: the groups achieved a good level of independence when programming. Most of the support was provided by the toolkit and the documentation, while the intervention of the researchers was mostly limited to solve connectivity problems.

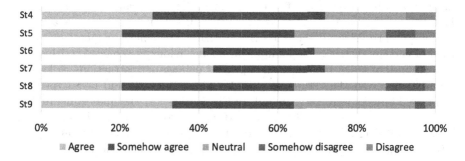

Fig. 3. Results of the questionnaire statements on the ability of the toolkit and the workshop to facilitate prototyping, allowing participants to work independently.

Proficiency in Coding and Prototyping – The guidelines for deployment and setup of the toolkit included all the steps necessary to prepare the Tiles devices and the development environment for the coding session. Such steps include (i) creating an application container from the development environment, (ii) adding a virtual handler for each physical Tiles, to be later used in the IDE when coding (iii) turning on the Tiles devices and pairing them with the mobile application gateway via bluetooth. The participants successfully completed in autonomy all the steps required. We assessed the proficiency in the coding paradigm analyzing the application code produced, the observations collected during the workshops and the answers to the test questions included in the questionnaire. We report in Fig. 4 the results relative to the five test questions. More than 80% of the respondents answered correctly to at least 3 of the questions, while almost 20% answered correctly to all of them.

IoT App Creation and Prototyping Outcome – The final application code delivered by all the groups was syntactically correct and consistent with the tasks addressed. Despite that, during the workshops we noticed that some groups experienced runtime errors when launching their application. However, the quick iterations between coding and testing on the Tiles devices allowed them to troubleshoot and fix the bugs without loosing too much time. The students were

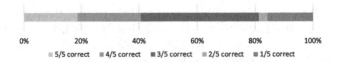

0%   20%   40%   60%   80%   100%

■ 5/5 correct   ■ 4/5 correct   ■ 3/5 correct   ■ 2/5 correct   ■ 1/5 correct

Fig. 4. Results of the coding test quiz.

able to augment the physical objects included in their application idea. In Fig. 6 shows the augmented objects used by a group, which employed a coffee cup and a computer mouse for their "smart cup" application. A Tiles Temp device was attached under a cup to sense the temperature of the coffee, while a Tiles Square was attached to a computer mouse. The goal of the application was to silently notify the user, without disturbing fellow colleagues, when the coffee was at the right temperature to be consumed. The application code intercepts the temperature input primitive fired by the Tiles Temp, and triggers a vibration output primitive on the Tiles Square when the coffee temperature drops below a certain threshold. This application behaviour is achieved writing less then 10 lines of code, including the optional debugging instructions to log the primitives received. The students who developed the code and prototyped the augmented objects were 14 years old. In Fig. 5 we report the questionnaire data regarding the perceived ability of the participants to create an IoT application. They generally agreed with the statements related to the ability to develop the IoT application concept. They were however less confident in declaring of being able to create other prototypes without help from the researchers, despite the

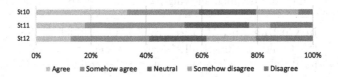

St10
St11
St12

0%   20%   40%   60%   80%   100%

■ Agree   ■ Somehow agree   ■ Neutral   ■ Somehow disagree   ■ Disagree

Fig. 5. Results of the questionnaire statements on the ability to create the IoT application.

Fig. 6. The Tiles Square and the Tiles Temp employed to augment the objects in the "smart cup" application.

fact that they successfully produced one or more IoT applications during the workshop. Triangulating this last statement with our observations, the low level of confidence might be explained if we take into consideration the technical interruptions experienced when interacting with the electronic devices. These connection issues slowed down the prototyping process and were temporary mitigated or fixed by the researchers in order to allow the participants to complete the coding tasks.

Learning Experience – In Fig. 7 the results of the questionnaire statements related to the learning outcome and experience are reported. The respondents were generally positive about the perceived enjoyment of the workshop activity and the learning experience. However, there seems to be space for improvements: a significant portion of the users remained neutral when answering the statements reported in Fig. 7. The participants were also asked what they thought they have learned. Several improved their knowledge of JavaScript or their coding skills, *"[I learned] more JavaScript"*, *"[I learned] a bit more coding"*, *"[I learned] what code means, not just copy-paste"*. Others instead experienced the learning as more related to the concepts of IoT and programming of physical interfaces, *"[I learned] how to program hardware"*, *"[I learned] programming to IoT, Tiles"*, *"I learned a lot about sensors and how they connect with each other. I also got a little bit more experienced with how to use them and how I write the code"*, *"[I learned] more about inventing new stuff and more coding"*.

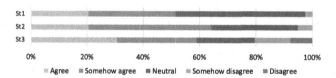

Fig. 7. Results of the questionnaire statements on perceived learning and enjoyment.

6   Discussion and Design Implications

Prototyping and Coding Proficiency – The participants understood and successfully employed the primitive based coding paradigm during the workshops. It was interesting to notice that after receiving the first physical feedback, some of the students started to code their own applications, discarding the tasks provided. While on one side this shift in focus interfered with the activity plan of the workshops, it was also an encouraging twist since suggested appropriation of the tools, interest, and excitement in experimenting with the input/output primitives. The pupils were confident enough to deviate from the guided script, eager to discover how the electronic devices and the objects would react to certain primitives. This motivated them to code an application making use of such primitives, even if they were not instructed to do so. These open ended, improvised activities might be an indication of technology appropriation and a confirmation of the low entry barriers of the platform, which are important requirements when targeting non-experts. In addition, the fact that open ended activities were preferred, might indicate that the toolkit can be useful to spark creativity in the pupils, and can be successfully utilized even without a predefined set of tasks or the supervision of an expert. Other aspects are also of great relevance when addressing non-experts, like the fact that the electronic devices are self-contained, compact, completely cable-free and do not require long or complicated deploy procedures.

Collaboration in Coding Activities – Observing the groups coding, we noticed how pair programming emerged to be a useful strategy for the prototyping phase. However, since the groups were usually composed by 4–5 students, some of them didn't find space to contribute in the development process. In order to maximize participation and engagement, and to avoid excluding participants from the workshop experience, groups of 2–3 students are more appropriate. A future extension of RapIoT might also explore collaborative coding from different workstations. The desire to code simultaneously was expressed directly by the participants, but was not confirmed by additional data. During the workshop, the best groups completed up to three coding tasks, creating at least a couple of IoT applications. The application example reported in Fig. 6 was developed by a group of 14 year old students, which were the youngest and less experienced among the participants. Given the non-expert background of the participants, the technology involved, and the time at disposal, the fact that at least one running application had been produced by all the groups can be considered an encouraging result, in line with the rapid prototyping approach and the research objectives reported in Sect. 1. Another emerging behavior was observed during the workshops: the appropriation of the application idea supported user's commitment. When they generated their own idea, deviating from predefined coding tasks, the students were more dedicated to turn it into a prototype, overcoming the coding challenges. This outcome is an important validation, and a point of strength, of the whole process supported by the Tiles toolkit, which spaces from the brainstorming and ideation phase, and connects to the creation of a prototype. Although the design and prototyping phases present a continuity path, the users preferred to have them as two separated activities, where the first one can feed the second, but do not frequently intertwine in a continuous feedback loop. They didn't spend much time, if any, going back and reviewing the idea represented by the cards, despite being a required step of a few of the coding tasks.

Providing Quick Feedback – We believe, given the dynamics observed during the workshops, that an additional simplification of the coding style could eliminate further barriers. This has proven to increase participation in collective activities [11], and could help to reduce even more the time needed to have the first lines of code running, getting a quick first glance over the physical effects on the objects. The time window between the start of the coding activities and the first feedback experienced on the physical object is critical to support adoption, engagement, and to motivate the users. The shorter the temporal window, the sooner the participants gain confidence about the prototyping process, receiving valuable feedback about the efforts put in coding the application logic. The results obtained are encouraging and validate positively the model used and the transition from idea to prototype. Advancing the technical infrastructure and creating a more robust and resilient framework, might allow to speed up consistently the prototyping process, enabling a workflow that is completely independent from the supervision of the researchers.

A Meaningful Learning Experience – Insights about the learning outcome were gathered through the questionnaire, from direct user feedback and from the developed IoT application. The students demonstrated to have acquired some basic programming skills in JavaScript, a language none of them mastered. The notions of IoT and programming of physical interactive objects were also part of the learning experience, as declared by the students. Creating an IoT application using RapIoT requires the understanding of the event based programming paradigm, used by its input/output primitives. This outcome was confirmed by the code produced, and reinforced by the results of the quiz test. Due to the collaborative nature of the workshop, other less technical skills were part of the learning process. For example, coordination skills were needed when pair programming, as well as to debug the application produced.

Lessons Learned and Guidelines – We summarize here a list of guidelines and lessons learned which emerged from our experience during the workshops, and might facilitate both future developments of the Tiles toolkit and similar activities involving technological applications in education.

Researcher – their role should facilitate the adoption of the technology, avoiding to intimidate the participants from too close, empathizing with their experience without disrupting their creative flow. They might nudge, spark creativity and curiosity, gently challenging the students into exploring how the tools can support their ideas, and stepping aside when not needed.

Teachers – they act as a social bridge between the pupils and the new experience, keeping them motivated and focused on the activity. They are almost always perceived as a recognized and trusted figure by the students, the same does not necessarily applies to the researchers.

Technology – for a time constrained activity, it's important to keep the technological access barriers low, providing a first feedback and insights of the toolkit capabilities early in the process. This strategy can quickly spark self motivation and curiosity in the pupils, pushing them to explore and experiment the solution space provided by the toolkit.

Organization – while the brainstorming phase has proven to be working best with groups of 4–5 students, the same is not true for the prototyping and programming phase. From the observations gathered during the programming phase, we reached the conclusion that a number of 2–3 students per group is an ideal trade-off to maximize collaboration and inclusion in the coding activity.

7   Conclusion and Future Work

We introduced in this paper an holistic approach to IoT application design, programming and prototyping for non-expert users. We presented the set of tools employed in such process, with special emphasis on the prototyping phase. We evaluated the learning experience and the technologies involved during educational workshops with 44 students aged 14–17. During the workshops, the participants deployed the technology and performed a series of coding tasks, which gradually guided them into the creation of a functional IoT application involving smart, connected objects. We analyzed quantitative and qualitative data collected during the workshops, and discussed the results in terms of acquired coding skills, prototyping proficiency, and learning experience. We elaborated on the approach employed and the lessons learned. Finally we distilled a set of guidelines useful to improve the workshop protocol and the prototyping platform. Future developments will be oriented to further simplify the programming approach and improve the robustness of the software framework. While the primitives are a flexible data exchange format, and are easier to use than a fully structured API, they are not part of a standard API, approved or adopted by internationally recognized organizations. Several IoT APIs and network protocols, like DotDot[4], oneIoTa[5] and W3C's Web of Things[6] have been proposed by different organizations, in an effort to standardize device interoperability. Adopting one of these standards, together with a visual programming language, might allow for better system integration, maintaining a comparable level of complexity for the users.

Acknowledgements. We thank the students who have contributed to the development of the framework and to its evaluation. The user study reported in the paper is co-funded by EU Horizon2020 under grant agreement No. 710583 (UMI-Si-Ed project, http://umi-sci-ed.eu/).

References

1. Angelini, L., Mugellini, E., Abou Khaled, O., Couture, N.: Internet of Tangible Things (IoTT): challenges and opportunities for tangible interaction with IoT. Informatics **5**(1), 1–34 (2018)
2. Ashton, K.: That "Internet of Things" thing. RFiD J. **22**(7), 97–114 (2009)
3. Bødker, S.: Third-wave HCI, 10 years later–participation and sharing. Interactions **22**(5), 24–31 (2015)
4. Botta, A., De Donato, W., Persico, V., Pescapé, A.: On the integration of cloud computing and Internet of Things. In: 2014 International Conference on Future Internet of Things and Cloud (FiCloud), pp. 23–30. IEEE (2014)
5. Brynskov, M., Lunding, R., Vestergaard, L.S.: The design of tools for sketching sensor-based interaction. In: Proceedings of the Sixth International Conference on Tangible, Embedded and Embodied Interaction, pp. 213–216 (2012)

---

[4] https://www.speakdotdot.com/.
[5] https://oneiota.org/.
[6] https://www.w3.org/WoT/.

6. Eris, O., Drury, J., Ercolini, D.: A collaboration-focused taxonomy of the Internet of Things. In: 2015 IEEE 2nd World Forum on Internet of Things (WF-IoT), pp. 29–34 (2015)
7. Fishkin, K.P., Gujar, A., Harrison, B.L., Moran, T.P., Want, R.: Embodied user interfaces for really direct manipulation. Commun. ACM **43**(9), 74–80 (2000)
8. Gianni, F., Divitini, M.: Designing IoT applications for smart cities: extending the tiles ideation toolkit. IxD&A **35**, 100–116 (2018)
9. Gianni, F., Mora, S., Divitini, M.: RapIoT toolkit: rapid prototyping of collaborative Internet of Things applications. J. Futur. Gener. Comput. Syst. (2018). https://doi.org/10.1016/j.future.2018.02.030
10. Greenberg, S.: Collaborative physical user interfaces. In: Communication and Collaboration Support Systems (2004)
11. Grudin, J., Poltrock, S.: Computer supported cooperative work. In: Encyclopedia of Human-Computer Interaction (2012)
12. Koreshoff, T.L., Leong, T.W., Robertson, T.: Approaching a human-centred Internet of Things. In: Proceedings of the 25th Australian Computer-Human Interaction Conference: Augmentation, Application, Innovation, Collaboration, pp. 363–366 (2013)
13. Koreshoff, T.L., Robertson, T., Leong, T.W.: Internet of Things: a review of literature and products. In: Proceedings of the 25th Australian Computer-Human Interaction Conference: Augmentation, Application, Innovation, Collaboration, OzCHI 2013, Adelaide, Australia, pp. 335–344. ACM (2013)
14. Kuniavsky, M.: Smart Things: Ubiquitous Computing User Experience Design. Elsevier, Amsterdam (2010)
15. Loomis, M.E.S., Shah, A.V., Rumbaugh, J.E.: An object modeling technique for conceptual design. In: Bézivin, J., Hullot, J.-M., Cointe, P., Lieberman, H. (eds.) ECOOP 1987. LNCS, vol. 276, pp. 192–202. Springer, Heidelberg (1987). https://doi.org/10.1007/3-540-47891-4_18
16. Maloney, J., Resnick, M., Rusk, N., Silverman, B., Eastmond, E.: The Scratch programming language and environment. ACM Trans. Comput. Educ. (TOCE) **10**(4) (2010). Article No. 16
17. Mellis, D., Banzi, M., Cuartielles, D., Igoe, T.: Arduino: an open electronic prototyping platform. In: Proceedings of CHI Extended Abstracts, pp. 1–11. ACM (2007)
18. Millner, A., Baafi, E.: Modkit: blending and extending approachable platforms for creating computer programs and interactive objects. In: Proceedings of the 10th International Conference on Interaction Design and Children, IDC 2011, Ann Arbor, Michigan, pp. 250–253. ACM (2011)
19. Mora, S., Gianni, F., Divitini, M.: Tiles: a card-based ideation toolkit for the Internet of Things. In: Proceedings of the 2017 Conference on Designing Interactive Systems, DIS 2017, Edinburgh, UK, pp. 587–598. ACM (2017)
20. Sadler, J., Durfee, K., Shluzas, L., Blikstein, P.: Bloctopus: a novice modular sensor system for playful prototyping. In: TEI 2015: Proceedings of the Ninth International Conference on Tangible, Embedded, and Embodied Interaction, pp. 347–354. ACM, January 2015
21. Sankaran, R., et al.: Decoupling interaction hardware design using libraries of reusable electronics. In: Proceedings of the 3rd International Conference on Tangible and Embedded Interaction, pp. 331–337 (2009)

22. Villar, N., Gellersen, H.: A malleable control structure for softwired user interfaces. In: Proceedings of the 1st International Conference on Tangible and Embedded Interaction, pp. 49–56 (2007)
23. Zehe, S., Grosshauser, T., Hermann, T.: BRIX–an easy-to-use modular sensor and actuator prototyping toolkit. In: 2012 IEEE International Conference on Pervasive Computing and Communications Workshops (PERCOM Workshops), pp. 817–822 (2012)

Out of the Box: Using Gamification Cards to Teach Ideation to Engineering Students

Christos Sintoris[1]([email]) (iD), Irene Mavrommati[2] (iD), Nikolaos Avouris[1] (iD), and Ioannis Chatzigiannakis[3] (iD)

[1] University of Patras, Patras, Greece
{sintoris,avouris}@upatras.gr
[2] CTI - Computer Technology Institute and Press,
and Hellenic Open University, Patras, Greece
mavrommati@eap.gr
[3] Sapienza University of Rome, Rome, Italy
ichatz@diag.uniroma1.it

Abstract. This paper reports on innovative teaching interventions in the frame of Internet of Things (IoT) design ideation classes. A card-based gamification approach has been applied in two different engineering masters courses. The participating students had already a good understanding of IoT technologies and they were asked to produce innovative designs by using them. We examine here the produced design ideas and the students' perception of the collaborative design process and tools. The paper discusses broader issues relating to applicability of design- and ideation-focused gamification methods in the context of engineering education and the effect they have on collaborative design and innovation.

Keywords: Internet of Things · Ideation method · Card-based design

1 Introduction

The general goal of engineering courses in Internet of Things (IoT) is to establish a clear view of the technological landscape of the Internet of Things. The range of technologies that students need to understand, from low-power embedded devices, low-power and long-range wireless networking, up to cloud environments, is vast. Engineering education should address the need for skills such as flexibility and ability to work in a broader multi-disciplinary perspective, which are recognized as key skills for the 4th industrial revolution [3]. Towards addressing this need, the University of Patras and the Sapienza University of Rome introduced design methods for ideation in different IoT classes, as part of course workshops. The aim was to investigate what engineering students gain from such design methods, and assess the weaknesses and strong points of such interventions in teaching design ideation. The workshops produced some interesting findings in terms of the applicability and usefulness of such methods,

© Springer Nature Switzerland AG 2018
A. Kameas and K. Stathis (Eds.): AmI 2018, LNCS 11249, pp. 221–226, 2018.
https://doi.org/10.1007/978-3-030-03062-9_17

with a particular perspective in the generation of innovative ideas, i.e. aiming to assess if this approach allows for 'out-of-the-box' design thinking. Design cards have been used extensively to guide the processes of ideation and negotiation, allowing introduction of new and different perspectives [2,4].

2   User Studies

The Tiles IoT Toolkit [5] (version 0.6) was used in the interventions presented here. The Toolkit contains 21 design *missions* cards, centered on human needs and desires, 25 *things* cards for connected and interactive technological artifacts, 9 cards on *human actions* and 9 on *feedback*, describing how people can interact with things, *services* (25 cards), with popular apps and online services for IoT communication, and finally 10 evaluation *criteria* cards. The rules were adapted in each intervention in order for the ideation activity to be constrained within the time limits of the workshop and to give a more playful character by introducing turn taking, and roles of defender and attacker of cards, as discussed next.

The Tiles IoT Tookit was used in design workshops in three separate occasions. Two of the workshops were organized in the frame of the graduate course 'Design of Interactive Systems' of the Combined Master's in Electrical and Computer Engineering of the University of Patras (UPatras), in two consecutive years, in the spring of 2017 and 2018 respectively [1]. In April 2018, a third IoT design workshop was organized in the frame of the 'Master's degree course in Pervasive Systems' in the Department of Computer, Control, and Management Engineering at Sapienza University of Rome (UniRoma). The use of the ideation toolkit and the design tasks differed in the two cases, as discussed next.

In the University of Patras, in total, 30 final year students participated in the workshops (ages 24–26). The first cohort (2017) had 12 students, in 3 groups of 4, while the second cohort (2018) provided data by 18 students, arranged in 4 groups of 4 or 5 students each. The design workshops had a duration of approximately 2 h.

The UniRoma workshop consisted of 31 (ages 22–30) students, split into 13 project groups. The workshop was organized in two sessions. Only data from the first session is included here, since the second session was focused on presenting and criticizing the designs of the teams.

Fig. 1. A typical design session with the Tiles IoT Toolkit.

Design task: The UPatras students were given the task of designing an innovative cultural heritage application or device. The 2017 cohort was asked to support visitors of an unspecified museum, without further specifying the type of device, or the characteristics of the museum. The 2018 cohort was asked to design an IoT application for the visitors of the archaeological site of Pompeii in Italy.

In the UniRoma workshop, unlike the UPatras workshops, each team individually determined its design task at the beginning phase of the workshop, however the students were more constrained in the use of the Tiles IoT Toolkit.

Procedure: In the UPatras workshops, each group used a full deck of Tiles cards and board (Fig. 1). The sessions were organized in phases: For every phase, each team member drew cards in turn, and when the player found one she thought was relevant, she argued defending it, while the rest argued for rejecting it. Teams were instructed to agree on 2–3 cards in each phase. In the first phase (50 min duration) they drew from the 21 *mission* cards in order to investigate possible design missions, then followed by 25 *thing* cards. Next, they used the *human actions* cards and corresponding *feedback* cards. Having selected the cards, they had to proceed with defining some scenarios of use for their design.

In the final phase of the workshop they had to use *criteria* cards for evaluating their proposal. Finally, they had to photograph the material and reflect individually on their design and prepare an individual report, to be handed in a week later. They were also asked to evaluate the tools and the group activity.

In the UniRoma workshop, the students were split in groups of 2–3 people. After an introductory discussion, the workshop facilitator handed to each group one or two *mission* cards, to reflect on context and to describe the subject area of the missions and what it can include (5–7 min duration). The workshop facilitator moved between them to stir ideas when they seemed stuck.

Next, each group presented the subject of their design task. As the presentations progressed, the facilitator wrote keyword-clouds on the board, linking different subject areas. Similarities between the groups emerged, on the basis of which, ten larger teams were formed. Next, selected *things* and *human action* cards were handed to the new teams. They were asked to continue brainstorming, with a more concrete scenario on their design task, to solve real problems with IoT application suggestions. The facilitator helped teams that seemed stuck by asking prompt questions. After 15 min of team brainstorm, they quickly presented their results to the other groups, aiming to cross-fertilize their ideas.

After the presentations, near the end of the two-hour session, the students were asked to individually evaluate the process and put their thoughts about the Tiles cards process in writing. These comments, along with the reports submitted by the UPatras cohorts, form the basis of the following analysis.

3   Designs

The UPatras groups produced the following design ideas: (a) A tablet and stylus device, through which the visitor can pick up the colour of a real object and use it to draw shapes on the tablet, inspired by the exhibit. (b) A smartwatch and headphones for a personalized guide in the museum. (c) An augmented reality glasses guide of the museum, that allows watching videos related to exhibits. (d) An immersive virtual reality application at various VR stations, providing experience of the site as it used to be augmented with avatars of current visitors. (e) Smart glasses presenting images of the exhibits, as they used to be, augmented with audio and text. (f) A head-mounted display and glass in a special room, providing virtual reality experiences of the site as it used to be. (g) An augmented reality application that allows the visitor to see the place as it used to be.

As one can observe, the produced designs lack in innovation and are mostly variations of the same idea, reflecting current trends and applications in museums and archaeological sites with virtual and augmented reality components.

The URoma groups produced the following design ideas: (a) Innovative authentication process using user's hardware and cloud resources. (b) A smart luggage that automatically checks its content and provides suggestions of what to pack and a reminder of when to pack. (c) A smart aquarium that can feed the fish and monitor their well-being. (d) Smart contact lenses that provide information about the emotional state of people around the user. (e) A smart bracelet that contains personal identification documents such as identity card, passport, credit card etc. (f) A device to record and manage track training exercise. (g) A neural computer-to-human interface that enhances human cognitive abilities. (h) An in-car sensing system for road pothole detection and reporting. (i) A bed with mechanical alarm that does not allow oversleeping. (j) A general architecture to integrate IoT hardware through a single interface. In the UniRoma case we have wider diversity as the task was not constraint by a specific problem, however some of the produced designs were either inspired by science fiction (e.g. neural-computer interface to augment human intellect) or smart devices (luggage, aquarium, bracelet) that sense the world and react to it, implementing more typical IoT applications.

The more diverse designs produced by UniRoma students reflect the fact that they were faced with an open design task.

4 Analysis

The students' comments were further analyzed following a structural coding approach [6], that allows the exploratory investigation of the participants' responses. After reviewing the students' feedback, an initial code list was developed, and used to code the responses. Subsequently, in two iterations, the code list was evaluated, revised and re-applied. The resulting list contains sixteen codes, ten of which express positive attitudes and six negative ones (Table 1).

The students made 137 comments (2.5 comments per student), 77% of which were positive, distributed uniformly across the two student groups (UniRoma 79% and UPatras 76% positive comments respectively).

Both groups agree on items 1 and 2, namely that the Toolkit supports fast ideation (65%) and that team brainstorming was perceived as effective (31%). Most of the comments are similarly distributed between the two groups.

Table 1. Coded responses of the 55 participants of the workshops (UniRoma N = 27, UPatras N = 28). Plus or minus signs denote positive or negative attitude respectively.

#	Code	All	UniRoma	UPatras
1	Fast ideation and rapid brainstorming (+)	36 (65%)	19 (70%)	17 (61%)
2	Brainstorming in teams was effective (+)	17 (31%)	8 (30%)	9 (32%)
3	The framework was limiting (−)	13 (24%)	3 (11%)	10 (36%)
4	Structured idea generation process (+)	11 (20%)	3 (11%)	8 (29%)
5	It is a useful tool to stimulate discussion (+)	9 (16%)	5 19%)	4 (14%)
6	Tiles toolkit provides flexible starting points (+)	9 (16%)	4 (15%)	5 (18%)
7	It has been an enjoyable experience (+)	9 (16%)	5 (19%)	4 (14%)
8	The tiles concepts are unfeasibile or unrealistic (−)	5 (9%)	5 (19%)	0 (0%)
9	Tiles cards do not lead to a design idea easily (−)	5 (9%)	3 (11%)	2 (7%)
10	Hones teamwork skills (+)	5 (9%)	5 (19%)	0 (0%)
11	The toolkit promotes speculative thinking regardless of technical limitations (+)	4 (7%)	2 (7%)	2 (7%)
12	Not enough time available for idea generation (−)	4 (7%)	0 (0%)	4 (14%)
13	Vague ideas, unfeasible or not realizable (−)	4 (7%)	2 (7%)	2 (7%)
14	Concrete ideas, feasible and realizable (+)	3 (5%)	1 (4%)	2 (7%)
15	Hones presentation skills (+)	2 (4%)	2 (7%)	0 (0%)
16	Brainstorming in teams was not effective (−)	1 (2%)	1 (4%)	0 (0%)

A negative comment, made by 24% of the students was that the framework was limiting (item 3). This was more pronounced in the UPatras group, whose design task was set by the workshop facilitators.

5 Discussion

Feedback from the students, indicates a positive view for both the approach used and the process of collaborative design. They commented that the tool supports fast development of new ideas, structures ideation, supports exploration of new design spaces, facilitates collaborative brainstorming. On the other hand, frustration was expressed on the time constraints and the feasibility of some of the mission cards allocated to them, in particular by students of UniRoma. Some explicitly mention in their comments that, because of training as engineers, they have not been taught rapid ideation in a team environment. Similarly, another student notes that, the real problem is that "we are engineers and it is very tough to be speculative." The complaints about time restrictions reflect the fact that engineering students are used to focusing on technical aspects of possible design solutions and not so much to exploring a design space horizontally. The produced design solutions were not very innovative, but were based mostly on existing applications. In particular the UPatras workshop designs were repetitive and of low innovativeness. This may be attributed in some degree to the fact that the students were not introduced to the requirements of the domain of cultural heritage, so ownership of the problem was low. There seems to be a contradiction between the positive view of the students on the tools and the process and the results of the workshops. Questions are thus raised regarding the motivation and ability of engineering students to use broad techniques and design ideation methods effectively, and, specifically, how they should ideally be trained in order to cope with broader thinking and adoption of multidisciplinary approaches.

Starting from specific mission cards may be the reason that the UniRoma students provided a wider diversity of scenaria. Indeed, 16% of the responses allude to the opportunities that the wide range of mission cards offer.

Broader issues are raised by these observations, as per the effectiveness of the educational curricula within which they are used, and on how engineering students are trained to utilize design methods effectively [1]. As the facilitators observed first-hand, and the students explicitly noted in their comments, background skills are missing from their (formal or informal) curricula, constraining their abilities to approach design problems from different perspectives, address the broader issues involved, and generate ideas from different starting points, an issue that needs to be further investigated.

Acknowledgements. The authors thank S. Mora, M. Divitini and F. Gianni of NTNU, for introducing us to the Tiles cards, and the students who participated in the workshops.

References

1. Avouris, N., Mavrommati, I., Sintoris, C.: Designing through ideation cards for internet of things: can cards help engineers out of the box? In: Proceedings of the 11th Panhellenic Conference with International Participation Information and Communication Technologies in Education (2018)
2. Chasanidou, D.: Design for motivation: evaluation of a design tool. Multimodal Technol. Interact. **2**(1) (2018). https://doi.org/10.3390/mti2010006
3. Glazer, L.: Google finds STEM skills aren't the most important skills (2018). http://michiganfuture.org/?p=9767
4. Hornecker, E.: Creative idea exploration within the structure of a guiding framework: the card brainstorming game. In: Proceedings of the Fourth International Conference on Tangible, Embedded, and Embodied Interaction, TEI 2010, pp. 101–108. ACM (2010). https://doi.org/10.1145/1709886.1709905
5. Mora, S., Gianni, F., Divitini, M.: Tiles: a card-based ideation toolkit for the Internet of Things. In: Proceedings of the 2017 Conference on Designing Interactive Systems, DIS 2017, pp. 587–598. ACM, New York (2017). https://doi.org/10.1145/3064663.3064699
6. Saldaña, J.: The Coding Manual for Qualitative Researchers. SAGE London (2009)

Supporting Students Through Notifications About Importance in Academic Lectures

Jörg Cassens[1]([⊠]) [iD] and Rebekah Wegener[2,3] [iD]

[1] University of Hildesheim, 31141 Hildesheim, Germany
cassens@cs.uni-hildesheim.de
[2] RWTH Aachen University, 52062 Aachen, Germany
rebekah.wegener@ifaar.rwth-aachen.de
[3] Paris Lodron University of Salzburg, 5020 Salzburg, Austria

Abstract. Identifying and extracting important information from monologic interaction is a difficult task for humans and modelling this for an intelligent system is a big challenge. In our work, we have previously used models that are grounded in semiotic, linguistic and psychological theories of multi-modal interaction. Here, we concentrate on academic lectures as a specific form of monologic interaction. Our goal is to support students through a system alerting them to important aspects of a lecture. In this paper, we outline the requirements that went into an early implementation of the system. We discuss a rich contextual model and what this entails for modelling requirements and system implementation. We provide an overview of the system and discuss our notion and role of context within the application domain.

Keywords: Modelling context awareness
Ambient intelligence education
Multimodal human-computer interaction

1 Introduction

The ability to take notes is by many educators considered to be one of the important competences students should exhibit [11]. One application area where note-taking skills are required is during lectures [2]. The ability to take notes is tightly linked to critical listening skills, and both are linked to student outcomes and success [4]. One key aspect of good note-taking skills is the ability to assess the importance of information presented. It has been shown that expert readers of lecture transcripts achieved good inter-annotator agreement on which parts of a lecture were considered important and which were not [10]. The same was not the case for students, who not only deemed large parts of the lecture as being of less importance, but who also achieved lower inter-annotator agreement.

Importance is a difficult concept to work with, and one that superficially could be replaced by concepts such as salience or prominence. There is an established body of research on detecting saliency in both video and audio data [6].

© Springer Nature Switzerland AG 2018
A. Kameas and K. Stathis (Eds.): AmI 2018, LNCS 11249, pp. 227–232, 2018.
https://doi.org/10.1007/978-3-030-03062-9_18

We argue, however, that retaining the concept of importance is crucial for making a distinction between the speaker driven concepts of salience and prominence and the contextual concept of importance.

The goal of the research presented in this paper is to support the development of student listening and note-taking skills by alerting them to important aspects of the lecture. In addition, the students should gain the ability to compare their notion of importance with the notions of experts in real time, providing crucial learning analytics. At the same time, the system should not add additional load on the lecturer, e.g. by requiring him or her to explicitly mark importance. The last requirement is that the system should not interfere with normal behaviour when listening in a lecture, in particular, it should not attract the focus of attention of students. Therefore, an ambient system that, on the one hand, observes lecturer behaviour for multi-modal markers of importance, providing a behavioural, implicit interface, and, on the other hand, delivers unobtrusive feedback to students, for example by tactile annunciation of times of importance and by ambient displays representing the "density" of importance e.g. through the use of colour, is an ideal solution.

Meaning making in human interaction is most often multi-modal and this feature can be exploited for dynamic, automated, context dependent information extraction. Drawing on semiotic models of expression, gesture, and behaviour; linguistic models of text structure and sound; and a rich model of context, we argue that the combination of these modalities to form multi-modal ensembles through data triangulation provides a better basis for information extraction than each modality alone. By using a rich model of context that maps the unfolding of the text in real time with features of the context, it is also possible to advance from notification about importance to producing real-time query driven summarization on demand.

This work is part of a wider theory-guided action research program that uses multi-modal markers of importance to automatically extract key information from lectures and summarises them as a step towards being able to identify and track contextually relevant importance in spoken language in real time. We base our contextual analysis on models we have proposed earlier [5,13]. Actual system development combines human-centred and feature-driven approaches.

2   Context

The system is to be used in a very specific setting. We can therefore make use of rich models of context and event structures, in particular systemic approaches to the specification of similarity and variation across contexts, which are useful for computational modelling [8]. For highly institutionalised settings (here defined as situations that have multiple and convergent coding for context) such as academic lectures, it is possible to state a Generic Structure Potential (GSP) [7]. These situations are less likely to be open for individual negotiation and more likely to have a recognisable and predictable structure.

The GSP is an abstraction that represents both the sameness (hence Generic) and the variation (hence Potential) of different situations instantiating the same context. While this model of the structure provides a generic and reusable model of the sequencing of a text in context, a rich model of the context provides prediction of the variation in the paths that a text might take through that GSP. This means that on top of the general model, we can represent variations across context and material situational setting. An approach to modelling context based on these findings is much more expressive and versatile than current approaches based on e.g. temporal sequencing alone.

In this particular instance, a more expressive model that integrates acoustic features such as prosody and intonation with a semantic model of behaviour, with facial expressions and gestures that co-occur with speech, has already been created in a preliminary analysis of samples of academic lectures [14]. Our work showed discipline specific variations in structure (field related), person-specific variations depending on the experience of the lecturer or the student level (tenor related) and variations according to time of day or semester (related to the material setting). It also showed that facial expression is related to the rhetorical thrust and that lecturer behaviour is potentially predictive of topic driven phase shifts in the lecture structure (e.g. moving from a definition to an example in the lecture). These findings are supported by recent research showing that gestures that co-occur with speech appear to provide important semantic augmentation of abstract concepts [9] and research in intonation suggesting that prosodic prominence is both identifiable and central to listening [3].

In Fig. 1, we can see a simplified depiction of the underlying Generic Structure Potential for academic lectures. The single lecture, while retaining individual variation, is an instantiation of the generic lecture. The single lecture is only one in a sequence of lectures, comprising a course. Those courses in turn form part of the overarching study program. What makes single instances of lectures recognisable as such is the GSP. While not part of every lecture, and varying in order, aspects like administriva, theory and examples form parts of recurring elements.

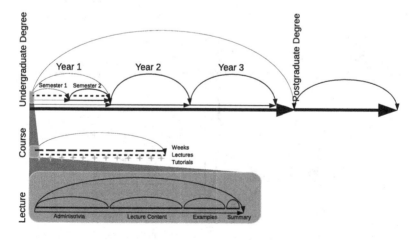

Fig. 1. Generic structure potential for a lecture.

3   Implementation

The system under development is an ambient real-time system that can be used to augment live lectures – providing students with the guidance they need to learn to listen critically during lectures. A schematic overview of the different system components and their relation can be found in Fig. 2. On the side of the lecturer, explicit user interaction is to be avoided to not distract him or her from teaching. When the system is running, the whole interaction with the lecture support system is through behaviour. On the side of the students, feedback is to be given in an unobtrusive manner. They can be alerted to important parts of the lecture through tactile feedback and get an overview of the importance of the current part of the lecture through colour coded ambient displays (either part of the lecture environment or through their phones). The system can also be used on captured lecture videos.

The computing pipeline (see Fig. 3) for detection of importance in lecture videos uses several types of input data. Video data is used to analyse the lecturer's behaviour (e.g. gestures, movement, gaze and visual target). Audio data leads information about their voice (e.g. prosodic markers, pitch, tone, loudness). Together, this can be used to identify flags that indicate targets of importance in the recording. The audience can then be alerted. Some information, like expert annotations or even transcripts, are likely only available during training. The pipeline is under continuing development.

During use, the system needs feedback from multiple stakeholders. The lecturer and potentially the teaching team need to provide feedback on accuracy. Did the system accurately capture what was important from the lecture? How important is this right now? How important is this over the course of the subject? The system also needs feedback from students. How effective was this system

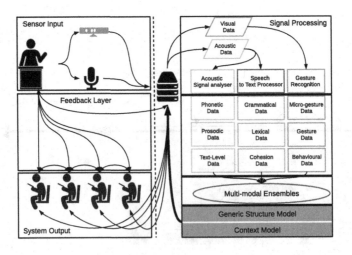

Fig. 2. Overview of system components.

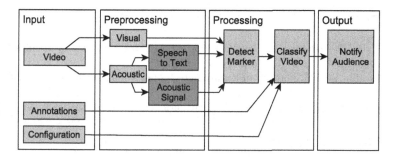

Fig. 3. Computing pipeline.

at helping me to notice important information during the lecture? How useful was the summary? Did I learn something from this interaction? Can I apply this to other domains? The system also needs feedback from the designers. What mistakes were made and why?

4   Conclusions and Further Work

We have outlined an ambient embedded system aimed at supporting students to improve their critical listening and note-taking skills. Key requirements are:

- No additional work for the lecturer, implying the need for multi-modal, implicit user interfaces based on user behaviour (verbal and non-verbal)
- No additional cognitive load for students, implying the need for unobtrusive notification e.g. through tactile signals like vibrating alarms
- Ability for the students to reposition themselves in the course of the lecture by getting an overview of the "density of importance" over a certain time as feedback if the students are momentarily distracted.

The pipeline to realize those requirements is currently under development [12]. Individual components have been tested successfully on recordings of videos, integration and test of the completed system on real-time data has not been completed. In terms of the phases of ambient systems research proposed by Aarts and de Ruyter [1], the system described is between context studies and lab studies while individual components have been used in lab studies.

Regarding future work, lectures are not the only domain where notification of importance and summarisation is useful. Moving from monologic (lecture) to dialogic situations, doctor-patient consultations are one of the next targets. Increasing in complexity, multi-participant situations such as team meetings (potentially including multi-language feature) can also be considered. Potential usage scenarios are mostly restricted by the applicability of the theoretic framework to a technical system, in particular a generic structure of such scenario.

References

1. Aarts, E., De Ruyter, B.: New research perspectives on ambient intelligence. J. Ambient. Intell. Smart Environ. **1**(1), 5–14 (2009)
2. Al-Musalli, A.M.: Taxonomy of lecture note-taking skills and subskills. Int. J. List. **29**(3), 134–147 (2015)
3. Baumann, S.: The importance of tonal cues for untrained listeners in judging prominence. In: Proceedings of the 10th International Seminar on Speech Production (ISSP), pp. 21–24 (2014)
4. Boch, F., Piolat, A.: Note taking and learning a summary of research. WAC J. **16**, 101–113 (2005). (Writing Across the Curriculum)
5. Butt, D., Wegener, R., Cassens, J.: Modelling behaviour semantically. In: Brézillon, P., Blackburn, P., Dapoigny, R. (eds.) Proceedings of CONTEXT 2013. LNCS, vol. 8175, pp. 343–349. Springer, France (2013). https://doi.org/10.1007/978-3-642-40972-1_27
6. Evangelopoulos, G., Zlatintsi, A., Potamianos, A., Maragos, P., Rapantzikos, K., Skoumas, G., Avrithis, Y.: Multimodal saliency and fusion for movie summarization based on aural, visual, and textual attention. IEEE Trans. Multimed. **15**(7), 1553–1568 (2013)
7. Hasan, R.: Situation and the definition of genre. In: Grimshaw, A. (ed.) What's going on here? Complementary Analysis of Professional Talk: Volume 2 of the Multiple Analysis Project. Ablex, Norwood (1994)
8. Hasan, R.: Dynamic view of context in language. In: Cloran, C., Butt, D., Williams, G. (eds.) Ways of Saying Ways of Speaking. Open Linguistic Series, Casell (1996)
9. Mittelberg, I.: Making grammar visible: the use of metaphoric gestures to represent grammatical categories and structures. In: Proceedings of the First Congress of the International Society for Gesture Studies: Gesture - The Living Medium, University of Texas at Austin (2003)
10. Schüller, B.: Understanding the identification of important information in academic lectures: linguistic and cognitive approaches. Bachelor thesis, RWTH Aachen University (2018)
11. Stacy, E.M., Cain, J.: Note-taking and handouts in the digital age. Am. J. Pharm. Educ. **79**(7), 107 (2015)
12. Ude, J., Schüller, B., Wegener, R., Cassens, J.: A pipeline for extracting multimodal markers for meaning in lectures. In: Cassens, J., Wegener, R., Kofod-Petersen, A. (eds.) Proceedings of the Tenth International Workshop on Modelling and Reasoning in Context, vol. 2134, pp. 16–21. CEUR Workshop Proceedings, Aachen (2018). http://ceur-ws.org/Vol-2134/#paper04
13. Wegener, R., Cassens, J.: Multi-modal markers for meaning: using behavioural, acoustic and textual cues for automatic, context dependent summarization of lectures. In: Cassens, J., Wegener, R., Kofod-Petersen, A. (eds.) Proceedings of the Eighth International Workshop on Modelling and Reasoning in Context (2016). http://www.ecai2016.org/content/uploads/2016/08/W17-mrc-2016.pdf
14. Wegener, R., Schüller, B., Cassens, J.: Needing and wanting in academic lectures: profiling the academic lecture across context. In: Chappell, P., Knox, J.S. (eds.) Transforming Contexts: Papers from the 44th International Systemic Functional Congress, Wollongong, Australia (2017). http://www.isfla.org/Systemics/Conferences/ISFC_2017_Proceedings.pdf

Author Index

Printed in the United States
By Bookmasters